CRITICAL MASS

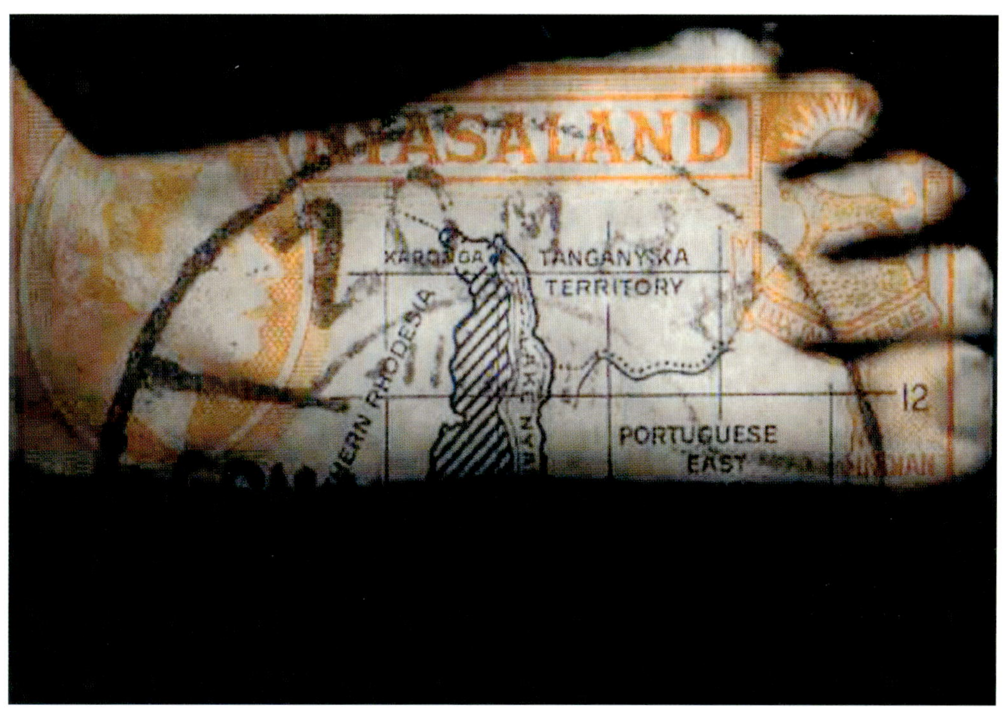

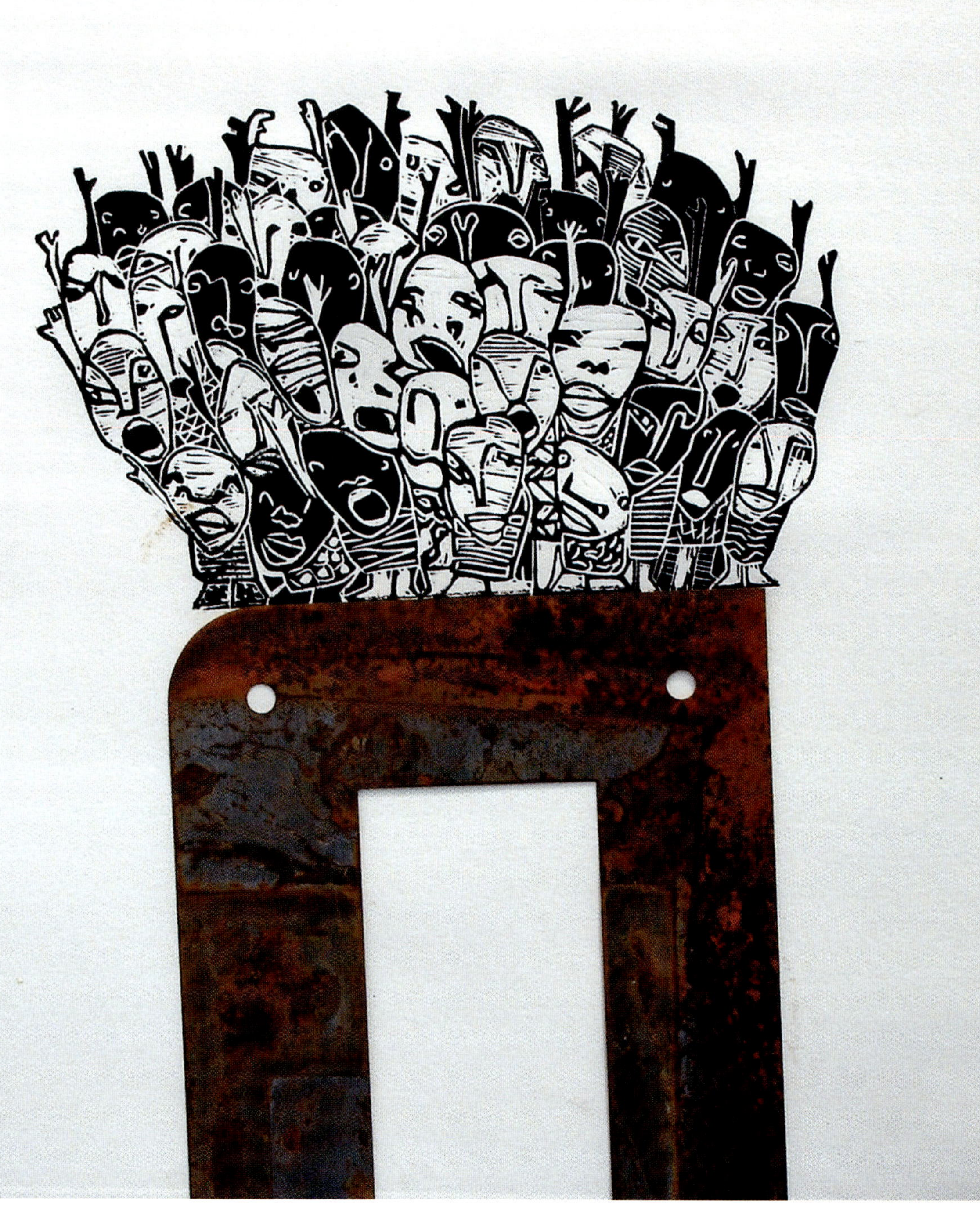

CRITICAL MASS

PRINTMAKING BEYOND THE EDGE

RICHARD NOYCE

DEDICATED TO PROFESSOR WITOLD SKULICZ
PRESIDENT OF THE INTERNATIONAL PRINT TRIENNIAL SOCIETY,
KRAKOW
1926 – 2009

A&C BLACK
LONDON

First published in Great Britain in 2010
A&C Black Publishers Limited
36 Soho Square
London W1D 3QY
www.acblack.com

ISBN: 978-14081-0939-7

CIP Catalogue records for this book are available from the British Library and the U.S. Library of Congress.

Typeset in Garamond Regular 10.5 on 12pt

Book design by Howard Whitley
Cover design by Sutchinda Rangsi Thompson
Publisher: Susan James
Copyediting: Julian Beecroft

Printed and bound in China.

A&C Black uses paper produced with elemental chlorine-free pulp, harvested from managed sustainable forests.

TITLE PAGE Shelagh Morgan, *Nyasaland (from the Landscapes of Exile series)*, 2007/08. Digital print on Magnani paper, size variable.

FRONTISPIECE Moises Yagües, *The Island*, 2009. Woodcut and collage, 56 x 38cm. 22 x 15in.

CONTENTS

ACKNOWLEDGEMENTS

I began the research and writing of this book in April 2008 and completed it in March 2010. During that time I received advice and information from many people in the international printmaking community, whose willing cooperation, advice and critical friendship assisted me in the completion of the book. The artists featured in this book were also generous in providing information and images, as well as suggestions of other directions for research, and I thank them all most warmly for their professionalism and their time.

My research journeys were helped greatly by the support and guidance of Lisa Bulawsky in Saint Louis, Ljiljana Cincul in Belgrade, Javier Martin-Jimenez and Sören Meschede in Madrid, Xenis Sachinis in Thessaloniki, Simeona Hoskova in Prague, Teresa Soliman in Kraków, Arūnas Gelūnas in Vilnius, and Chang-Soo Kim in Seoul: my grateful thanks to all of them for their continuing friendship.

The professional assistance of Susan James at A&C Black, London, during the research and writing of this book, and her colleagues during its production, has been of great assistance, and it continues to be a pleasure to work with them.

Finally, I thank my family, and especially Fiona, for their support and tolerance during the research and writing, and for their understanding.

Wales, March 2010

INTRODUCTION

This book follows on from *Printmaking at the Edge,* published by A&C Black in 2006 and reprinted in 2008 and 2010, which documented some of the many changes which the arts of printmaking had undergone in the preceding decade, and highlighted the work of 43 artists in 16 countries. Since completing that book in 2005 I have continued to explore the world of contemporary printmaking, travelling to a number of countries to meet artists, see exhibitions, speak at conferences and give lectures and seminars at a number of university art departments. I have been continually encouraged, and frequently surprised, by the work that is being produced by artists who use printmaking mediums in their practice, often extending these mediums into new areas and combinations. One enduring certainty is that printmakers continue to embrace with enthusiasm, just as they always have done, new developments in technology, new materials, new processes and new means of communication.

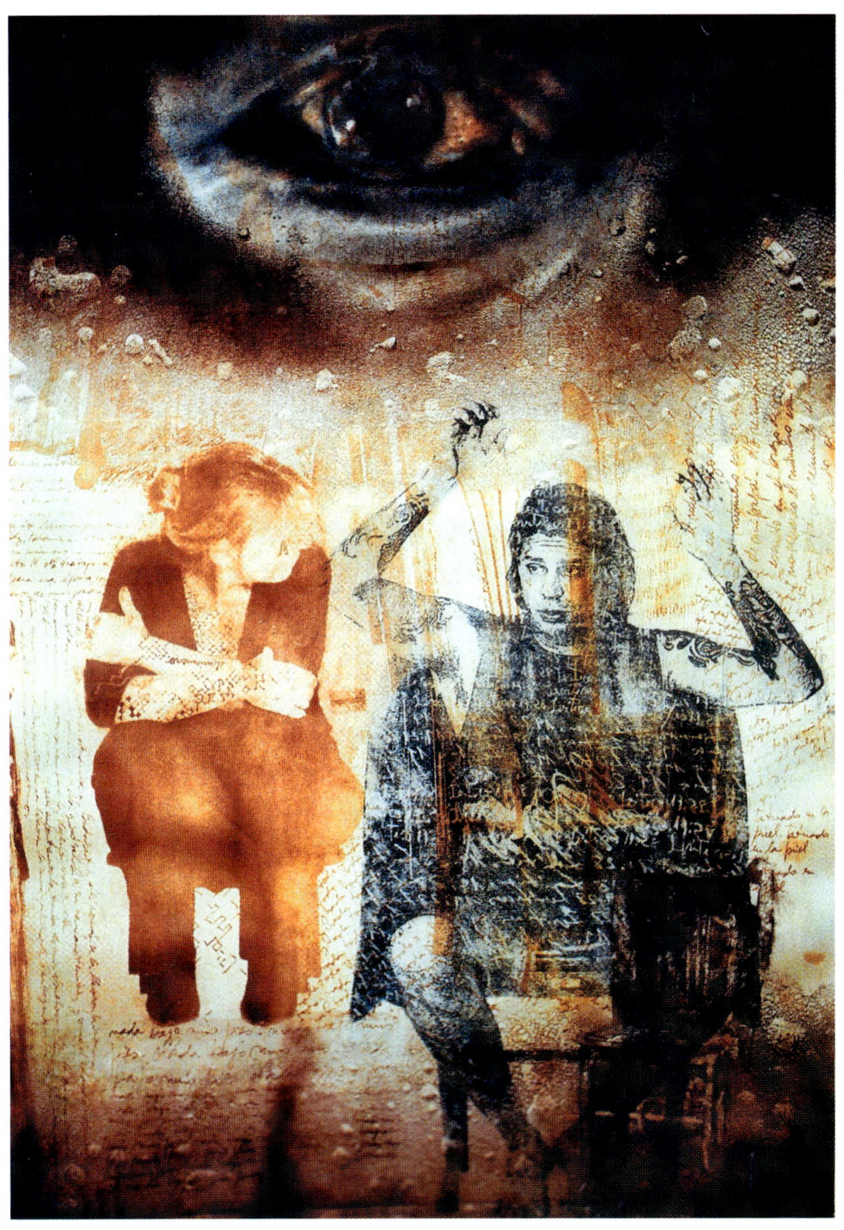

Mirta Kupferminc, *Written on my Body, 2007.*
Photopolymer and metal etching, 65 x 80cm. 25.5 x 31.5in.

This book documents my continuing exploration of this most fascinating part of the contemporary art world. In pursuing my research in both the real and virtual worlds, it has become clear that the nature of 'the edge' is continually shifting; it is not a single, fixed edge, which was in any case never going to be open to precise definition, but an evolving set of edges. Some are philosophical in nature, being considerations over what constitutes a print in a contemporary art world that is itself moving from certainty to uncertainty; some ask questions and provide interim answers of a kind. Some are factual, dependent on the consideration of specific traditional techniques and the extent to which new processes and materials allow them to develop; yet others are growing from the continual mutations of the new technology, which offer hitherto unimagined possibilities for the creation of reproducible images and the means by which they can be shared. The edges are many and various, offering wide scope for academic discussion, polemical statements and constant reconsideration. There is now a spectrum of edges that ranges from the most traditional, such as woodcut and etching, to the most experimental, such as those offered by the new technology. It seems sometimes that no sooner has an edge been defined or described than it has changed direction, folded in on itself, or moved on towards another horizon. Artists are practitioners at such edges, making use of what they find there in their quest for the means to express the emotions, desires and experiences that make them the artists they have to be, driven by the same motivations that have driven creative minds since the making of the earliest human art.

The dynamic nature of the international printmaking community continues to surprise many, and reinforces in me the belief that what is happening in that community has relevance far beyond its immediate confines. Contemporary printmakers are the heirs of all those artists, across the millennia of global cultural development, who have invented and developed techniques – using their hands, or mechanical devices, or more recently electronic equipment – to enable the production of reproducible images that convey ideas and dreams, reflections of the imagination and the potent exposition of human experience.

This book includes concise profiles of and examples of work by 52 contemporary artists from 27 countries across the world, and from across the generations; there are brief references to other artists and groups. It also considers the role of a number of organisations that include and make use of the work of printmakers. I also set out my own view of the changing nature of contemporary art against some of the broader political, social and technological changes that are currently taking place. Particular aspects of contemporary printmaking, as they manifest in the work of the artists included in the book, are also considered. There are references to new techniques and the technology that generates them, as well as to the welcome persistence of traditional techniques, and due consideration is also given to some of the means for sharing and exhibiting these new forms of printmaking.

The selection of artists is necessarily a personal one. There are many other good artists I have met, or whose works I have encountered, who warrant a place alongside those selected, but unfortunately, for reasons of space, I have not been able to include them. Between the completion of the book in March 2010 and its publication, it is inevitable that I will encounter many more whose work excites and stimulates me. These facts point to the validity of my assertion that the field of printmaking, in all its manifestations, is the most vibrant and stimulating in the contemporary visual arts, one that will continue to grow and reveal yet more of its great potential. The 'critical mass' of artists and their work that constitutes this book is therefore the record of another stage in a long and eventful journey, one that points the way towards the rich variety of printmaking that will develop in the future.

Wales, March 2010

CRITICAL MASS

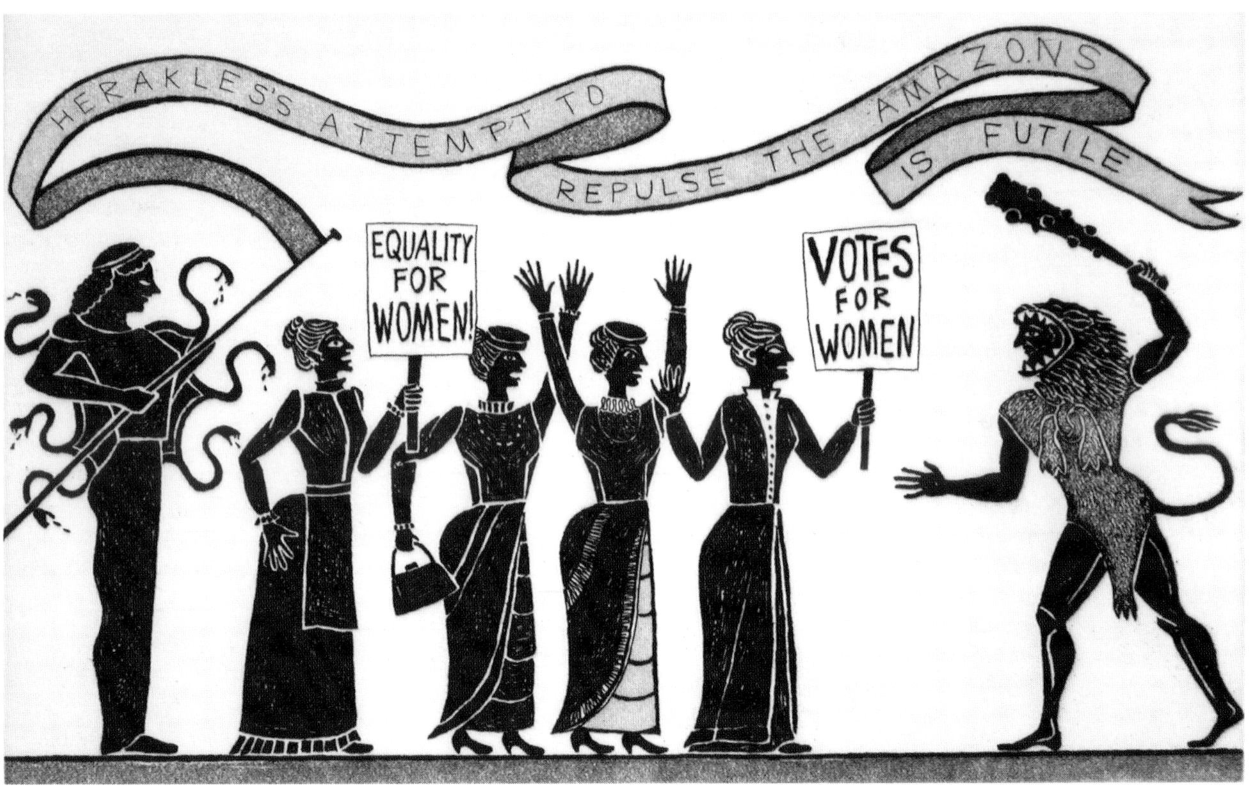

Marian Maguire, *Herakles' Attempt to Repulse the Amazons is Futile, 2007.* Etching, 12.2 x 19.5cm, 5 x 8in. (plate) on 35.5 x 38cm, 14 x 15in. (paper).

THE GLOBAL CONTEXT

othing is forever. The pace of change in world society is increasing. The nature of change itself is changing, and the unpredictable is now to be expected. In the past two centuries the evolution of social organisation has been far-reaching. Industrialisation, urbanisation and more recently globalisation have resulted in a society that has greater potential access to education and the products of culture than at any time in the past. We can move further and faster than ever before, and are changing the planet on which we live in ways that may not be reversible. We are more and more dependent on each other for survival, and yet we have still not learned to live in harmony with others and with the environment in which we live. Social, political, religious and territorial conflicts continue, interlinking to create a complex web within which the rights and welfare of individuals sometimes seem to count for very little. We rely to an ever-greater extent on the information we receive through the media in order to attempt to make sense of the world in which we live. Much of our knowledge of that world comes to us through our computers, which more and more of us rely upon to enable easy communication with others, and to share information. The electronic interdependence of the increasingly wired-up world is intensifying, and we submit ourselves to it with varying degrees of willingness.

Those who edit, often with idiosyncratic selectivity, the rolling television news channels that broadcast for 24 hours a day every day of the year, and which are also transmitted live across the internet, are the mediators of our knowledge of world events and their implications. As television becomes ever more self-referential, it is increasingly difficult to disentangle fact from fiction. A look at programme schedules reveals a high proportion of so called 'reality' television productions, soap operas, makeover programmes and increasingly bizarre game shows; updates on some of these programmes are even, bizarrely, given during mainstream news bulletins, contributing to a change in the nature of reported reality. It is becoming harder to work out what the priorities are for the broadcast media, when the latest events in a television talent (so-called) competition take precedence over news of a major natural disaster, a famine or another bloody conflict. By contrast, informative programmes on the arts, and programmes that discuss the role of culture in our lives, even in the broadest terms, let alone in serious, thought-provoking terms, are few and far between, mostly relegated to minority digital or satellite channels. The quality and content of tabloid newspapers become ever more disheartening, an impression amplified by the content and sheer number of celebrity and gossip magazines, into which some of the tabloids seem to have morphed. It is difficult to argue with the oft-stated opinion that the press and broadcast media are being dumbed down for consumption by a docile, compliant public that is at the same time becoming less well informed and educated. And yet attendance at art galleries, for instance, has never been higher, and the range and number of art publications such as this one never greater; not to mention the burgeoning number of people studying and being able to make a living from an arts practice of one kind or another. On top of all this we are under increasing surveillance of one sort or another for, we are told, our own security. The increase in shopping malls patrolled by security staff, and the rise of gated communities as desirable places to live are further symptoms of our changing social world. Small wonder then that people living in urban societies feel increasingly alienated.

Despite, or perhaps because of, that sense of alienation, those same societies, both urban and rural, go on producing culture that reflects their hopes and anxieties in ever-greater abundance. Culture is made up of a 'set of shared attitudes, values, goals, and practices that characterises an institution, organisation or group' and 'an integrated pattern of human knowledge, belief, and behaviour that depends upon the capacity for symbolic thought and social learning'. (Definitions from Wikipedia).

Culture can also refer to the creation of works of art, literature and music, covering the full range from popular culture, with its music, fashion, graffiti and rapidly evolving styles, to the applied arts and the fine arts. Applied more broadly, the notion of culture has also been extended to encompass sports and leisure activities, folk dancing and customs, the construction of the built environment and the changes wrought in the natural environment through the intervention of human beings; the word has also been hijacked into contexts such as, 'a culture of violence' and 'the culture of despair'. The hoary old cliché, 'When I hear the word "culture" I reach for my gun' mutated into 'When I hear the word "culture" I reach for my chequebook', and has now perhaps mutated again into 'When I hear the word "culture" I reach for the TV remote control'. Culture, in the traditional sense in which it was used when referring to the arts, sadly is not really very fashionable these days. Culture, as a substitute for religion among the secular middle classes is another matter. The huge popularity of blockbuster exhibitions at Tate Modern and elsewhere is an indicator of what is sometimes an uncritical following of the visual arts. Much of what is offered to the general public by the press and broadcast media is, like much of the news and current affairs, reduced to a basic minimum of challenge, with the target audience reduced to a low common denominator. When the Brit artists Jake and Dinos Chapman took a genuine original edition of Goya prints and altered it by the addition of crudely drawn comic details, it was a signal that the barbarians had taken over the establishment asylum. Further evidence of this came with the cynical financial-market shenanigans and tabloid feeding frenzy that accompanied the exhibition of Damien Hirst's diamond-encrusted platinum skull, *For the Love of God*, which dragged the showbiz end of the contemporary art scene even further down: the public at large mocked it with well-deserved laughter and an ill-disguised measure of contempt.

For all this, and despite all the pessimism and gloom that pervades so many areas of human life on the planet towards the end of this first decade of the 21st century, artists go on making art, because that is what they do, and what they have to do.

Printmakers are artists, and contemporary printmaking is contemporary art. Printmaking is not something other: it feeds, and feeds on, the same things as other forms of visual art; it is just another medium through which someone's ideas, passions, fears, desires and emotions are expressed in a visible form to be shared with others.

THE UNHOLY ALLIANCE

During the 20th century, particularly in the later decades, as far as the new breed of whizz-kid 'gallerists' and the newly rich urban generation were concerned, the visual arts mutated into just another commodity to be invested in and traded, no more important than pork-belly futures, abstract financial products or scarce minerals on the other side of the globe. Increasingly astonishing prices were reached at auction, and suddenly wealthy investment bankers and post-soviet oligarchs bought art by the truckload. Vast amounts of money changed hands – both real and notional – and the fortunate few among artists became very rich indeed. Inextricably linked with the financial markets whose bubble of expectations had been inflating throughout the previous decade, the art market would go on to suffer along with every other sphere of economic activity when the bubble burst spectacularly in late 2008.

Shortly before it did, Robert Hughes, writer and art critic, made a film, *The Mona Lisa Curse*, for Channel 4, the British television channel, which documented how the art world and the financial world had become incestuously intertwined since the exhibition of Leonardo da Vinci's *Mona Lisa* in New York in 1962/3. In this polemic, delivered in his characteristically trenchant style, Hughes challenged many of the assumptions of those living in the art/finance bubble, and highlighted the risks of this unholy alliance. At the end of the film he said, 'If art can't tell us about the world we live in, then I don't believe there's much point in having it. And that is something we're going to have to face more and more as the years go on, that nasty question that never used to be asked, because the assumption was always that it was answered long ago: what good is art? What use is art? What does it do? Is what it does actually worth doing? And an art which is completely monetarised, as it is these days, is going to have to answer these questions, or it is going to die.' (Robert Hughes, in *The Mona Lisa Curse*, for Channel 4 Television (UK), September 2008).

'Apart from drugs, art is the biggest unregulated market in the world, with contemporary art sales in the region of $18bn a year.'

Robert Hughes, *The Mona Lisa Curse,* **Channel 4 Television (UK), 2008**

Not long after the film's first transmission in Britain the financial market in the United States ran into serious difficulties, and then crashed, with repercussions that spread rapidly around the globe, causing unprecedented suffering in many countries. As ever, the arts, which have always been an easy target for cuts, were one of the first publicly funded areas to suffer.

While parts of the contemporary art world, particularly auctions and art fairs, have been adversely affected by the global financial downturn, and while this in turn has had something of a dampening effect on some of the enthusiasm for the sale and purchase of paintings and sculpture as a trading commodity, printmaking seems to be weathering the storm with greater success. The reasons for this are several, but one is that printmaking has always been as resilient as it has been innovative and even revolutionary. Despite the problems elsewhere in the art market printmakers have continued to sell their work, and individuals and museums have continued to buy prints. However, until very recently, many gallery directors, curators and critics have considered printmaking to be a marginal medium, subservient and supplementary to what they considered to be those noble fine arts of painting and sculpture. Michael Schneider, a Viennese artist and academic, posed a question during a panel discussion at the Southern Graphics Council conference in Kansas City, Missouri, in 2007. He asked, 'Why do some mainstream art dealers still not trust printmaking? Is it because they know it is revolutionary and therefore untrustworthy?' He had a point: anarchy isn't about making money.

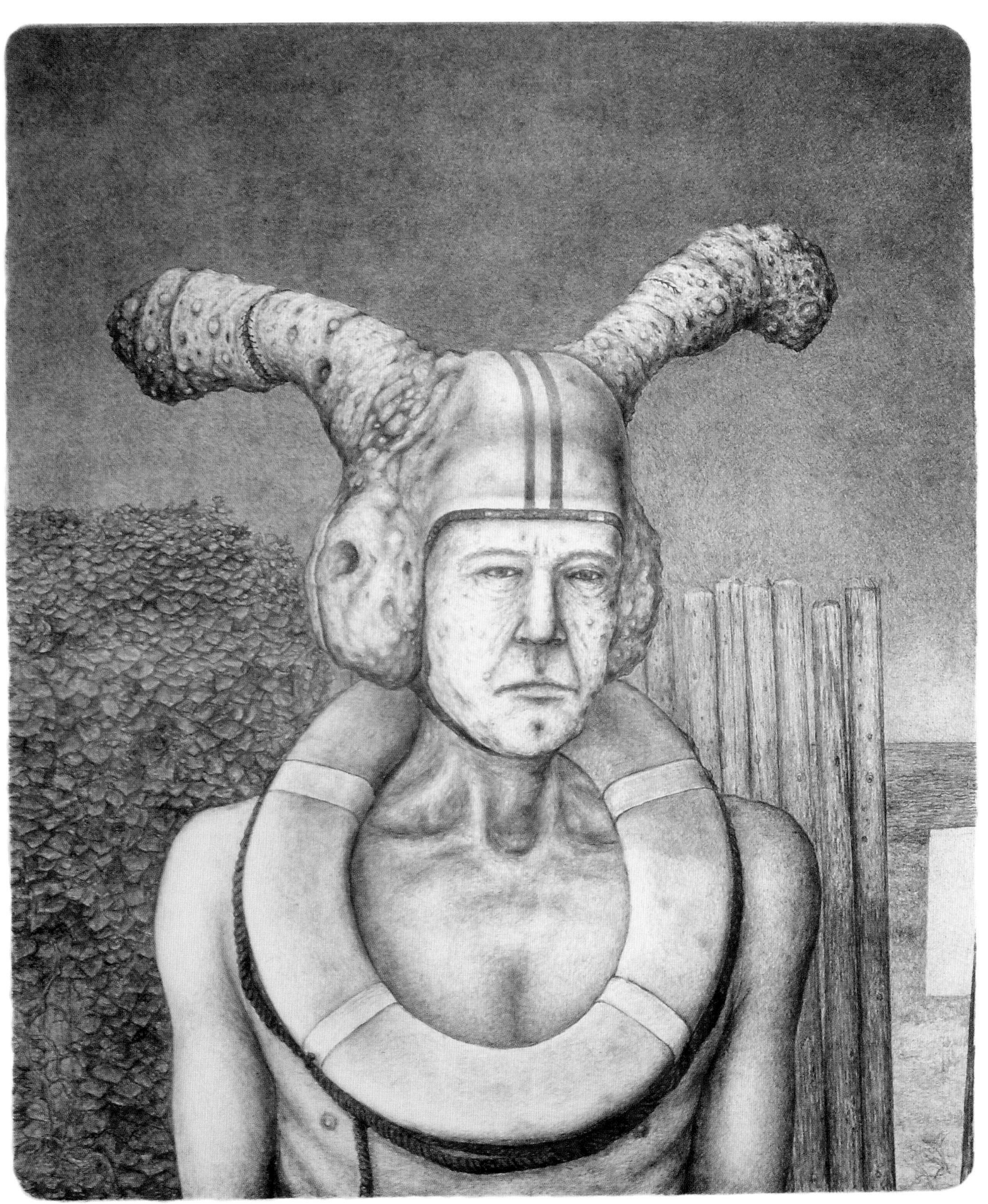

Michael Barnes, *The Mariner, 2009*. Lithograph, 56 x 46cm 22 x 18in.

CHANGE IS THE NAME OF THE GAME IS CHANGE...

One thing that has struck me about the contemporary printmaking world in the past few years is that not only is it growing rapidly, but in several ways it is also changing focus and expanding its position. There is a noticeable shift toward work that engages directly with social and political concerns, and not just aesthetic ones. There is nothing new in this, perhaps, because the graphic arts have a long history of social and political engagement. Consider the enduring impact of work by, amongst others, Gillray, Rowlandson, Hogarth, Goya and Daumier, as well as many Polish poster artists from the 20th century. The role of the graphic arts, including printmaking, in the agitprop of the 20th century likewise had an effect that has not been diluted with the passage of time. Art and politics have long been intertwined in one way or another, and the new technologies have become a major motive force for a determined thrust in this direction.

'Art perpetually rewires society whether anybody wants it or not. If society refuses it or loses the ability to react to it, that society forfeits its own energy and will die.'

Jeff Nuttall, *Art and the Degradation of Awareness*, Calder Publications, London, 2001

The range of works that can now be considered as constituting parts of the constellation of printmaking is also changing, and there seems to be a growing acceptance of new mediums and techniques across the printmaking world. Historically, the emergence of new forms of printmaking has always been controversial. The technology that allowed the printing of books in a range of languages caused problems within the Christian Church that led to the Reformation. The Church had long maintained its monopoly in the recording and transmission of permitted knowledge through handwritten books in Latin, which by the late Middle Ages was a language that only existed in written form, and thus was available to the clerisy but excluded the ordinary man. Stone lithography was once an upstart technique, as was the plate lithography that followed. Engraving allowed for the mass dissemination of scurrilous and satirical works, and later enabled images derived from early photographs to be included in newspapers. The appearance of new chemical colours and high-volume commercial lithographic printing in the latter part of the 19th century encouraged the emergence of the new brash poster work of artists such as Toulouse-Lautrec. Photolithography played its part in the establishment claim that painting as a medium was under threat, and yet painting has still not died. Screenprinting, developed firstly as a reproductive method for commercial art and advertising, became a mainstay of the Pop Art of the 1960s and helped to launch Andy Warhol from an obscure advertising post to his pre-eminence as the first pop-artist star. Despite some initial controversy and argument it did not take very long for any of these techniques to become accepted by the printmaking establishment – albeit that there are still some who mutter darkly about the illegitimacy of screenprinting as a medium for making fine prints.

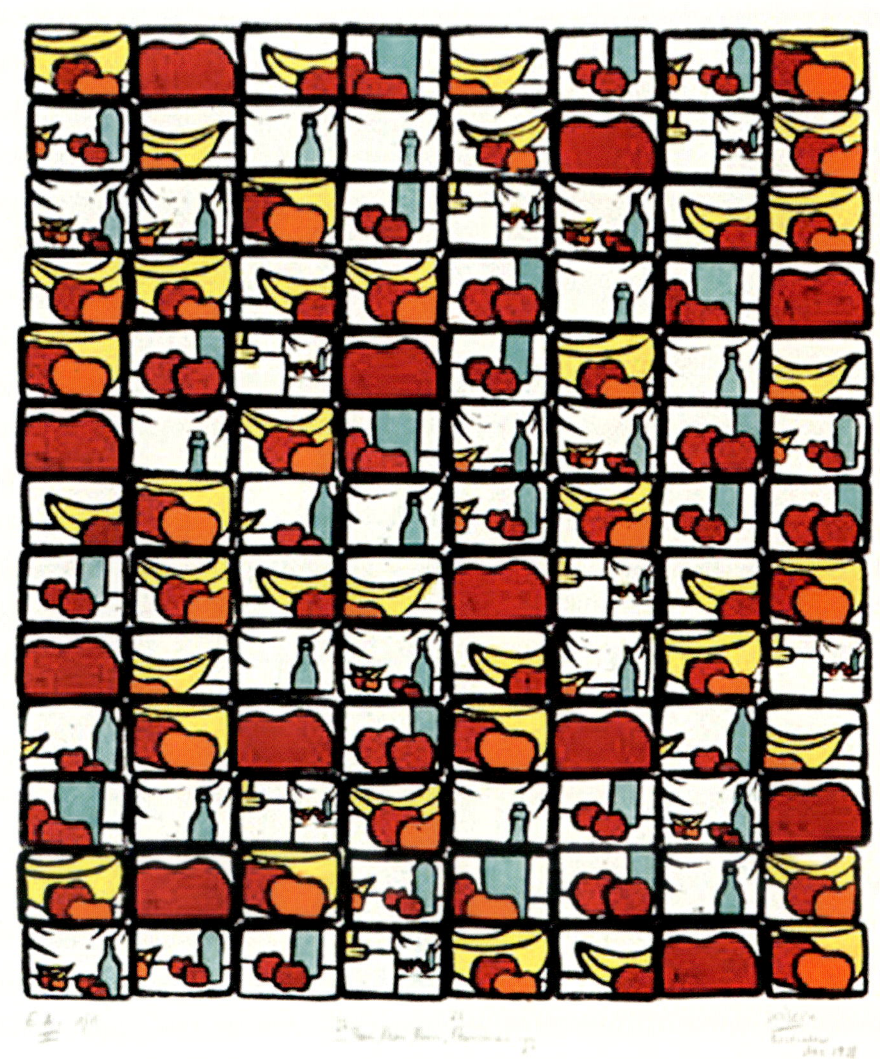

Kikie Crêvecoeur,
Improvisation, Pommes, 1988.
Gum print with colour, size unknown.

The emergence of digital image making and the digital printmaking that followed caused similar heated debate in the printmaking world, and much discussion about the nature of the print as an object. The inevitable spread of digital printmaking, and the fact that it is one of the most generally accessible techniques, has led to its becoming acceptable in all but the most traditional of international printmaking competitions and exhibitions. For most printmakers (except the hardest of hard-line traditionalists) digital processes have now become just another technique, to be picked up or discarded, used alone or in combination with other printmaking techniques. Also, the development of non-toxic printmaking methods and the emergence in recent years of new materials has brought about a great deal of change in the ways in which printmakers work, and the resulting works now have a greater vitality and range than ever before.

The new cutting edge of techniques of reproducibility began, as many other techniques have in the past, with new industrial technology. Ink-jet printers that print at very large scale, or on deep three-dimensional surfaces, allied to new substrates that include transparent plastics and fibrous fabrics, extend still further the possibilities for image making. There is even a commercially available, and affordable, ink-jet process for transferring images of any variety onto the icing on cakes and cookies, enabling the personalisation of confectionery in a hitherto unimaginable variety: your birthday cake can have not only your name but also your face on it. Industry and commerce have long had a symbiotic relationship with the visual arts, and computer technology has pushed this to new levels. It is inevitable that artists, particularly those who continue within the tradition of the artist-as-rebel, will embrace such possibilities and will change still further what can be done in the name of art: and with the ease of electronic communications their work will very quickly come to influence others.

Growth and change after all are natural concomitants to the whole business of being a human being, and particularly the business of being an artist. I suggest that this inevitable growth and change is moving printmaking towards a stronger position in the contemporary arts world, and towards a situation in which it will take on a more dominant role. It may be that at some time in the future printmaking becomes a less distinctly identifiable and separate medium, or range of mediums, and will incorporate itself quite naturally within the main body of contemporary art. While traditionalists will resent this and pull in the opposite direction, I believe there is a high degree of inevitability in the far-reaching changes that are coming. The nature of the visual arts even ten years hence may well be very different to what is familiar in 2010, and how it will look in 2050 is beyond safe prediction. To validate this assertion, we need only look back to the visual arts (and printmaking) in 1950, and then consider the point they had reached a mere 50 years later, at the turn of the millennium. The rate of change and technological progress has increased greatly even since then.

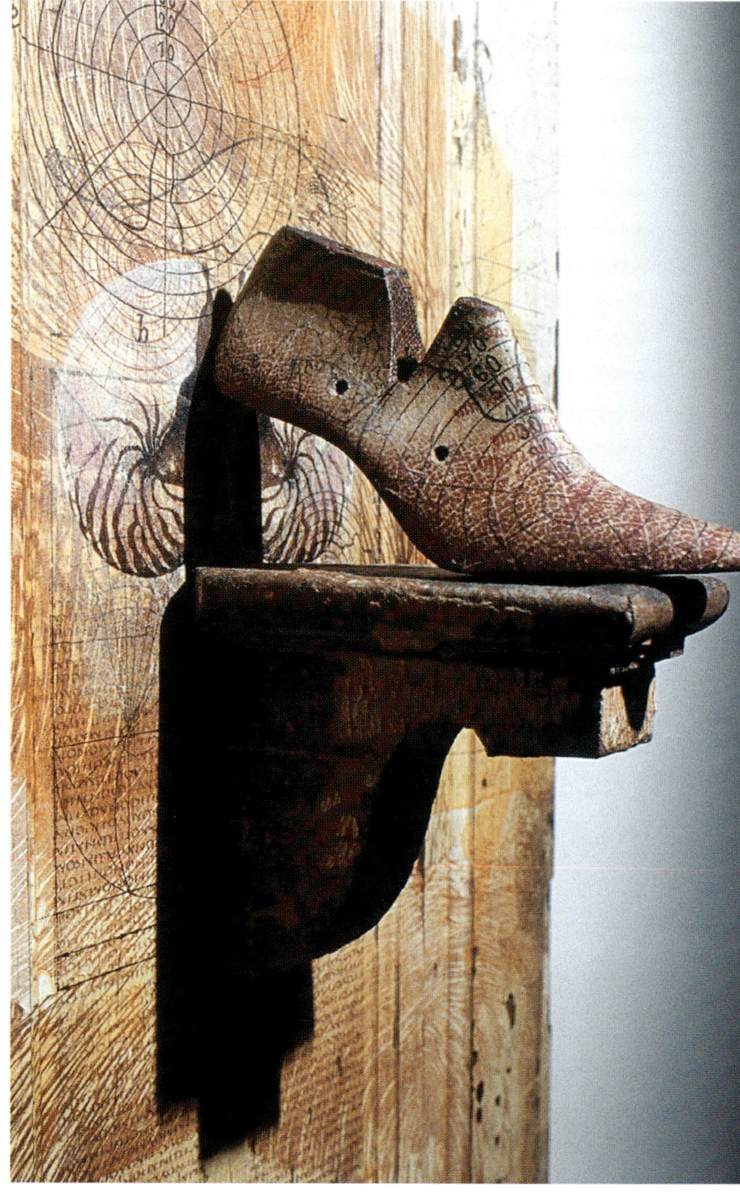

Patricia Olynyk, *Bound (detail), 2001.* Print and hand colouring on paper, laminated onto salvaged wood, 203 x 96 cm. 80 x 38in.

CRITICAL MASS

The term 'critical mass' derives from nuclear physics, and refers to the smallest amount of fissile material needed for a sustained nuclear chain reaction, whether to enable a weapon of mass destruction or for power generation in a nuclear reactor. The term is also used in the study of sociodynamics to describe the existence of sufficient momentum in a social system such that the momentum becomes self-sustaining and fuels further growth. In the latter instance the usual example given is of what happens when one person stops in a street and looks up, but nobody really takes notice – until a second, then a third, then more all gather and look up, by which time other passers-by will join them, until there is a crowd, all staring upwards, looking for something. Both these references have a relevance to the world of printmaking that, despite all the less welcome influences of a society going through many radical changes, continues to offer a deep insight into the ways in which committed artists can engage with that society, celebrating, criticising and illuminating it. Printmaking offers a wide range of views to the growing numbers of artists and art lovers who find that this area of contemporary culture does indeed offer a rich universe of mediums and styles, as well as shared working practices.

In relation to printmaking, 'critical mass' can also be considered in other ways. It can be thought of in parallel with the two definitions given above: as a number of artists working in a similar way whose collective work would sustain continuation and expansion of the discipline along the same lines; or as a group of artists, sufficient in number, whose work has broadly similar qualities and is exhibited or distributed in such a way as to attract the attention of a growing number of onlookers. But a further possibility can be considered: a critical mass of printmakers can be thought of as a number of artists whose work shares similar aims and intentions to criticise or comment on social injustice, inequalities, ecological and environmental threats, abuses of human rights, and so forth. Such a group – a mass that is critical – does not have to be concentrated in one place; indeed it can be thought of as being even stronger if dispersed across a number of countries or locations. An additional way of thinking about the term could be a group of artists whose work is of such importance as to deserve critical attention and acclaim. All these definitions can be applied, in various ways, to the artists featured in this book.

**Leonard Cohen, in 'Anthem',
on Live in London, 2009**

Printmakers are not generally amenable to being placed indiscriminately in affinity groups, due largely to their inherent position, now and historically, as innovators and, to a greater or lesser extent, outsiders or rebels. It is certainly true that printmakers tend to get together for the purpose of sharing workshop space and equipment, and through this there is a tendency toward collaboration on portfolio projects, exhibitions or print exchanges. It is equally true that, because of this, printmakers are perhaps more likely than painters or sculptors to be gregarious, gathering together at conferences and symposiums to share knowledge and learn from each other, or meeting up at the social events that accompany major print festivals and competition exhibitions. This natural gregariousness has created the international printmaking community and sustains both its current strength and continuing growth. For example, in 2009, the annual conference of the Southern Graphics Council, held in Chicago, attracted over 1800 participants, including many from countries beyond the USA. The wide range of panel discussions, presentations, workshops and exhibitions, as well as the numbers attending such events, demonstrated beyond question that printmaking and its allied fields has become a major interest to a lot of people. In future years this annual event will be billed as the SGC International Conference.

Allied with such shared activities are the print journals, some local, others national or international, through which word spreads. More recently there has been an exponential growth in online information about printmaking through dedicated websites, social networking sites and the like. The internet, in printmaking terms at least, is 'recreating the world in the image of a global village', as Marshall McLuhan described it in the 1960s, long before the development of personal computers and the internet, whose growth as a resource for printmakers, as with every other sphere of human activity, has been considerable. Two examples will serve to highlight how it can be used. *Printeresting* is an internet blog, based in the USA, about a wide range of issues and concerns about printmaking and associated matters; *Tradigital* is another blog, emanating from Scotland, which specialises in matters linking traditional and digital printmaking. Both are regularly updated and contain well-organised archives, as well as a good range of links to other websites of interest to printmakers.

The rise of social networking sites and the occasional concerns raised by them continue to be a subject of interest and comment in the print media. Two in particular are dedicated to printmaking. *Inkteraction*, a networking site dedicated to the work of printmakers, was initiated in 2007 by Cerisse Palalagi, a Māori printmaker living in New Zealand, and in the short time it has been online has gained well over 3,979 members (as of December 2009). As well as acting as a showcase for the work of artists all over the world it is proving valuable as a forum for discussion, and as the source of information on forthcoming exhibitions, competitions and events. In addition it is a powerful means for enabling artists at all levels to become part of a widespread international community of interest. *The Art of Democracy* website is more specialised: growing from the website of the same name, which was begun by Art Hazelwood and others in California, and fuelled by a growing sense of discontent and frustration during the dying years of the George W. Bush presidency, the site now has a relatively small (211, December 2009) membership, primarily in the United States, but offers interesting insights into printmaking. This networking site and the associated website give access to a wide range of images of prints and other materials that raise important questions about the nature of democracy and the role that artists can play in highlighting its failings and successes.

It is significant that the internet played a crucial role during the aftermath of the elections in Iran in the summer of 2009. While the broadcast networks found difficulties in reporting the protests and events, mobile-phone technology allowed for instantaneous transmission of still photographs and video clips into networking sites such as YouTube and Facebook, where incidents could be plainly seen almost as they happened. The death of Neda Soltan, captured on video by someone with a mobile phone, rapidly became a cause célèbre around the world, sparking further protests in many countries. One of the forms of protest was a web-based graphics program that allowed the creation of images not dissimilar to those produced by Shepard Fairey during the 2008 election campaign in support of the candidacy of Barack Obama as President of the United States. The *Printeresting* website carried a short section on this subject in July 2009 in which the term 'Metaprint' was used to define this new generation of images. The text included the following:

'Downloadable political prints… bring up some interesting issues. At the risk of overusing the 'meta' prefix, the Internet seems to be creating an era of Metaprint. Historically, images had to be distributed by physical means to affect change. The strategy of the political print was clear and simple: make a bunch of prints and get them out into the world so that your message reaches an audience. Now, distribution is executed through an electronic network and the message reaches the audience without a printed component. The print (if there is one) is the last step, a step farmed out to the audience as an optional souvenir.'

This is a point well made, and one that will doubtless continue to be controversial for some time to come. While it is not being claimed that images produced through means such as these constitute printmaking of the highest order, it is certain that they do contribute to a changed and changing context within which serious artists work and by which they are, to a greater or lesser extent, influenced.

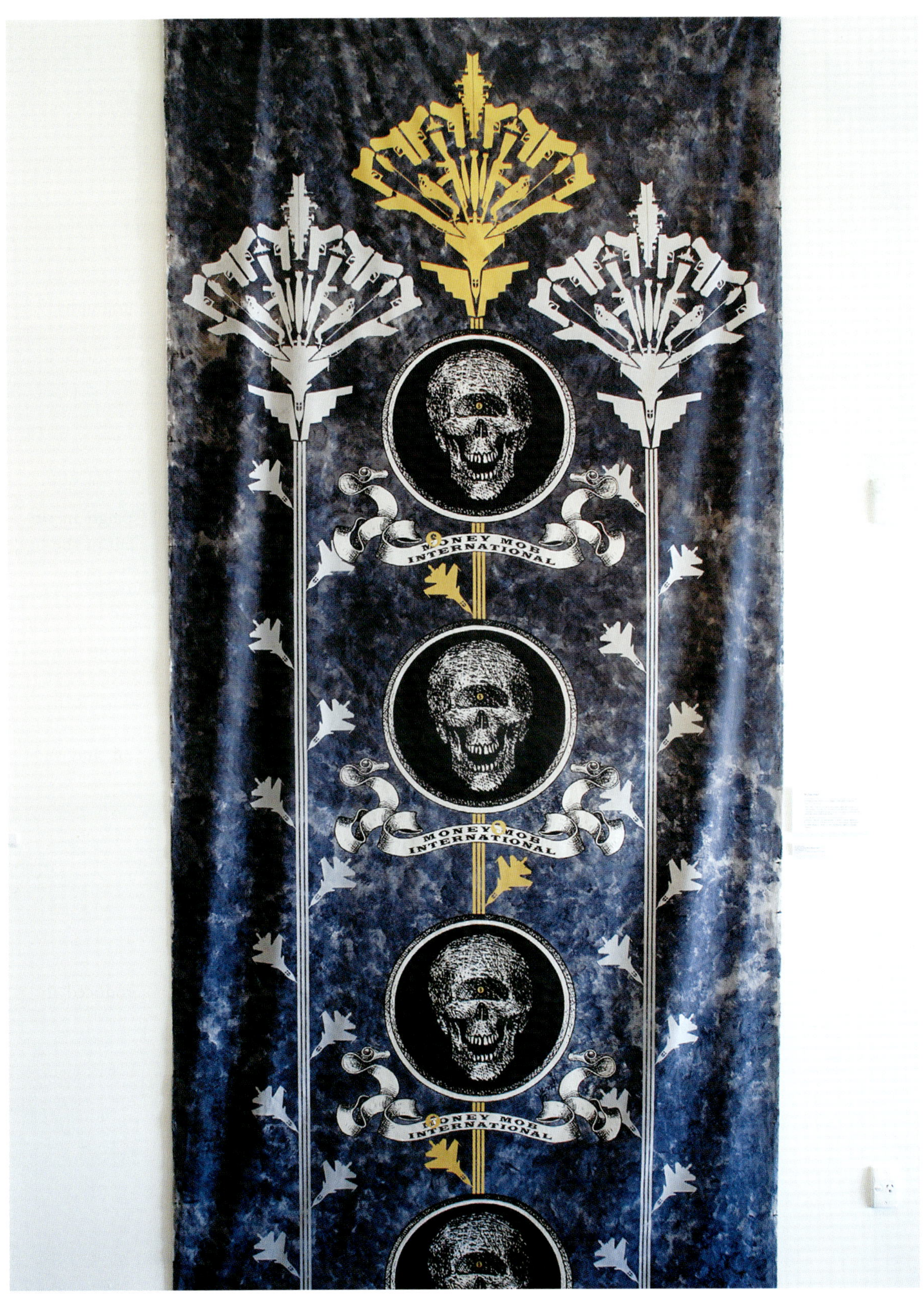

Michael Reed, *Money Mob International (from Drapes for Real Men series), 2009.*
Screenprinting, stencil and painting on textile, 1600 x 450cm.

THE CONTINUING METAMORPHOSIS

Not all contemporary printmakers are overtly critical in their work of the social and political situations around them, or indeed in other parts of the world. Some prefer to locate the centre of their work in other concerns: the striving for perfection of technique; the better articulation of an impression, an emotion or a real-world experience; a fusion of excellence in concept, execution and final image. The diversity of forms of expression and the continuing metamorphosis of those forms and mediums of expression are among the factors that make contemporary printmaking so continually fascinating.

While raw numbers alone cannot give a full picture of any situation, they do indicate levels of interest in events and educational courses. For example, the bare statistics of the entries for the 2009 Kraków International Print Triennale demonstrate that there is still a high level of interest in this major competition. The total of works submitted for consideration in the first (electronic) phase was 5467 works by 1643 artists; this was reduced to 1884 works by 599 artists by the qualification jury; the selection jury reduced it still further to 344 works by 227 artists (from 49 countries) to be included in the Kraków exhibition, leaving the awards jury the task of selecting 20 prints, each by a different artist, to receive recognition in the form of an award. It is significant that the general standard of works considered at the selection and awards juries stage was very high. The lengthy and rigorously democratic process of selection led to just over 6% of the total works submitted being shown in the exhibition, with less than 0.4% of them receiving an award. Such slender chances do not seem to deter artists from submitting work for this prestigious and long-established competition.

'Our world is increasingly left brain while we work and in our daily interactions, and no brain at leisure. Where does this leave the dreamy, intuitive, playful, creative right brain? For most people, their right brain is rafting a rough sea; shipwreck is likely.'

Jeanette Winterson, writing in the 'Books' section of The Times, London, August 2008

A country's education system is as subject as any other part of its infrastructure to increased economic pressures due to the global financial situation. In some places courses are being reduced or cut entirely; in others the pressure of interest is such that an increase in available places is being considered. For example, in one European academy of fine art in the summer of 2009, fewer than 16 applications were received for the course in sculpture, and fewer still for ceramics and or textiles, compared with nearly 60 for the course in printmaking. Of some interest is the fact that the majority of applications were from young women, a statistic repeated among printmaking courses in many other parts of the world. Again, such raw figures can give little more than an indication, but they are significant when taken in conjunction with the increasing numbers of people taking courses in printmaking centres and workshops around the world, or pursuing their own individual studies. They are evidence of an increasing level of interest in the medium, which shows no sign of diminishing. The reasons for this are many, but at a time in which (despite the numbers of tourists whose itineraries include a visit to a major gallery or blockbuster exhibition) interest in and support for some areas of the visual arts would seem to be waning, it is worthwhile noting the increasing support for printmaking. A combination of the range of available techniques, the alchemy by which a negative matrix can be turned into a positive print, the increasing range of materials and the prospect of producing an edition must all contribute to the medium's allure. So too must the need to work in cooperation with others, not only to learn but to produce the end results – a social factor that renders the making of a print a very different exercise from the essentially solitary business of making a painting or sculpture. To engage the creative half of the brain in a collaborative setting is clearly an attraction in a society whose citizens seem to be fighting an increasing sense of alienation.

Predicting the future is an increasingly risky business. Predicting the future of the visual arts is perhaps even more hazardous. A major feature that I was commissioned to organise and edit for the *Grapheion Yearbook 2008*, entitled 'The Memory of the Future', gave 47 artists and writers from 22 countries the opportunity to predict in word or image where they thought printmaking might be in the year 2028. The general consensus was that printmaking would still be alive and well, flourishing perhaps in different ways in a changed society, but still essentially an important part of the way in which human beings create works that communicate with intensity their hopes and fears, and their delight in the act of living in a challenging world.

The artists included in this book share that vision, approaching the making of prints in many different ways. They are from countries with different identities and cultural heritages, and from a number of generations. But while they have very different backgrounds, and their approaches to the making of art are wildly divergent, they share the conviction that the making of art, using techniques derived from printmaking, is quite simply what they have to do. The evidence of their commitment to this imperative is presented in this book.

DIVERSITY

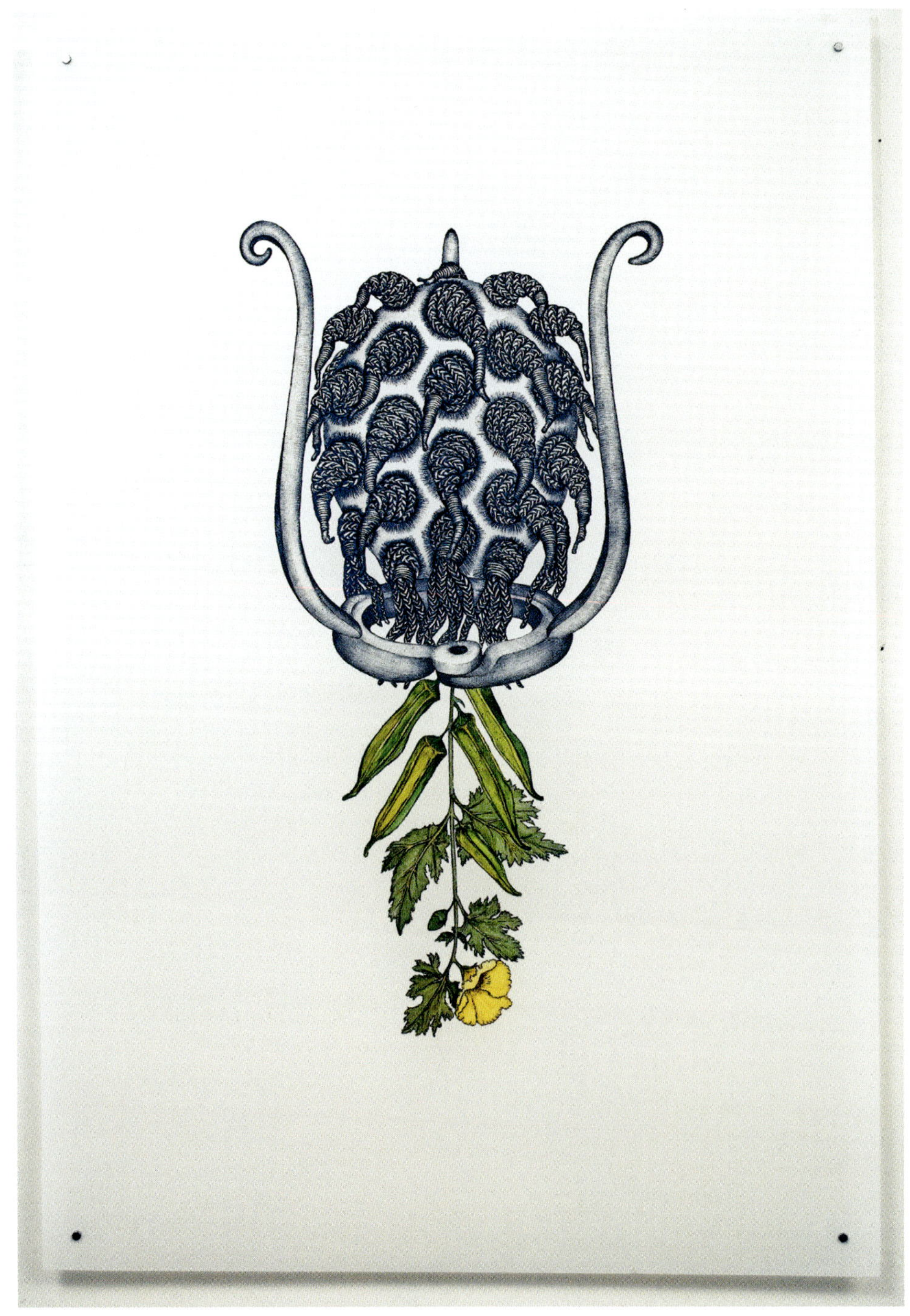

Joscelyn Gardner, *Hibiscus esculentus (Sibyl), 2009.*
Lithograph, with added watercolour, 91x 61cm. 36 x 24in
Photo: Norm Colton.

THE ARTISTS AND THEIR WORK

There is a growing diversity of approaches and works in printmaking at the current time. Attempting to categorise printmakers and their work is, to use a cliché, like trying to herd cats. While there are certain distinctions, mostly connected with the traditional techniques (by which, for example, a certain artist can be described as a wood engraver if that is her primary working technique), in the majority of cases printmakers in the early 21st century are far less easy to put into neat categories. In fact it is true that many people described by others as printmakers do not even see themselves in this way, but more as artists who just happen to use printmaking techniques as their main working practice, or as one technique among many that they use to convey their ideas. However, in order to give some form and direction to the selection of artists represented in this book, it is necessary to propose certain headings under which the wide range of their work can be considered.

The following part of the book sets out the scope of those headings, so as to give indications of the background to the artists' work. The headings are interspersed with anecdotes about some of the places visited during the research for this book, in whose cultural life printmaking is an important component. The artists whose work is described appear in alphabetical order according to their first name, reflecting the spirit of informality and cooperation that pervades the international printmaking community. At the end of the section on each artist is a website reference, where available, and a note of the main headings under which their work might be placed; other categorisations are, of course, equally valid.

It is intended that this part of the book should illuminate the complexity and diversity of the contemporary printmaking world, and offer ideas for further exploration. It is certain that the edges approached by contemporary printmaking are fluid and continually evolving – such is the richness of this area of the contemporary visual arts – and therein lies the challenge for anyone who wishes to explore it further.

NEW USES FOR OLD TECHNOLOGY

The principle of recycling is nothing new in the world of printmaking, as its history reveals. New techniques have been introduced throughout the development of the medium, driven partly by developments in technology and partly by developments elsewhere, including those in the social sphere, and in some cases because of a desire among artists to find a new means of expression. But the introduction of a new medium has not meant that older mediums disappear – far from it. On the contrary, new mediums have tended to lead to new ways of using or incorporating older techniques. While fashions in preferred printmaking methods come and go, and will continue to do so, there will always be artists who find a fascination in reviving older techniques, and perhaps in using them in new ways. Moreover, artists have a natural desire to experience the tactile qualities of materials and processes, and an equal propensity toward breaking rules whenever appropriate, if to do so enables a desired result to be achieved.

It is significant that the continuing exponential growth of digital printmaking techniques has not resulted in older and more demanding techniques fading from view: far from it. Many younger artists are finding out for themselves the pleasures and challenges of working with venerable and time-consuming techniques, and teachers report that students are showing new levels of interest in stone lithography, mezzotint and linocut, using them to express ideas that are – naturally enough – very different from those usually encountered with these processes. At the same time innovative ways are being found to use techniques in new combinations, with results that are tending to blur the once-clear divisions that made categorisation so much more straightforward. This can be seen as a healthy sign, as it allows artists a greater freedom in selecting the appropriate technique. What remains important, of course, is that all techniques should be thoroughly taught and learned; this is a continuing challenge for printmaking education.

One of the problems with established techniques such as etching was that the processes used were based on toxic chemicals, resulting in levels of risk that are unacceptable under current health and safety laws. As a response to these risks non-toxic methods have been developed, such as those investigated in depth by Nik Semenoff, and the development of the Solarplate™ technique by Dan Welden. Far from diminishing the appeal of traditional approaches these new developments have led not only to their continuation but also to the expansion of the available languages of expression that they offer. In the case of Solarplate™ there has been a widening of the appeal of etching and relief techniques through the ease with which this process can be used, as no chemicals are involved, and as the processing of the image requires only ultraviolet light and water. The rise of digital imaging has also brought about a revival in screenprinting, allowing this accessible technique to be used with complex images and more painterly approaches: once again, technological development has assisted the evolution of a working process.

New materials have always enabled innovative developments in printmaking. In recent years there have been many important changes, and a growing range of more sophisticated papers with specific attributes are being produced for all mediums. One particular growth area has been in the availability of papers from Japan, China, Korea and elsewhere, produced by hand using traditional methods but incorporating new textures and fibrous structures; and also produced on a more industrial scale but replicating some of the characteristics of handmade paper. Many of these are produced for specific purposes, including traditional papers made for use in ink-jet printers. Other forms of substrate have been brought to a high level of development and availability, including fabrics and plastic films that can be used across the range of techniques. There is also a growing interest in papermaking, and many artists are now making their own with specific purposes in mind that are directly linked to their work as a whole. This new synergy is very promising. At the same time new formulations of non-toxic inks, mediums and solvents have enabled a widening range of effects to be achieved, with longer guarantees of lightfastness and durability. The end result of all these developments is that artists now have access to a wider range of techniques and materials than ever before, enabling a continuing evolution in the ways in which printmaking can be used to express ideas.

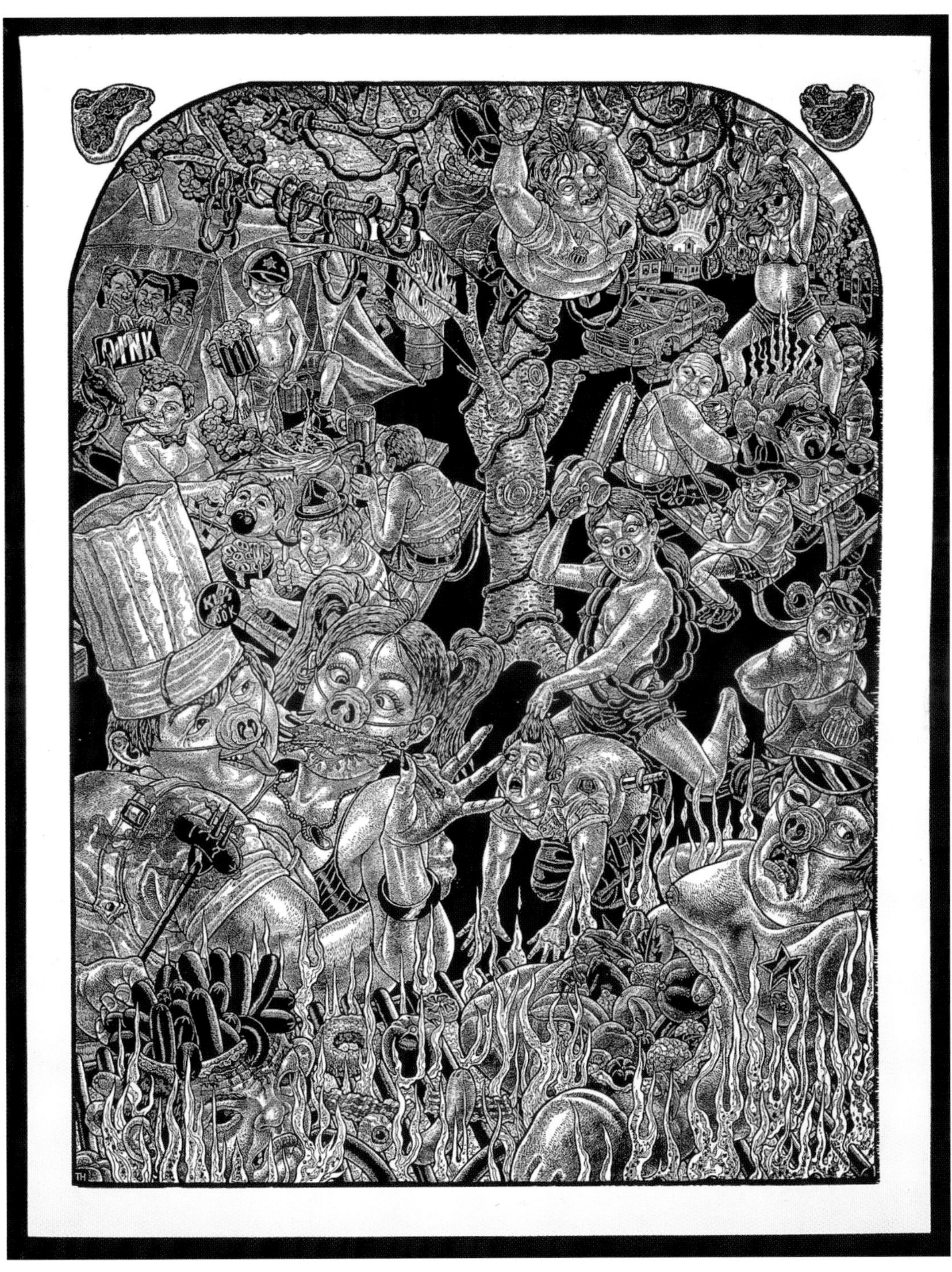

Tom Huck, *Pork Chop Suey: Oinktoberfest, 2007.* Woodcut, 132 x 100cm. 52 x 39in.

NEW TECHNOLOGY

The contentious debate as to whether or not digital printmaking could be considered legitimate, together with the arguments about the validity of digital images, has now largely receded. For most people involved in the printmaking world digital has become just another technique, as capable as any other of being used and developed on its own or in combination with other methods of making reproducible images.

A wide range of approaches to an increasingly adaptable technology has increased the accessibility of digital printmaking, and it is now firmly established across all sectors of the medium. Technology never stands still, and new developments continue to inspire artists. Rapid prototyping, for example, intended initially as a process for producing prototypes of objects and components in industry, has become a new area for artists to explore. Put at its simplest, the process is an evolution in ink-jet technology that applies a series of thin layers of material, usually plastic, to create a three-dimensional form. The possibility of utilising the process to produce three-dimensional prints has understandably attracted the attention of artists, and this is an area of research in a number of places. For example, at the Centre for Fine Print Research at the University of the West of England, processes being investigated include CNC (Computer Numerical Control) modelling derived from the world of engineering, which utilises laser and other cutting machines linked to computers to cut complex images in a variety of surfaces, including thick and layered papers; and 3D printing using plaster, or a powder and glue mixture or, more recently, ceramic to create large forms. CNC modelling is an ideal process for producing large-scale woodcut matrices for subsequent printing, or even as autonomous objects, which are infinitely and precisely reproducible. For example, Mike Lyon, in Kansas City, Missouri, works with a CNC router and a self-designed combined press and storage system to produce woodcut prints in sizes up to 190 x 114cm (75 x 45in.), and also works with CNC drawing techniques.

At the other end of the physical scale of prints is printmaking at micrometer scale. This involves a natural progression from the production of silicon chips for the electronics industry, and Erik Brunvand, working in Salt Lake City, Utah, is exploring the potential for making digital images on the spaces between the components on 1.5 x 3.0mm silicon chips, with 'drawn' lines of 0.5µ width (compared to the width of a human hair at 100µ). The apparent colour in the image depends on polarised light, but the images can only be seen after extreme magnification.

The comparative ease with which digital images can be produced has led some printmakers to investigate the possibilities of digital animation, for transmission across the internet, for projection in public places, or for distribution in the form of DVD discs. With these developments has come the possibility of incorporating live music and performance, extending the definition of printmaking into hitherto unthought-of directions. All such processes are mechanically reproducible in exact detail, and capable of production on demand, or in theoretically unlimited editions. With the rapid changes in technology, sophisticated 3D film production and projection is fast becoming a reality. The first consumer digital camera capable of producing 3D images became available in September 2009, and domestic 3D television is not far away; it is also inevitable that artists will continue to embrace with enthusiasm all such processes in an effort to find new ways of creating images.

There is a problem, however, within the confines of the traditional printmaking community, as artists known to be practising printmakers embrace new technologies and use them to produce works that are connected to and derived from their work in the more conventional mediums, but essentially so distinct as to constitute what diehard traditionalists would consider to be 'non-print'. This problem does not exist if printmakers position themselves, or are positioned, as artists: as such, all means of making art are possible and valid. In the end it is a matter of personal choice, and the answer to the problem will depend on whether or not you think there is a problem in the first place.

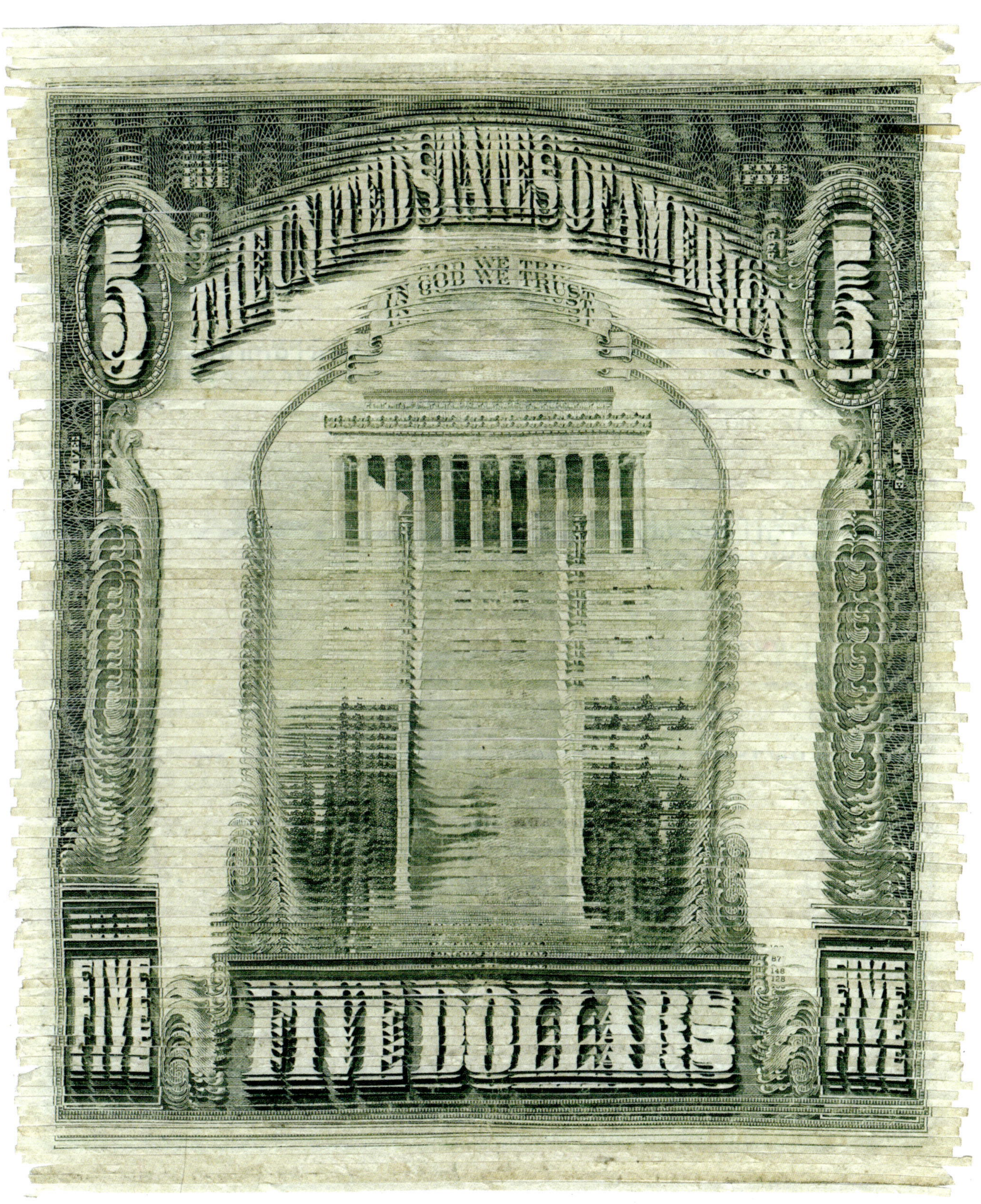

Curtis William Readel, *Stairway to Heaven, undated.* Collaged shredded US currency, size unknown.

St Louis, Missouri, USA

I am looking at the Mississippi River, 190 metres below me, from the top of the Gateway Arch on a Sunday in March. The river level is high and the water is brown; I can see why its nickname is 'The Big Muddy'. The surface wrinkles and shifts in the sunlight. A few hours ago I left a grey and cold Chicago; it was snowing on the way to the airport and the taxi driver was lamenting the unending winter while at the same time praising President Obama. Warm sunshine and a good friend, Lisa Bulawsky, greeted me when I arrived in St Louis, and I am now looking out over the city from the top of the Gateway Arch, an extraordinary stainless-steel parabolic arch, with Illinois across the river in one direction and Missouri stretching out across the plain in the other. Later that evening I eat with friends at Blueberry Hill, the celebrated bar and restaurant. As I go in I pass a showcase containing a famous guitar, and inside the walls are covered with memorabilia and amazing collections of all sorts. The excellent meal is as good as the conversation, and we talk about printmaking and life in St Louis. I am told that Chuck Berry, 83 years young, still plays there one Wednesday a month, appropriately enough in the Duck Room. I find myself wishing that it was Wednesday.

A tourist guidebook refers to Chuck Berry as one of the two great St Louis poets, the other being T.S. Eliot, a personal favourite, who was also born in the city. His grandfather was one of the founders of the city's Washington University, where I will be going to meet students and artists and to give a lecture. Later I will be visiting some artists in their studios in the former industrial area of the city. Overall, it is a short but memorable visit to one of the great cities of the Midwest. There is a strong sense of history there, and a vibrant arts life. As I leave Blueberry Hill later that evening I already begin to feel at home: some places are like that.

The printmaking department at the university is far-sighted and adventurous, and the standard of work that I am shown by the students is very high. Traditional and innovative techniques are used with equal enthusiasm, and there is no sign that they are following a predominant style. The influence of the professors is clearly good, encouraging the students to think and work in different ways, and it is clear from the conversations I have that they appreciate this. What is also interesting, and somewhat unusual, is that the department has for many years been the base of the Island Press, which was started by Peter Marcus during his time there and is still running with great success. The principle is that professional artists can spend time in the department to produce an edition of work, with some of the students working with them as assistants. In addition to this the press that is used is capable of producing very large prints. Unable to find a suitably large press, Peter Marcus designed and built one himself, and this design has now resulted in ten or more such presses being constructed, some of which can be found in the studios of other St Louis artists.

The demands of editioning very large prints are considerable, especially when the artists using the facilities of Island Press are working with techniques of printing and subsequent construction that are challenging in their own right. I am told that it is not unusual for the student assistants to work with the artist until well after midnight, but also that these students relish the experience.

The day after my lecture I am on the plane back to Chicago to catch the flight back to Britain. The broad river plain is in bright sunlight. The geometric fields are intersected by highways, and the watercourses show through as a palimpsest: the old land as it was before the settlers made their way westwards is still clearly visible, with the streams and rivers that drain towards the Mississippi standing out darkly beneath the ordered imprint of settlement and agriculture. Descending towards Chicago the high-rise towers of the downtown area are etched in silver against the deep blue of Lake Michigan.

LARGE-SCALE PRINTMAKING AND INSTALLATION

t was once the case that prints were of a size suitable for framing and hanging in a modest domestic interior, or for storage in folios, Solander boxes or cabinets, awaiting the loving gaze of a connoisseur. In recent years there has been a trend to make prints on an increasingly large scale, placing them far beyond the sizes that can be accommodated in the average home, and taking them into the realm of galleries and museums, as well as site-specific works for public locations. This change has brought about a led to a redefinition at many levels of the printmaking community of what a print can achieve. Scale, of course, is not everything, and my experience on international competition juries has shown that in many cases large size is all a print has. Nonetheless there are artists producing large-scale prints with both aesthetic value and contextual meaning.

The technical challenge of producing prints increases exponentially with size: while a small relief block can quite easily be used with a baren (burnisher) to produce prints by hand, larger and more complex prints require a traditional mechanical press. The limitation on the size of print that can be made depends on the roller width and the bed length, and while very large presses are available, they are also expensive, and so are more usually found in collaborative workshops or institutions. Extremely large prints require other means of production, such as a road roller. This method – which has been used in a number of places in the United States in recent years, and was first used in the UK at the Sidney Nolan Centre, near

Presteigne in Wales, in August 2009 – enables artists to explore the production of prints that can be as wide as the width of the roller (usually around 96cm/38in.) and whose length is limited only by that of the block or the available paper. Larger prints can be produced by combining separately made sections. At the University of Montana, Missoula, steamroller printmaking has become an annual public event, the 'Day of the Dead' being celebrated with the making of prints and their subsequent parade through the streets as a popular spectacle.

In the area of digital images it is possible to produce prints on an architectural scale. These often take the form of advertisements printed by light-jet machines on transparent micro-perforated vinyl, which are subsequently installed on the outside of high-rise buildings, or as self-clinging transparent sheets on the interiors of the windows. Artists are now beginning to use this technology, which holds the promise of further development.

In terms of gallery or museum installation there are many examples of artists using print techniques as part of their practice, combining smaller elements such as adhesive message notes and rubber-stamped images as ways of producing large images. In some cases projected images are used, produced through printmaking techniques and using the interior (or exterior) of a gallery as part of the process. Taken to an extreme such installation events in the open air can enter the realm of entertainment – a very long way indeed from the traditional print.

THE THIRD DIMENSION

Just as large-scale printmaking has led to new forms and approaches being used, so has the tendency to employ printmaking as part of the process of producing works in three dimensions. Some of these works take the form of sculpture, while others are elements in sculptural installations. It is possible through the use of the new technologies to produce prints that can be transferred to three-dimensional surfaces, or to produce images through the use of a printed matrix and etching on glass, combining these transparent elements to create sculptural forms. The use of printed colour images on glass and light transmitted by the display lighting can add another element to an artist's work.

Other artists using papermaking as part of their technique have developed ways of printing on and manipulating that paper, with or without other elements, to produce large-scale works that are truly three-dimensional, and subject to variation in their overall size on account of their flexibility and the methods employed in mounting them on walls or other surfaces. The techniques used to light such works can introduce a further variation in the ways they can be experienced or perceived. The mixing of mediums has liberated new ideas and new forms of engagement – with possibilities for considerable further exploration.

Paper arts in general offer different challenges to artists, in the form of pop-up books, three-dimensional tableaux and also machines that introduce the element of autonomous movement. All of these have a long history, usually mass-produced and incorporating traditional commercial printing methods. But with the growing international popularity of the making of artists' books (which in many cases include elements of printmaking) there are fresh possibilities for artists, and the opportunity to engage with new forms and ways of communication. Of interest to those printmakers who are used to making works as limited editions is the range of the forms of production and distribution that these three-dimensional mediums offer.

Belgrade, Serbia

I am boarding the JAT flight to Belgrade at London's Heathrow Airport, on my way to speak at the symposium organised by the Galerija Graficki Kolektiv as part of their 60th anniversary celebrations. I look through the window of the boarding tunnel at see that the plane carries the livery of Air Ivoire, and wonder where I will end up. It is clearly not a new plane, but the safety instructions on the backs of the seats are, reassuringly, in Serbo-Croat and English. The in-flight catering is basic and unmemorable. The flight path leads down to Belgrade across the broad flat plain of the Danube. The sun is in the west and reflects off the river, turning the blue of the river of the famous waltz into fiery gold among the darkening fields. Far below the fields make a patchwork of geometric strips in shades of green, bisected by a modern highway. It was across this landscape that NATO warplanes flew between March and June 1999 as part of the Kosovo campaign. Ten years later I am crossing the same landscape to meet artists and talk about printmaking. It is the first time that I have been so close to a place of recent conflict, and I feel uneasy.

I am met at the airport and immediately swept into a round of warm hospitality that is to last throughout the few days I will spend in Belgrade. I am driven to the hotel in the centre through a city in transition, with shiny new hotels among buildings from the recent and more distant past. My own hotel, which is in need of refurbishment, reminds me of similar establishments in Poland in the 1980s, echoing with physical reminders of another era, another century.

On the final day of my stay I am in a taxi, returning from a fascinating morning. Enthusiastic and friendly artists have taken me to visit FLU Centre for Graphic Art and Visual Research, a unique and dynamic centre for printmaking, followed by a visit to the University of the Arts, Belgrade. In rundown buildings among the green parklands outside the city centre the printmaking students – who are talented and optimistic – produce excellent work in a department that is certainly in need of greater funding. I am told that those students who wish to work with digital techniques have to work on their home computers, and then bring the work in for appraisal; the department desperately needs a digital studio.

Together with other speakers from the symposium who shared the same visit I have had a very good lunch at a restaurant whose name translates as 'The Printer', rather than 'printmaker'. On the way back to the centre the taxi crosses the river and passes a street with a number of buildings, among them the former army headquarters, still bearing the gaping holes caused by bombs and missiles in the 1999 attacks. A little further down the street we pass the United States Embassy; it resembles a fortress. Again I feel uneasy: there are poignant contrasts between the creative energy of the students and artists on the one hand, and, on the other, the political uncertainty that accompanies the evidence of a destructive past.

Later that evening we go to see the studio of Zoran Todovic, a well-established artist in Serbia, at the top of a high-rise building in Novi Beograd, out near the airport. He tells us that when such buildings were constructed in the former Yugoslavia the authorities determined that each such building should have one or more studios for artists; he also says that this no longer happens with new high-rise apartment buildings. There is a terrace from which there are far-reaching views out over the River Sava toward the city centre in one direction and across the Danube plain in the other. We spend some time looking at his work and talking about the present-day art scene in his country: he seems generally optimistic, despite the problems that artists face. Later we descend in the old-style elevator and walk to the next high-rise, only to ascend in an identical elevator to the apartment of the photographer and artist Branimir Karanovic and his family, where we are entertained to supper with great hospitality and warmth.

On the flight back to London I think about the contrasts I have seen. It would seem that the wounds in that country have not yet completely healed, and that there is still some political distance to be covered before Serbia becomes a full part of the new Europe. Despite the unease I felt at times, I have been impressed by the high standard of printmaking I have seen in the country, encouraged by the positive energy and the warmth and good humour of the artists and students that I have met, and enveloped in their generosity. From the evidence of even a short visit, it is apparent that the rapidly developing printmaking scene in that country deserves to be much better known.

POLITICS

There is a centuries-long and honourable tradition linking printmaking with politics. The natural function of the medium for making reproducible images enabled the production and distribution of prints that were critical of, or protested against, the perceived wrongs in society. The British tradition of caricature (the work of artists such as Hogarth, Gillray and Rowlandson), the biting satire of Daumier's prints, and the agitprop posters of the early years of Soviet Communism, among others, all either condemned what was considered bad or praised what was deemed desirable by social reformers (in the first two cases) or political rulers (in the last). The graphic strength of these works endures in spite of the passage of time. Just as the early Christian Church patronised the work of anonymous medieval artists in stained glass, and later the work of artists it favoured from the early Renaissance onwards, to convey Biblical messages to the largely illiterate congregations, so too has the work of artists been harnessed more recently to convey ideological messages across borders in simple forms requiring little use of language.

It is not surprising, therefore, that many artists in the 20th and 21st centuries have used the accessibility of printmaking to comment on or criticise the world in which we live. One of the most striking aspects of the successful campaign to elect Barack Obama to the US Presidency was the use made of the work of Shepard Fairey, whose strong and simple graphic images of Obama rapidly became iconic, and a source of great inspiration to many of the voters who had in earlier years felt alienated by a system that appeared not to value them.

For a long time, and during the past 50 years in particular, the arts have been used to an increasing degree by organisations and individuals seeking change in society. A strong example of this is Art for Humanity, based in Durban in South Africa. The work of AFH grew from the campaigns of Artist for Human Rights, which led to the production of the Images of Human Rights print portfolio, exhibited in venues across the world, and the subsequent development of the Artist Proof Studio, which sought to empower members of all communities in the country through the arts and in particular through printmaking. Powerful use was made of the work of printmakers and poets in the campaign to raise awareness of the AIDS epidemic, combining image and text (one inspired by the other) on large billboards throughout the country. AFH now works on a wide scale to take this work further, with a major project and conference planned to coincide with the 2010 Football World Cup in South Africa.

There is no doubt that the links between the visual arts and politics will be strengthened by the pervasive presence of the internet and the ease with which complex messages can be transmitted, enabling them to be quickly comprehended in the Babel that is 24-hour rolling news and the media inundation of contemporary life. A picture, truly, can be worth a thousand words, and does not need translation.

POST-COLONIALISM

European imperialism in the 18th and 19th centuries, boosted through the period of the two world wars and then more or less abandoned by the end of the 20th century, has left a deeply rooted legacy in many countries, among which are Australia, New Zealand and former dominions such as South Africa. The political shifts in these countries following the fading of empire, and the rise in the determination of their indigenous peoples to reassert their rights to the land and their own culture, constitute a strong force which has found its voice through the arts. The determination of the Aboriginal nations, the Māori and the nations of black Africa to take their rightful place in their countries of origin, to gain education and a political voice, and to re-establish themselves as rightful owners of their traditional lands, has led to major initiatives in the dramatic and musical arts, and a strengthening presence in the visual arts. This is part of the movement for peace and reconciliation. Such reassertion and striving for equality is to be warmly welcomed as it goes some way to righting the many wrongs of empire.

At the same time as this has been happening there has been an increase in the consciousness of their ethnic identity among many artists of European origin, and others with roots far beyond the countries in which they now live. Their awareness of and identification with the rights of the indigenous first-nation peoples has been important in encouraging them to find their own place in the multinational cultures of these countries. At the same time many artists, in all mediums, have questioned the history and the contemporary politics of the countries in which they live, and many have sought through their work to find some sort of catharsis, and some deeper understanding of the environment around them.

The well-known and deeply respected identification of first-nation peoples with the natural environment, and its place in their mythologies and belief systems, has inspired artists of European and other immigrant origin to re-examine the ways in which they relate to the landscape and the environment. In those countries with a colonial legacy, the descendants of the colonists have sought to find ways to reconcile themselves with the history of their ancestors, and its profound and often corrosive impact on the history and culture of the original inhabitants. The situations in which they work, and the degree to which their art can explain and illuminate the nature of their identification with the countries in which they now live, offers a new experience to help those who live in Europe and elsewhere to their own understanding of the nature of empires in general.

At the same time it is clearly evident that the shifts in consciousness of both the native and the incoming peoples has led to a spirit of sharing skills, ideas, knowledge and positive cooperation on cultural projects, in all mediums of the arts. Such changes have a deeply political aspect, but are also derived from a sense of shared humanity, and the need to finds ways to coexist and prosper in the globalised society to which we all now belong. For all who encounter such work, there is the invitation to re-examine their own identification with the history and culture of the places in which they themselves live. The history of colonialism, like globalisation, affects all countries and peoples, and a growing awareness of shared histories and challenges offers positive hope for development in the 21st century.

Viinistu, Estonia

I am in the capital of Estonia for the Impact conference in October 2007. Tallinn has a wonderful medieval old town where ultramodern interiors are fitted into the well-conserved exteriors of historic buildings in ways that seem totally appropriate. Estonia is the smallest of the Baltic States, and its capital city offers a unique view into the history of this far northeast corner of Europe. Traces of previous centuries and occupations are clearly visible as remnants of the past. I take a short and easy walk from a modern hotel past relics of the soviet era, as well as buildings dating from 18th and 19th centuries, and into the medieval centre: few other cities can offer such richness within such a small area. Just outside the centre is the park where Peter the Great built the Kadriorg Palace for his mistress Marta Skavronskaya, the serving girl who later became Catherine the Great. Close by is the new Kumu Art Museum at which the Impact 5 Printmaking Conference is being held. At the same time this ultramodern museum is hosting Political Poetical, the 14th Tallinn Print Triennale. The conjunction of the two events produces a high level of interest and activity over the five days of the conference, which is being attended by artists and writers from all over the world. It is another occasion when the international printmaking community comes together to celebrate the arts of print, to share ideas and techniques and to discuss some of the issues affecting world printmaking.

On the Sunday of the conference I join the excursion by bus with other delegates to the village of Viinistu on the edge of the Baltic, where there is a unique arts centre, less than an hour's journey by road from Tallinn. There are probably no other arts centres in the world housed in the remnants of a Soviet fish-processing plant, as is the case here. The centre is the result of the vision, energy and financial support, of Jaan Manitski, who was born in the village in 1942 but subsequently spent most of his working life in exile, for a major part of that time as the financial manager of the pop group ABBA, before returning to his birthplace after the fall of Communism. He decided to buy up the site of the collective farm and fish-processing factory, to demolish some buildings so as to open out a view of the sea, and to convert others for arts use. The former storage and factory buildings now house a gallery of Estonian painting, a space for drama and music performances, a hotel and a restaurant, all filled with 20th-century and contemporary Estonian art. I spend some time in two former water tanks, huge iron cylinders converted with track lighting to show exhibitions of prints. These prints are from the second half of the 20th century, including works by celebrated Estonian artists such as Silvi Liiva, Henno Arak and Evi Tihemets, the last of whom is a senior artist who had the day before taken me on a personal visit to an exhibition of her continually evolving and innovative work in the Parliament House. There are interesting distinctions in the work on display in Viinistu – those from the Soviet era convey a different sensibility from works produced since 1989 – but throughout there is a high level of skill and vision.

Fascinating though the visit is, we are not there just to look at art: there is work to be done. Loit Jõekalda, one of the conference organisers, has decided that a maze of stones should be laid in the design of a spiral labyrinth, an installation intended to mark the Tallinn's hosting of the conference; the work of laying out the stones is to be rewarded with lunch. The site is on a raised level area close to the edge of the sea. A circle of deep, gritty sand some ten metres in diameter has already been laid and levelled. There are large piles of stones, some fist-sized, others the size of small boulders. We set to work; some of the stones can barely be lifted. Loit directs operations, and also carries enormous stones from the piles to the platform to encourage us by example. The late October air is clear and cold, the sky a piercing blue and the sea calm and silent, all the way across the sea to Finland: it feels like an edge of the world. In what seems a short time the labyrinth is laid out, needing only slight adjustment to create the spiral that winds from the edge to the centre and back again. The builders of the maze – along with those who took the photographs and those who made the video – walk in a line to the centre and back again, along the interlaced curves of the spiral, treading the sand into a pathway. The work is done, the lunch has been earned and we leave the prints of our feet in the sand.

SCIENCE

Although science and art have at times in the past been treated as two separate realms of human thought and activity, they are in face close together, and in fact can be considered two parallel disciplines, with the distance between them varying from very close indeed to somewhat further apart, depending on a range of circumstances. The depiction of science by artists is not a rare thing – consider, for example, Joseph Wright's painting, *Experiment with an Air Pump*, which captures much of the essence of the Age of Reason. In addition the work of scientists has at times had a strong influence on the direction of the visual arts, as happened in the mid-19th century with the discovery of aniline dyes. These were intended primarily for the fabric industry, providing vibrant new colours to catch the eye of fashion in Europe. This was a time of great optimism, with the successful exploitation of the spoils of imperial expansion, such as cotton, giving Europeans a sense that their culture was superior. But the new dyes also led to the manufacture of a brighter range of oil colours, which were sold in what at the time were revolutionary metal tubes that allowed artists greater freedom to work en plein air: the rapid rise of Impressionism was one of the main results of this development. In the early 20th century the achievements of science and technology became a source of fascination for artists, leading to the work of the Futurists and the art of the Jazz Age, with its connections to modernist architecture, mass-produced furniture, the excesses of the automotive industry and the burgeoning world of civil aviation. Artists in considerable numbers also responded to the destruction of the technologically driven wars of the 20th century: science and art were never really that far apart.

Artists are explorers of the visual world and are therefore drawn to other areas of human research and the scientific exploration of the natural world. The development of photography in the early decades of the 19th century is one example of this connection that, far from signalling the death of painting, has subsequently been one of the central driving forces in the visual arts, with printmaking being prime among the mediums so driven. Photography is after all a form of printmaking in itself, an important generator and manipulator of images and an active constituent of mixed-medium practice. Recent developments in computer imaging have accentuated the relationship between photography and printmaking, becoming one of the main integral factors in the making of digital images.

There are connections between art and medicine that extend back over centuries into the past. Anatomical studies were central to a classical art education, and life drawing, for which a good understanding of human anatomy is essential, still forms a major part of the structure of academically based art education. More recently, artists have been drawn to the artificial worlds of science fiction, to the science/art interface of cybernetics and cyborgs, and to a fascination with prostheses and other scientific means for enhancing human performance. The role of artists such as H.R. Giger in establishing the new canon of science-fiction films has been of major importance. The synergy between art and science looks set to continue.

ENVIRONMENT

The visual arts have an important advantage over other forms of expression in dealing with the environment. Just as global environmental issues are at the forefront of much debate, both academic and political, so too are the means by which the arts are mobilised to protest about or deal with such issues. The visual arts have a distinct advantage over, say, literature or theatre, in that they are not dependent on a verbal or written language, being comprehensible across frontiers. It is therefore of little surprise that much of the visual art dealing with environmental matters uses a symbolic or illustrative language to communicate ideas. The graphic arts, printmaking foremost among them, have much to contribute to this important area of international discourse.

But outside the realm of protest and polemic the environment is also a rich source of ideas for artists, as it has been since the emergence of art as a form of ritual, celebration or communication more than 40,000 years ago. Sensitivity to the creative process carries with it a strong likelihood that artists will draw inspiration from the natural world around them. The history of the depiction of landscape and of human intervention in that landscape is one of the most extensive archives in the visual arts. Contemporary artists are continuing that process, sometimes in radical ways, sometimes using their art to comment on environmental matters, and sometimes as an act of homage or reverence to the planetary ecosystem upon which humankind depends (and upon which humankind continues to wreak much havoc).

Depicting the landscape can be a simple act without any deeper meaning, or it can be a metaphor for the problems we encounter in living with each other. It can highlight environmental issues, or celebrate the joys of the turn of the seasons or a journey through the landscape. It can describe the dilemma of coming as a stranger to an already ancient land and attempting to reach an understanding of what went before, and through this of finding a way to coexist with the past.

Depictions can be literal, or abstract, or symbolic, taking the form of figurative depictions or abstract derivations. Depictions can also be in the form of diagrams or maps, those symbolic representations that are predicated upon the need to know our location in space as well as how to get where we want to go.

It is unsurprising that one of the primary means of illustrating landscape is through the medium of photography, or a process derived from this, as it is through the medium of photographs – principally, the holiday snaps – that many people record where they have been, in an attempt to remember not only what they saw but also what they felt while they were there. This seems to be a basic desire among the majority of people who travel to other places for recreation or vacation. For those who inhabit the landscape, often in remote parts of the world, such depictions are unnecessary: being of the land they have an intuitive understanding of the landscape and need no visual reminders. But for those artists who travel to such places, reminders are necessary, and the knowledge and beliefs of the people they meet in such places can be a powerful source of inspiration. Thus it is that depictions of the landscape can be literal or symbolic, metaphorical or illustrative, creating links and making commentary, sharing experience with those who choose to share. Water flows and the land abides; the artist is the traveller who pauses in reflection before making some record of where she or he has been, so that others may know. In some ways this is not so very different in essence from those who know the landscape like the back of their hand because it is part of their Dreaming.

Thessaloniki, Greece

Thessaloniki is a city by the sea. It clings to a series of hills on the northern edge of the Thermaic Gulf of the Aegean, sheltered by the hills of Macedonia to the north and Halkidiki to the east. This major city, the second largest in Greece, has the reputation of being the country's cultural centre. Rising from the edge of the gulf to the Byzantine walls above the Old Town, Thessaloniki has been of strategic importance since the time of Phillip II of Macedonia. Thirty miles or so to the west of the city across the plain of Thessaly is the major archaeological site at Vergina containing amongst other things the remains of Phillip's tomb. A museum celebrating the life of this extraordinary historical figure, and containing a wonderful array of artefacts, has been constructed beneath the tumulus in which the tomb was discovered. To see the tomb and some of its contents, dating from the King's assassination at the wedding of his daughter Cleopatra in 336BC, is to be brought into close and moving contact with this distant point in history. Since that time the region has been a crossing place and a meeting point for many cultures, and Thessaloniki contains a remarkable range and number of historical sites and buildings, Greek, Roman, Byzantine and beyond. The nature and history of the city has created a melting pot of culture, including a celebrated local cuisine that blends many national characteristics.

In October 2008 the sun is still warm enough for me to enjoy the city and its delights. I am visiting this part of Greece for the first time, to be part of the jury for the inaugural Thessaloniki Printmaking Triennial. This event has been organised at the Helios Printmaking Centre in the Neapolis district of the city under the direction of artist and professor Xenophon Sachinis, a tireless and enthusiastic promoter of international printmaking exchanges. The triennial exhibition has the title Bridges Between the Mediterranean and the Baltic, and links these two seas through the work of a wide variety of artists and printmakers. The Helios Centre sits on the main road through Neapolis, and is readily distinguished by the street-art mural that covers the outside of this former industrial building. The competition, and the resulting exhibition, is a great success, with the opening evening event being thronged by a predominantly young, student audience. Thessaloniki is a major university centre, and later that year and into early 2009 the city would be rocked by the riots that broke out in several Greek cities. But that evening is about a celebration of printmaking; there is enthusiasm, and congratulations for the organisers from everyone – students, art lovers and municipal authorities alike. The municipality has been generous in its support for the triennial, and the Mayor is delighted by the outcome.

Returning to the hotel by car the following evening our host is surprised by the throng of police and security guards outside. It turns out that the entire team and officials of the Panathinaikos Athinai football team are staying there before their match against PAOK FC at the Toumba Stadium the following day – an important event in the wider culture of the city. The hotel is very secure that night. The match will be a goalless draw.

On another day I conduct a seminar for the printmaking students at the Aristotle University: their energy and the high quality of their work is gratifying, and it is clear that great steps forward have been taken in developing a challenging and wide-ranging course. One of the students I speak to is from Estonia, now spending a semester at the university under the Erasmus programme of the European Union: she is enthusiastic about the value of exchanges and has already fallen in love with the city. This department is no place for a goalless draw – the achievements already mark it as a winner.

As the aircraft rises into the sky on the flight back to London the geographic location of the city becomes clear, with the blue hills surrounding the wide plain at the edge of the sea. I can also see two major football stadiums. Mostly I am thinking about the long cultural history of the city at the edge of the wine-dark sea of legend. The work of the students at the university, and the works shown at the Triennial, are bold and welcome steps into the future.

MEMORY

Printmaking, by its very nature, is a process-driven form of creation, through which an intended image is converted into a matrix from which one or more prints can be made. In this sense it can been seen as operating in a similar way to the cognitive and psychological processes involved in turning experiences into memories, from which recollections or records may be made: memory becomes the matrix.

The making of art, in whatever the chosen medium, is a means whereby an experience and the memory of that experience can be shared with others. For centuries this has been one of the main driving forces for artistic creation, a process accentuated by the development of photography, which some thought would be a shortcut but which instead has proved to be more complex, becoming a medium through which the experience can be mediated before being shared through the medium of print or transparency or, with the coming of digital media, a computerised image. Those who assert that printmaking has to involve a high degree of manual labour and drawing skills, as well as the transfer from matrix to substrate – and that photography cannot therefore be included either directly or in any other way, may by using these very narrow criteria have a point. But since photography usually (but not always) involves the production of a print from a matrix (the negative or the digital file), it has in recent years become admissible as a form of printmaking in a number of international competitions.

The making of art can also be an act of remembrance, or celebration. In this manifestation it can achieve a powerful potency that reaches from the heart of the artist's mind directly to the heart and mind of the observer, communicating directly and without the need for explanation. It can achieve an immediacy that fulfils the sense of the Greek word 'methexis' ($\mu\varepsilon\theta\varepsilon\xi\iota\varsigma$) – meaning the 'moment of becoming one', with the word, the music, or in this case the image. One specific example of this is the power that can be achieved through images relating to a profound human experience, for example some of the images produced in response to the Holocaust.

Another aspect of memory in art comes through the use and depiction of palimpsest. This term was originally applied to a manuscript, such as those written on papyrus or parchment, on which more than one text has been written, with the earlier writing incompletely erased. The term can also be applied to the experience of landscape, where evidence of the past can be perceived in, for example, crop marks; or to a drawn, painted or printed image revealing something else beneath its surface. Palimpsest and memory go naturally together, as newer memories supplant those that lie beneath, rendering them less easy to recall. The visual arts can make powerful use of this concept, and printmakers frequently use palimpsest within their work, enhancing the nature of the surface through the creation of visual depth.

THE NEW GENERATION

The work of printmaking is characterised by collaboration in a way not found in other areas of the visual arts. The need to share equipment, due among other factors to the high cost of presses, leads naturally to the sharing of techniques and tricks. There is also the relationship between the artist/printmaker and the master printer or technician, whose skills have been developed to a high level. Add to this the relationship between the student and the teacher, and the strong link between different generations becomes clear. While in earlier times there existed a form of teaching based on the 'do as I do' approach, in recent years there has been a growing tendency for the teacher to become the enabler – to echo the words ascribed to Buddha, 'not the way, but the finger pointing the way'.

The strict academic process, based on the idea of master and apprentice, formed the mainstay of the art education process in some countries for many hundreds of years. Students would follow a general course in the early part of their studies before making a decision about which professor or professors they would choose to guide those studies to completion. In Poland, for example, this allowed for something akin to a family tree to be constructed, whereby through the details of a artist's CV, in which credit was accorded to the professor from whose studio the artist graduated, a continuous link could be traced back to the end of the 19th century – for example, to the painter Malczewski and to his teacher, Matejko. This traceability of influence has all but disappeared, as noted by Professor Witold Skulicz, the Director of the Krakow International Print Triennale, in his notes in the web bulletin of the Triennale in reference to the 2006 Grand Prix of Young Polish Print. He wrote, 'We have witnessed a definite end of the school of master professors whose artistic shadow was cast over the semester and even graduation work of their students. Quite recently we have also witnessed the end of the primacy of professors creating (sometimes intentionally) their artistic schools in order to boost their own prestige.'

This change was inevitable, as students in many parts of the world are now identifying with very different methods of communication. Rebecca Beardmore, a professor in Australia, remarked at the Southern Graphics Conference in Kansas City, Missouri, in 2007 that many of her students showed no real interest in the concept of exhibiting their work in galleries, preferring to use the online communities offered by MySpace and Facebook, within which works can be exhibited and shared with an immediacy and international reach not offered by conventional galleries. Such changes are inevitable and the increase in electronic mobility provided through the internet will only lead to the expansion of such developments in the future. But while some students will reject, as they always have, the frameworks of the past, others are showing a real desire to learn what some might have considered are techniques outmoded by the promise of digital printmaking. In 2007 a student at Capilano College in Vancouver, Canada, took me to task following a seminar in which I had extolled the promise of digital printmaking, telling me that I was wrong. Asked which medium she worked in, she pulled open a drawer and showed me a masterly set of mezzotints. This interest in the more traditional techniques is noticeable in many other institutions. Nothing, it seems, is as predictable as might have been thought, and change is to be expected in unexpected ways.

This new generation of artists (as with all new generations before them) has the right to choose what to accept and what to reject: they are the new avant-garde. The difference is that they live in a world in which the 'new electronic interdependence' that Marshall McLuhan wrote of in the 1960s has truly 'recreated the world in the image of a global village'. Printmaking continues to be a good indicator of the directions in which the contemporary arts are heading as we move into the second decade of the 21st century.

Seoul, South Korea

The flight from Manchester to Dubai is uneventful. The plane lands at Dubai around midnight and I join the other passengers to disembark, board a bus, drive across the sand-strewn airport to the terminal building, only to have to check in for the next leg of the flight, pass through security to a waiting lounge before boarding another bus to drive back across the airport and board the plane for Seoul. The plane has a camera in the fuselage pointing directly downwards, linked to the entertainment screens on the backs of the seats. I watch as the camera shows the Himalayas far beneath, lit by the rising sun. The images of the mountains are spectacular – clear blue on the night side and golden yellow on the sunrise side. I watch the screen for nearly an hour before drifting back to sleep. Later the plane descends in gathering darkness over the Yellow Sea to the huge airport at Incheon.

The hour-long journey through the dark to the city is along a broad highway that leads to a city centre full of light. Despite the exhaustion of a long journey I am fully awake as my first impressions of an Asian city flood in – the colours, the signs in Korean and English, older buildings glimpsed between the glittering new high-rise towers. Over the next week the impressions accumulate and the richly visual culture of the city emerges, as I am guided by the artist Chang-Soo Kim through the art world of Seoul to see exhibitions and meet artists, and to give some lectures. I watch the changing of the guard at the palace at Deoksugung, with the bright traditional costumes, the drums and flutes, the flags and banners, and the ritual shouting of orders all performed in front of the ornate and beautifully conserved gateway with its sweeping roofline; and then I watch the guard march off with military precision, only to wait patiently for some minutes at the road crossing with all the other pedestrians until the lights change.

On a day of soft rain I visit the Royal Palace at Gyeongbokgung, a vast enclosure of parkland, lakes with pavilions, walls and buildings, all laid out with precision in compounds beneath the mountains that surround the city and at the foot of Bukhansan mountain that rises behind. Even on a dull day the colours of the pavilions and surrounding walls are striking – soft reds and greens, enlivened by vivid blue, yellow and pink, with ornate carving, decorated tiled roofs, and all combining to give a pervasive feeling of calm and a strong sense of the centuries of history and intrigue that evolved within the buildings in the heart of this busy city. I am taken to Insadong, a bustling street of antique dealers, traditional teahouses, and art materials shops with amazing displays of pigments and brushes and ink-stones and paper, and souvenir sellers with astonishing varieties of products. The teahouses provide oases of calm, and the myriad restaurants of the city demonstrate the wonderful variety of Korean cuisine. Museums are visited: the Seoul Museum of Contemporary Art with its impressive collection of contemporary Korean and world art, the Seoul National Museum that contains a world-class collection of exhibits in a new building that redefines the museum experience, and the Museum of Photography on the upper floors of the Hanmi Tower, at which is being staged an exhibition of the 'Further' portfolio of prints generated by the artists in my book Printmaking at the Edge. I look out from that museum over the city to the mountains beyond, with the Olympic Park beneath me, with the Freedom Gate and the surrounding semicircle of international flags lit brightly in the autumn sunlight.

The vitality and variety of Korean printmaking is beyond doubt, with high levels of skill matching highly original creativity. It is clear that the high standard of teaching printmaking and art within the universities has much to do with this fact. The city and its long culture provide a powerful context for work that links tradition to innovation, matching perfectly the Korean sensibility that honours the Confucian traditions while at the same time driving forwards at the cutting edge of technology. On the return journey there is a longer stopover at the airport in Dubai but somehow, after the experience of Seoul, there is little that attracts.

When I land in Manchester, it is raining.

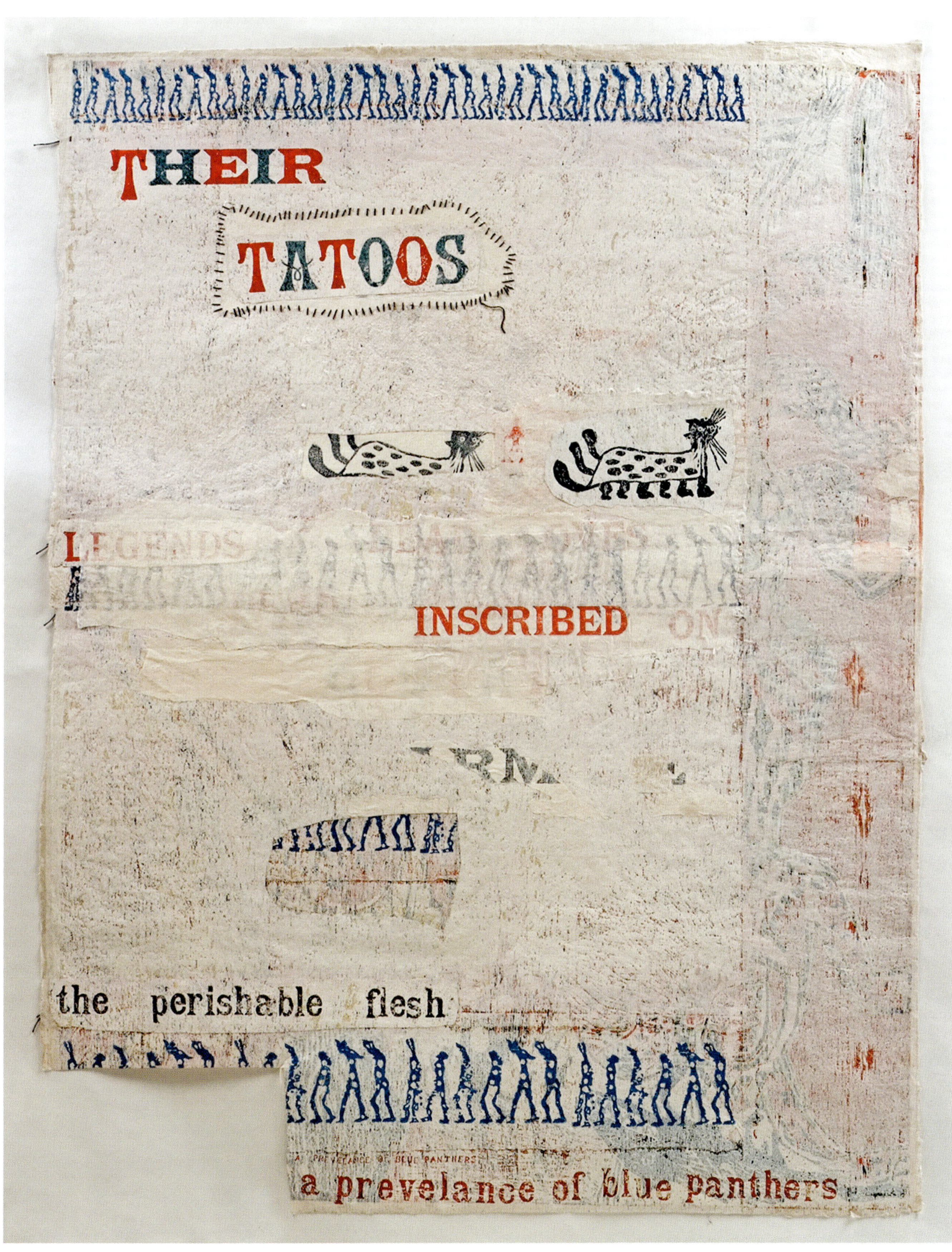

Sandy Sykes, *Their Tattoos... (from the Manuscripts series), 2007/08.*
Hand-rubbed woodcut and mixed media on handmade paper,
150 x 100cm. 59 x 39in.

52 ARTISTS

Aistė Morkvenaitė (Ai Mo)....................Lithuania
Amy Sterly ....Wales/USA
Ana Maria Pacheco................................England
Anne Heyvaert ....Spain
Ardan Özmenoglu..................................Turkey
Auksė Petrulienė ....Lithuania
Bodo Korsig ....Germany/USA
Brian Jones ....Wales
Chiara Giorgetti ....Italy
Christina Hallström ....The Netherlands
Curtis William Readel ....USA
Diane Victor ....South Africa
Eglė Kuckaitė ....Lithuania
Gaia Persico...Wales/Italy
Geraldine Berkemeier............................Australia
Guntars Sietiņš ....Latvia
Helena Horálková ....Czech Republic
Igor Benca..Slovakia
Jan Davis ....Australia
Janet Curley Cannon.............................England
Jelena Sredanović..................................Serbia
Jeoungeun Lim......................................South Korea
Jesús Pastor...Spain
Joan Hall ....USA
Joanna Pavlopoulou..............................Greece
Joscelyn Gardner ....Barbados/Canada

Kikie Crêvecoeur ....Belgium
Klavs Weiss..Denmark
Konstantinos Kissas..............................Greece
Ksawery Kaliski ....Poland
Leonie Lane...Australia
Lina Rica...Croatia
Liz Ingram...Canada
Małgorzata 'Malwina' Niespodziewana ..Poland
Marcus Rees Roberts ....England
Marian Maguire ....New Zealand
Marina Núñez ....Spain
Michael Barnes......................................USA
Michael Reed ....New Zealand
Michael Walker ....Brazil
Michael Wegerer ....Austria
Mirta Kupferminc ....Argentina
Moises Yagües..Spain
Myeong-goog Jung ....South Korea
Nathaniel Stern ....USA/South Africa
Patricia Olynyk ....USA
Paul Croft ....Wales
Rūta Spelskytė ....Lithuania
Sandy Sykes...England
Shelagh Morgan ....Australia
Tom Huck...USA
Xenophon Sachinis................................Greece

AISTĖ MORKVENAITĖ (AI MO)

Transhumanism and its manifestation in art was the subject for Aistė Morkvenaitė's thesis, accompanying the prints that formed her graduation project at the Vilnius Academy of Fine Arts in Lithuania in 2008. Wikipedia defines transhumanism, as 'an international intellectual and cultural movement supporting the use of science and technology to improve human mental and physical characteristics and capacities.' Proponents of this movement look to science to counter what they consider to be unnecessary and undesirable aspects of human existence, such as disability, disease and ageing, through the use of biotechnology and cybernetics. Much of the thinking in the movement comes from the realm of science fiction, and artists such as Orlan, Patricia Piccinini and Stelarc have explored the interface between technology and the human form in their work. Like them, Ai Mo positions her work at the far boundary of contemporary art, but uses conventional techniques to explore the themes and ideas surrounding transhumanism. In an e-mail to me she wrote, 'With my creations I want to join science and art together and to talk about the importance of science. I think anything can be explained with the language of science sooner or later.'

The dystopian genre of cyberpunk fascinates her and has been her primary inspiration, with its often-bleak absorption with themes of death and eternity, terminal angst and pessimism. Her favoured musical genres include post-punk and deathrock, and she has a strong interest in the early films of John Waters, David Lynch and Stanley Kubrick. At the same time she views transhumanism as being optimistic, a glorification of science and rationality, in addition to which she has a commitment to healthy diet and fashion. As such her interests reflect one of the underlying themes of contemporary culture, as she seeks to reject the conventional formal separations between art, science and daily living, and the admonishments of those who see technology as a threat, instead embracing a way of living that promotes a symbiotic relationship between art and science.

Ai Mo's printmaking uses conventional techniques that have been at the heart of Lithuanian printmaking for many years. In her monochrome etchings she combines finely controlled lines with tone, setting out her vision of a future world in which the natural structure of the body is combined with the world of electronics. In *Brains* she depicts the convolutions of the surface of that organ, with the lines and folds familiar to many through diagrams in science texts,

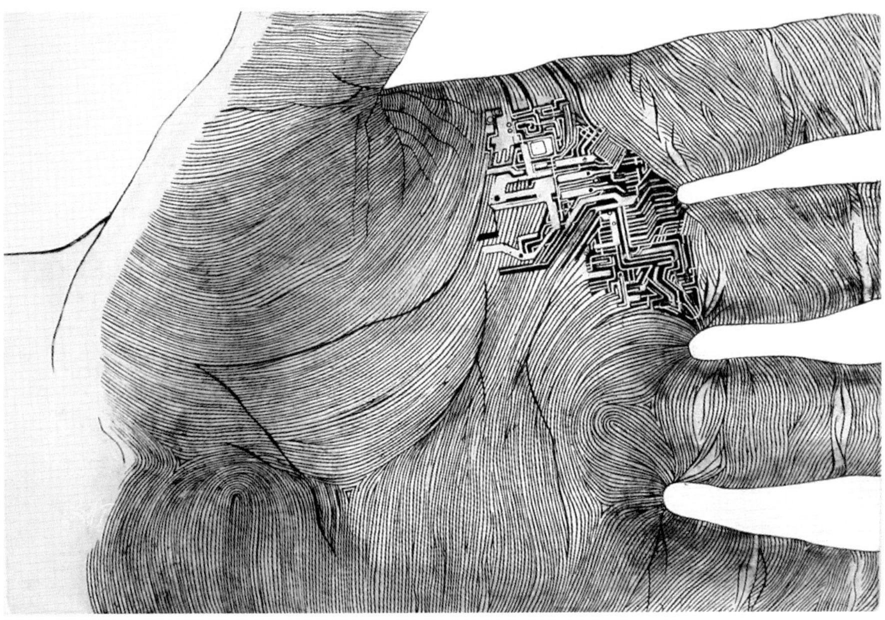

Aistė Morkvenaitė,
Hand, 2008. etching, 43 x 60cm. 17 x 23.5in.

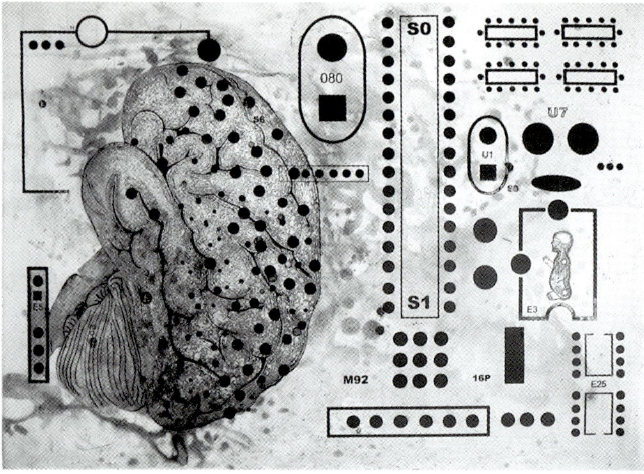

Aistė Morkvenaitė,
Brains, 2008. Etching,
45 x 62.5cm. 18 x 24.5in.

but with tones in the background to suggest the spillage of cranial fluid. This naturalistic image is overlaid with a formal, diagrammatic representation of electronic circuitry, one part of which contains an equally diagrammatic representation of a section through a human torso. The physical reality of the brain – that most mysterious of human organs – is contrasted with the strict mechanical formality of circuit diagrams. In *Hand* the contrast is established more simply, with a diagrammatic representation of the lines on the skin of the open palm of a hand – those lines that through their unique patterns give each of us a personal identity – combined with an equally diagrammatic representation of part of a microchip. The contrast is clearly established, and through the image comes the suggestion of the fusion of flesh and electronics that defines the cyborg. In the third image, *Heart*, that most complex and vital human organ, poetic seat of emotion and romantic longing, is reduced to a hard-edge diagram, such as is used as an interim stage in the construction of a three-dimensional model created on a computer. The added elements of tone and suggestions of external pipes distance the poetic nature of the heart still further from this depiction. By contrast, Ai Mo's work in colour, as shown in the frame from a series of digital colour images prepared for a Latvian publication, 'Comix', seeks to tell the story of the creation and experience of a robot girl, and through this narrative takes the opportunity to comment on the potential for conflict between the raw world of human desires and needs, and the cool and rational predictability of a cybernetic creation.

Aistė Morkvenaitė does not depict a comfortable world, and is not satisfied by the pursuance of conventional ideas about human relationships and the interface between natural and artificial worlds. The pursuance of art as a medium for exploring her ideas and attitudes and for depicting her hopes and desires is central to the way she lives. Printmaking and graphic forms offer the most appropriate medium at this early stage in her career, and while the results may not be comfortable (and are not intended to be) they are clear evidence of a creative person's search for the best means for expressing her developing beliefs in human potential.

www.myspace.com/ai1mo
(Science, New uses for old technology, The new generation)

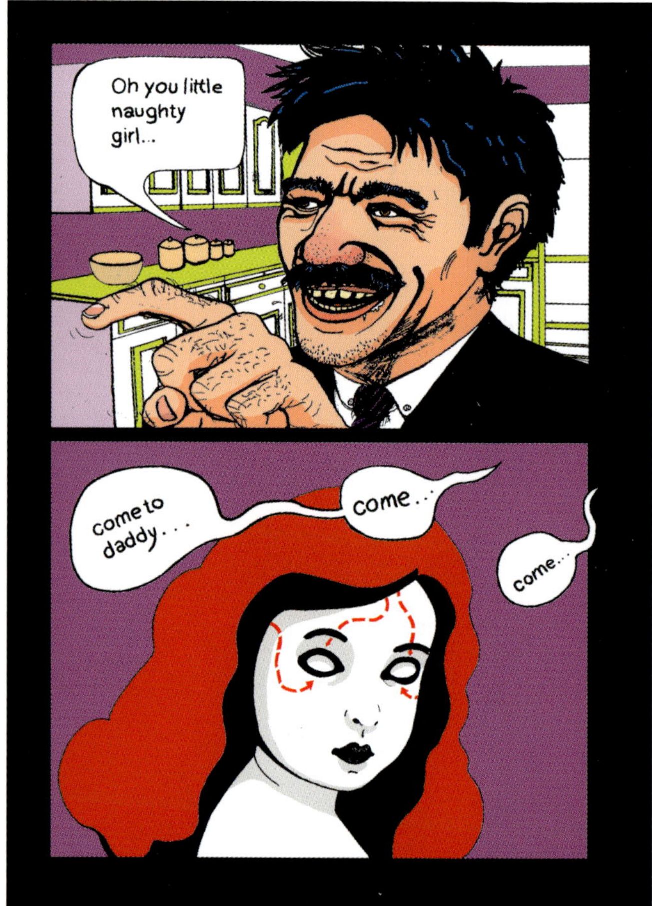

Aistė Morkvenaitė,
Comix (Oh you Naughty Little Girl), 2009.
Digital print, 24 x 17cm. 9.5 x 8in.

AMY STERLY

The contrast between the high-rise urban environment of Chicago and the rolling green landscape of rural Wales could not be more extreme. But it is this contrast that is central to the work of Amy Sterly. She was born in the USA and gained her degree in fine art from Rockford, Illinois, some 85 miles west of Chicago. In the early 1990s she moved to Wales, and she now lives in an isolated cottage in Mid-Wales. Her work is in printmaking – primarily drypoint, drawing and sculpture – and she has exhibited extensively, in one-person and group exhibitions, in the USA and the UK, as well as in Bulgaria. In addition she writes on contemporary art matters for a number of magazines, and has experience of working in a number of art-related fields, currently at an art foundry in North Wales. She participated in the Interventions 2009 festival in Llanfyllin, which brought together artists from Wales and Denmark to create a series of site-specific works in and around that small town.

In a statement about her work she sets out the main concern behind all the visual art forms she pursues: 'The forms that make up our modern landscape – the building, tower, skyscraper. The forms in which we live, love, work, communicate. They define who we are. We communicate through them. They have a relationship to us and the landscape.' Her connections with Chicago are relevant in this respect. There the downtown cityscape is dominated by skyscrapers, some of them iconic American landmarks, and a rich heritage of late 19th-century high-rise buildings. It is a city beside Lake Michigan, from which the mist rolls in and cold winds blow, a manmade landscape at the mercy of the weather. Sterly admits that these skyscrapers were her original influence, but now feels that they belittled and overshadowed all human life around them, existing on their own terms, seeming to have 'sprung out of the ground and staked their claim to the land, and no one could oppose them'. She also quotes as part of her inspiration the poetry of Carl Sandburg, especially the lines, 'I loom in the smoke/And the stars/And have a soul.' (From: 'Skyscraper').

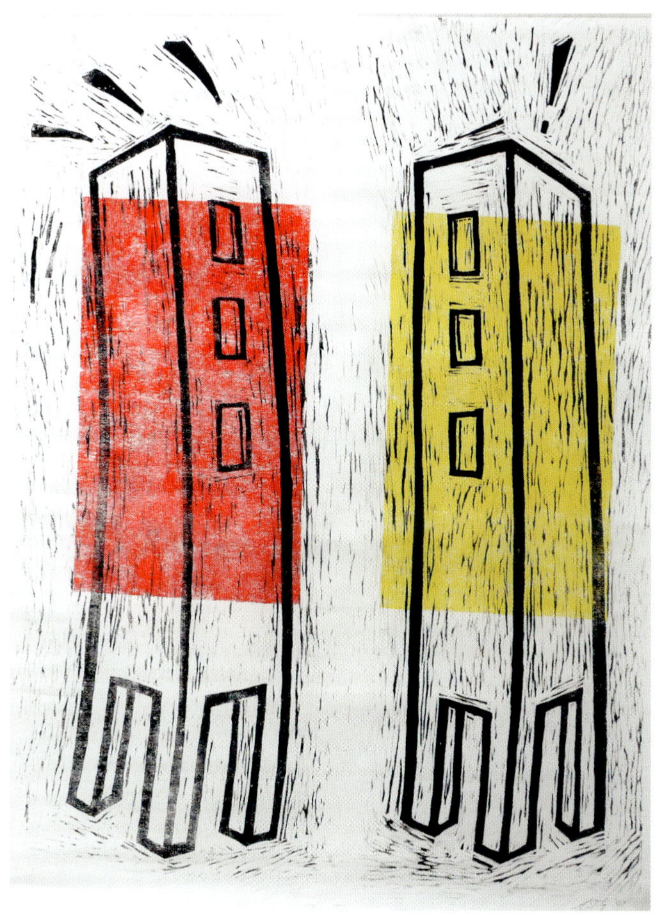

Amy Sterly,
Two Towers, 2009.
Woodcut for
steamroller print,
152 x 100cm.
60 x 39in.

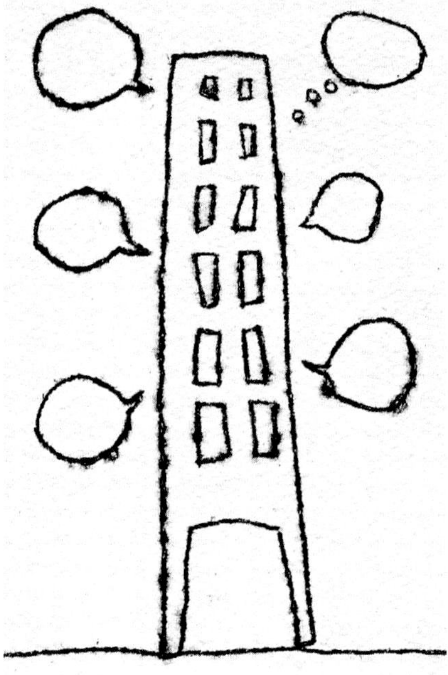

She writes that despite now living in rural Wales it has taken her a long time to realise that the images of skyscrapers are part of her and that, as an artist, she doesn't have to conform with parochial expectations and make pictures of some rural idyll. This realisation has enabled her to develop an idiosyncratic world of images in which the icon of the skyscraper is transmuted into something other than shiny glass and metal. She reaches for abstracted forms that communicate something more universal about the nature of human relationships, with ideas of home and shelter, utilising a visual language that owes something to comics and graphic art – simple lines, little depth of field, direct undecorated images with clear shapes that need little decoding. Her drawings and small-scale linocut or drypoint prints – usually in small editions – have an undeniable humour, but one with an uncomfortable edge, sometimes with simple added colour, and with speech bubbles that are usually devoid of text. The visual language is simple, direct and universal, and the buildings and forms can easily be seen as symbols of the success or failure of human communication. In some the towers have grown stumpy legs, anthropomorphising them so that the artist can use them as characters in the brief dramas that she sets up to express a range of human emotions and responses. Within her repertoire of forms and words she can set up oppositions, tensions between organic and industrial, as well as playful and menacing – a sense of threat in some of the works that subverts the initial response of a smile.

There is nothing romantic about her work, however it may at first appear. Instead, like a skilful conjuror, she presents what seems obvious and then, through misdirection, turns it round to offer something entirely different. But the threat within the work is not without humanity. It is always contained, preferring to communicate through hint and suggestion rather than direct assault. Her work in sculpture likewise subverts the form: working with bronze – conventionally seen as a material for monumental sculpture – she produces three-dimensional forms of towers, often in relating pairs, but at a small scale that would fit in the hand. In 2009 Amy Sterly took the opportunity of participating in the first steamroller-printing event to be staged in Britain, and produced a print of her iconic two towers, but on a much larger scale. The magnification in size, and the shift from linocut to woodcut, produced prints in which the monumental scale worked to perfection – a powerful questioning of the dominance of the urban world.

www.flickr.com/photos/amysterly/
(Large-scale printmaking and installation,
The third dimension)

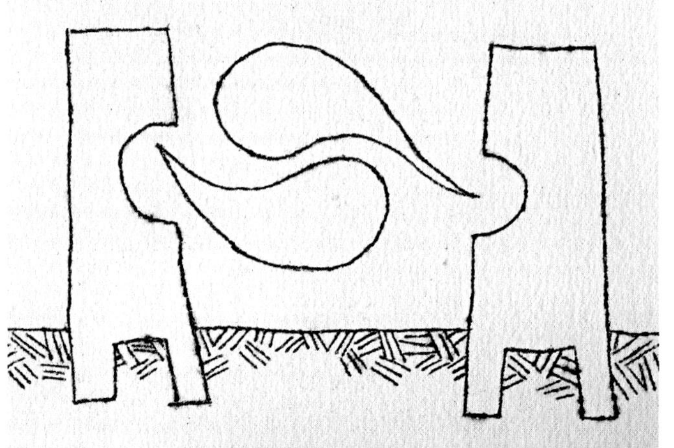

ANA MARIA PACHECO

Born in Goiânia in central Brazil in 1943, Ana Maria Pacheco has lived and worked in the UK since 1973. She has degrees in both music and fine art and has taught in both disciplines. Her work encompasses sculpture, paintings, drawings and prints in a wide range of mediums, and has been widely exhibited to high critical and public acclaim. In the years 1997–2000 she was Associate Artist at the National Gallery in London, resulting in a well-received major exhibition.

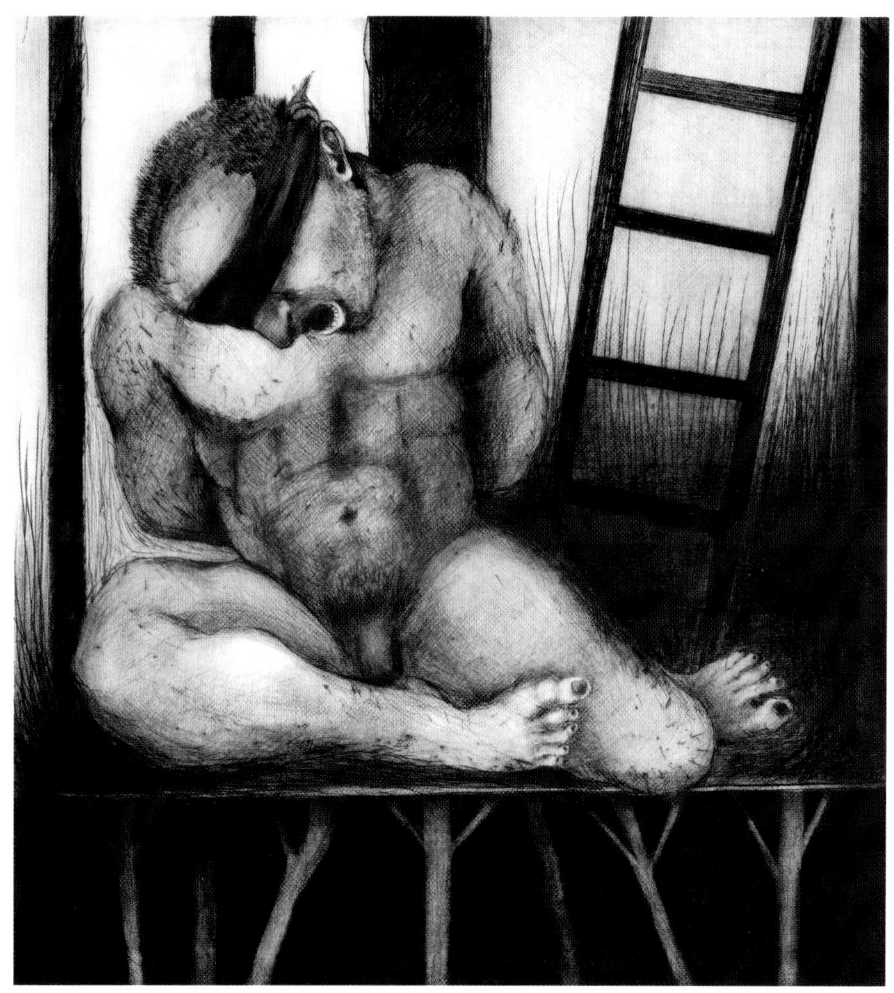

Ana Maria Pacheco, *Dark Event Plate III, 2007.* Drypoint on Somerset Textured Soft White paper, 68 x 60.7cm, 27 x 34in (plate) on 77 x 68.2cm, 30 x 27in. (paper). Printed by Martin Saull. Photo: John Slater, courtesy Pratt Contemporary.

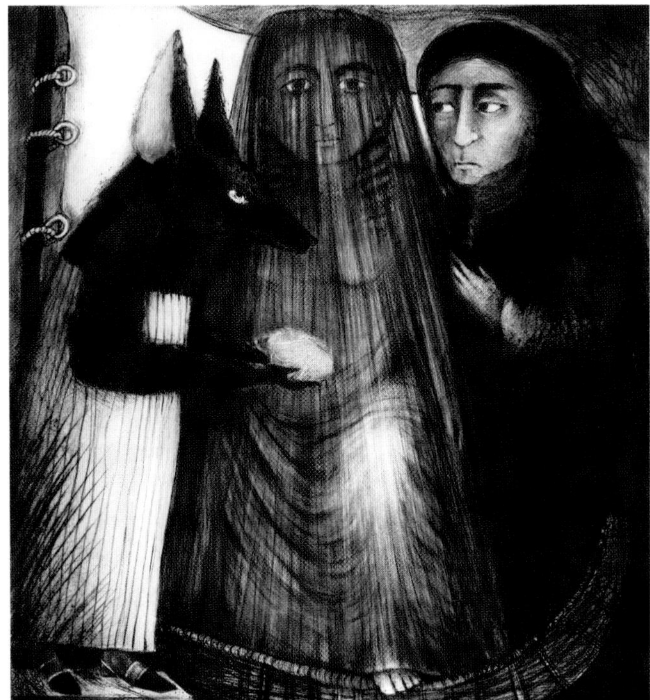

The roots of her work lie in the confluence of cultural strains that meet in her place of birth: the imagery of the strict colonial Roman Catholicism brought by the conquerors from the Iberian peninsula, with its iconography of hope and despair, and the animist beliefs of the native peoples that are strongly linked to the environment in which they live. The common thread between these seemingly disparate faiths is one of mysticism, woven through with fables and parables, derived from the quest for light in a world in which darkness contains the fear of the unknown. Pacheco addresses both realms in her output, creating unforgettable images that relate to the archetypes of world mythology and religious belief, sensed subconsciously (even if not always immediately comprehended) by all those who encounter her work.

Drawing and printmaking have for a long time been integral to her work in sculpture and painting, providing the means by which she can explore imagery and relationships, but at the same time resulting in a body of work distinct in its own right. Her skills in all the mediums in which she works are highly developed, even masterly. The tableaux of life-size or even larger figures are carved in hardwoods, then polychromed using traditional materials and techniques, providing the double image of sculptures overlaid with paintings, rather than being painted in a style such as to emulate reality. When these large-scale tableaux are installed in galleries the intention is that the visitors should be able to walk among the figures, becoming transient participants in the dramas depicted, and relating on a close personal level with the various characters. This is an unusual opportunity, and one that some are reluctant to take. But the concept has great relevance to the artist's work in other mediums. In Pacheco's painting, for example, the finish is absolutely smooth, devoid of the brush marks that have for many other artists since the Impressionists been an integral part of the surface: the image itself is the important thing for this artist, not the evidence of its making. To this end she works in oil on gesso, building up layers of smooth glazes, then rubbing down the final surface with a very fine glasspaper before waxing it to a high gloss. This, she says, permits the viewer to have a direct relationship with the image, and to enter into complicity with it.

When Ana Maria Pacheco first came to the UK as a British Council scholarship student at the Slade School of Fine Art from 1973–75, she was inspired by the guidance of Stanley Jones, who encouraged her to explore printmaking methods as a way of breaking the creative impasse that she had reached. As a printmaker Pacheco has for many years worked in close association with Pratt Contemporary, a workshop and gallery that has, under the guidance of Bernard and Susan Pratt, become a beacon for excellence in British and international printmaking. Over the long period of her association with the workshop, she has produced an extensive series of portfolios of prints and artist's books using etching, lithography, drypoint, woodcut and screenprint, each one involving a deep exploration of aspects of the human psyche, world mythology and religious beliefs. The figures in the prints have a sense of otherness, a quality that links them to medieval satire, religious mysticism and folk narratives, even to some aspects of Outsider Art. Masks, tumbrels and boats can be found in her work, as well as angels with trumpets and other, more sinister beings, plus a medieval Don Quixote encountering a modern Dulcinea, and a whole theatre of bizarre and tragic figures caught up in fates beyond their control.

In her most recent portfolio, *Dark Event (2007)*, Ana Maria Pacheco presents seven drypoints in which a mysterious drama unfolds: there is childlike innocence set against superstition and threat, harrowing images that encapsulate the torture and brutality of both historic and contemporary regimes; there is compassion and slender hope, redemption and, in a darkly strange final image, a veiled central figure with another resembling Anubis and a third like the dark figure of Fate or a grieving widow. These prints are by an artist at the height of her powers, ambitious in their reach and international in their relevance.

www.anamariapacheco.co.uk
(Memory, New uses for old techniques)

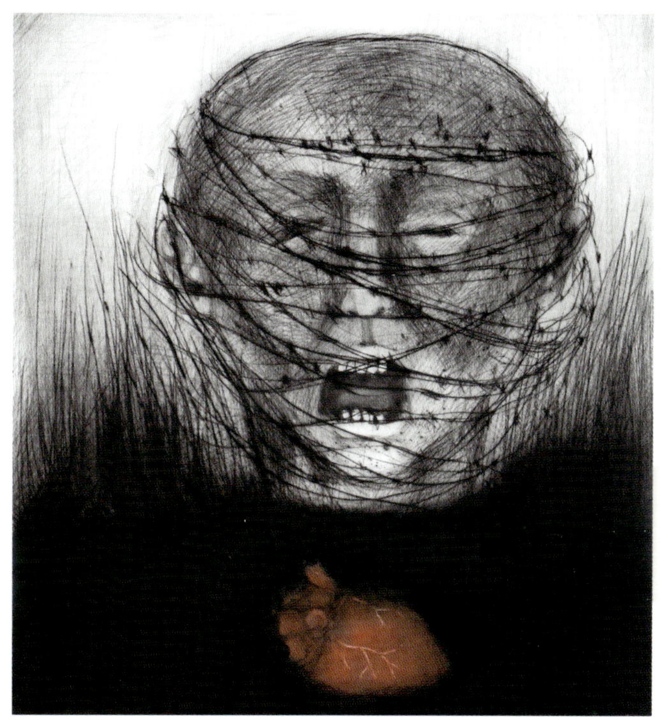

Ana Maria Pacheco, *Dark Event Plate VII, 2007.* Drypoint on Somerset Textured Soft White paper, 68 x 60.7cm, 27 x 34in. (plate) on 77 x 68.2cm, 30 x 27in. (paper). Printed by Martin Saull. Photo: John Slater, courtesy Pratt Contemporary.

ANNE HEYVAERT

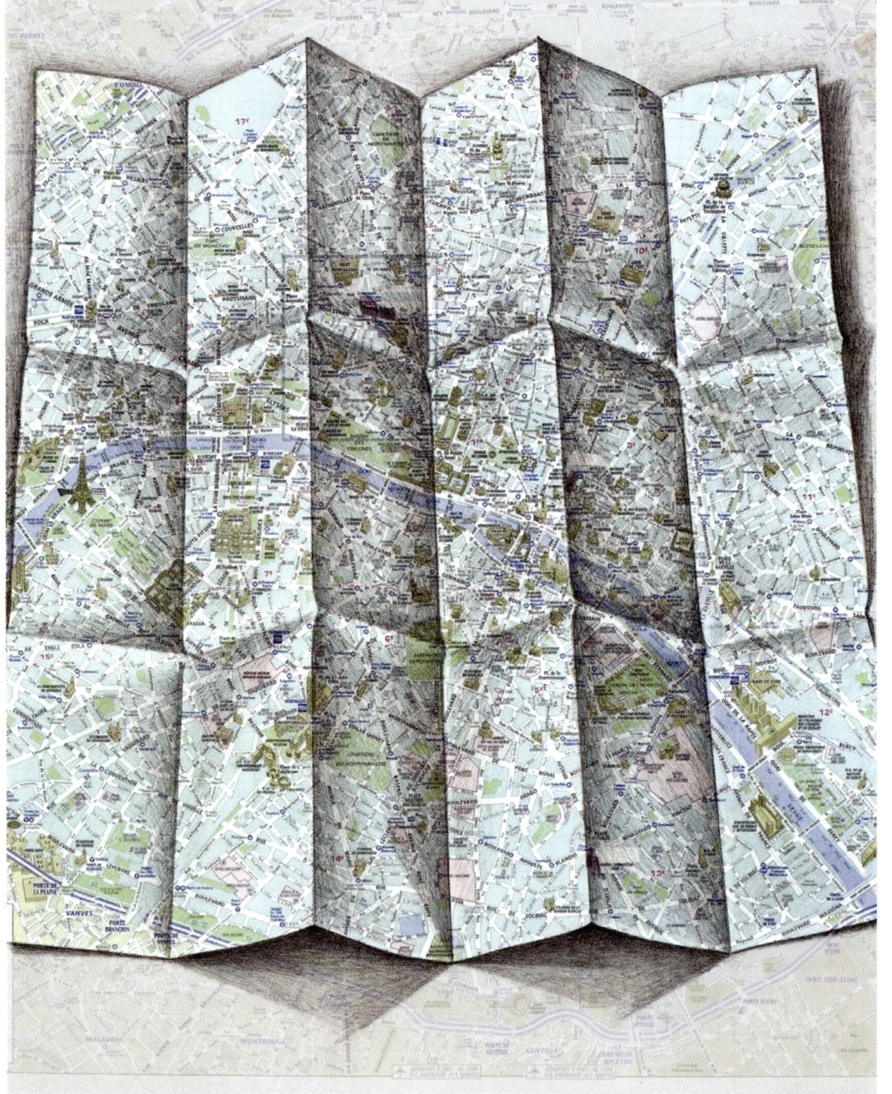

Anne Heyvaert, *Déplié, Paris, 2008.*
Lithograph on inkjet on paper,
76 x 56cm. 30 x 22in.

This artist, born in Memphis, Tennessee, and brought up in France, with studies firstly in France and latterly in Spain, now lives and works on the Atlantic coast of Galicia in the northwest of that country. Having moved home frequently, it is not surprising that the nature of place and the means by which we locate and relocate ourselves should have become the major preoccupations in her work. Cartons, wrapping paper, books and maps are recurrent themes, and with them a preoccupation with the nature of reality and the means by which it may be depicted. The region of Galicia is the antithesis of most preconceptions of Spain: it has a culture with Celtic roots, a lush green landscape, a wild and windswept coast (including Cabo Fisterra or Finisterre, the end of the earth, the most westerly point of Spain, and Europe) with a heritage of seafaring; it is rich in architecture, including the cathedral at Santiago de Compostela, with its shrine of St James, located at the end of the ancient pilgrim trail.

Anne Heyvaert's work is deceptive: at first sight it appears to be straightforward, depicting literally, and with apparent ease, elements that are familiar to travellers and to those who have moved house. What emerges after consideration is that she is also depicting illusion, and in so doing is questioning the nature of our perception of reality, and the means by which it can be copied, or duplicated, or represented (and re-presented).

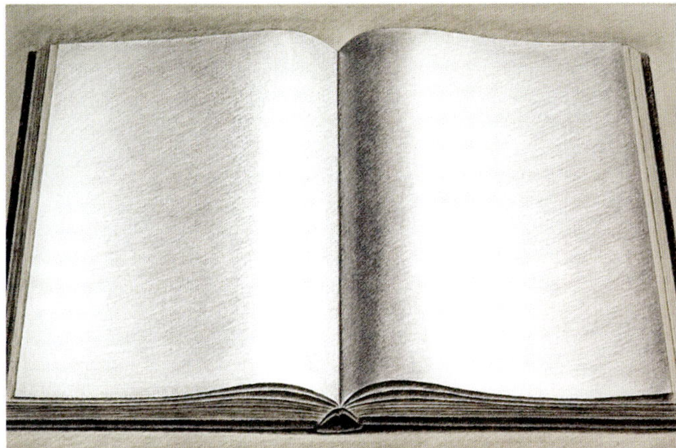

Anne Heyvaert, *Livre Blanc, 2007.* Etching, soft-ground etching and drypoint on paper, 33 x 50cm. 14 x 29in.

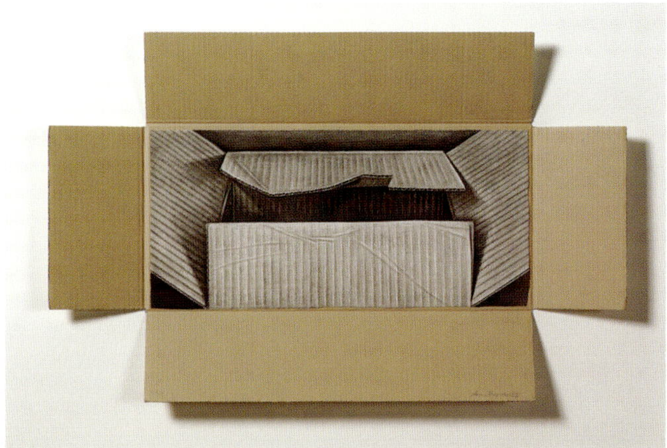

Anne Heyvaert, *Carton sur carton, grande ouverture, 2004.* Etching, aquatint and drypoint on paper, mounted on cardboard, 47 x 73cm. 18.5 x 29in.

There are elements of trompe l'œil, created with precision but always with just enough hint of their duplicity to suppress any impressions of absolute perfection. The question arises: is the subject matter real, or a version of reality, and what then is the nature of the reality from which the works are observed? There are elements of the trickster in Heyvaert's work, the games of cunning and deceit that are themes common to many world mythologies, the Celtic world being a prime example, in which the assumptions of reality are challenged and the unexpected is to be expected. This element also has strong relationships with psychology and 20th-century philosophy, and in any event is apposite to the changing and uncertain times in which we live. Ultimately those who encounter this remarkable work must decide for themselves what they choose to believe when looking at the images through which this artist explores the world.

The image of an opened book of white pages, depicted in etching and drypoint with soft varnish on grey paper, offers a clue: presented in two dimensions with the illusion of a third, it is a volume yet to be written, an unuttered text, intimating the fourth dimension – time. In another series of lithographs there are depictions of folded sheets of blank paper, creased by the unseen hands that manipulated them. Earlier work in drypoint shows the paper used to wrap delicate objects when packing them in cartons for moving home, some showing the objects and others the form left behind once the objects are removed. These and a major series of works beginning in 1996 and continuing to 2004 explore the packaging with which we move our belongings from place to place, the transient evidence of a familiar experience that is seldom noticed, those ghosts of the enclosures within which the accumulation of the objects of our lives are kept secure. In some of these prints (in etching, aquatint and drypoint) the images of folded cardboard, taped and seamed, are themselves mounted on the cardboard of cartons, offering a further layer of illusion.

Anne Heyvaert's work from 2006 onwards has been much involved in a major ongoing series, From Memphis to Finisterre, in which maps and plans are depicted with great assurance. In some there is a return to the theme of the book, but in this case they are depictions of the pages of an atlas, the maps curved with the open fall of the pages. Others in the series are folded diagrams opened to our view, with shadows beneath them creating illusory space: these lead to depictions in etching, aquatint and drypoint, of folds and creases superimposed on digital reproductions of diagrammatic maps and city plans, creating the illusion of one map laid upon another identical to the first. But the illusion is not complete, as it becomes clear with study that the lines creating the streets and urban areas themselves do not follow the illusions of fold and crease. This technique continues to perfection in later works, in which the image of a fanned-out folded map, or an unfolded map, is superimposed on a digital reproduction to create the final illusion of a map that is itself merely a representation of part of the three-dimensional world in which we live our four-dimensional lives.

http://issuu.com/anneheyvaert/docs/anne_heyvaert_memphis_finisterre_doblar_real
(Environment, Memory)

ARDAN ÖZMENOGLU

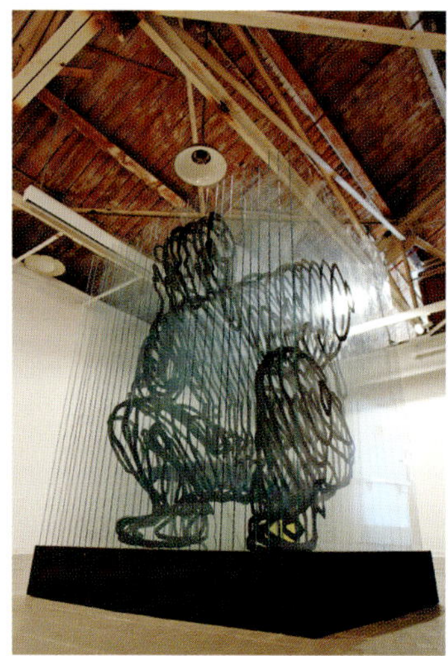

Ardan Özmenoglu,
Oturan Adam, 2007.
Screenprint on
30 pieces of glass,
70 x 90 x 120cm.
27.5 x 35.5 x 47in.

Graduating in 2006 with an MFA from Bilkent University in Ankara, Turkey, Ardan Özmenoglu's approach to the making of art through printmaking mediums crosses conventional boundaries and explores a territory somewhere between print, installation and sculpture, between permanence and transience. The country in which she lives is itself in transition, but with a history that stretches back as far as the Ottoman Empire and then beyond to one of the most ancient of cultures. At the same time Turkey, recreated by Mustafa Kemal Ataturk in the early 20th century as a secular state, but one in which Islam remains the dominant faith, is a now rapidly developing country with ambitions to join the European Union. It is in this transitional society that Özmenoglu lives and works. She writes that her work is 'contemporary in the extreme', and that 'my investigation into image coexists with gestures that challenge, provoke and invite'. The mediums provided by printmaking, most usually that of screenprinting, allow her a route into the multiplication and repetition of images as the elements from which she builds up her works. The basis of her work is 'the idea of repetition as it investigates the process of image consumption, history, and permanence in relation to mass production, ritual and accompanying psychological states.' In addition to these themes, the artist is clearly concerned with making reference to the male-dominated history of her country to allow consideration of the changing nature of Turkish society.

Ardan Özmenoglu's solo exhibition at the Galerie IAC in Berlin in April 2008 included the installation *Out of Season*, and comprised a grid of papers printed with negative silhouettes of branches, upon which yellow and green leaf forms were collaged; the papers were fixed to the wall along the top edges, allowing the bottom corners to curl. Suspended in front of the wall was a branch, which also bore collaged leaf forms, and on the floor was a pile of yellow and green Post-It® notes, bearing screenprinted images of silhouetted leaves. The installation carried with it notions of impermanence and temporal shift, alluding to autumn in a springtime exhibition. On another

wall in this exhibition was the installation 1 birds, 2 birds, 3 birds…, which also comprised a multitude of Post-It® notes in multiple colours, predominantly pink and blue, bearing screenprinted images of silhouetted branches, some with birds. The density of this installation, filling two walls from floor to ceiling, also alluded to impermanence, as over the course of the exhibition some of the elements curled away from the wall and some fell to the floor.

A further installation work in Turkey in 2008 also utilised the technique of screenprinted Post-It® notes, but this time on the exterior wall of a shop. *Padisah Post-Itleri* presented a densely packed collage of images of sultans and photographic images of 20th-century politicians, randomly arranged so as to create lines and curves of colour from the papers, with faces relating in equally random ways, curling in the air, subject to removal by passing pedestrians, or falling from the wall to reveal the painted surface beneath, as if the faces from history were brought into contact with each other, only to be dispersed by the passage of time. In all these examples the works now exist only in documentary photographs of a past event: another level of impermanence.

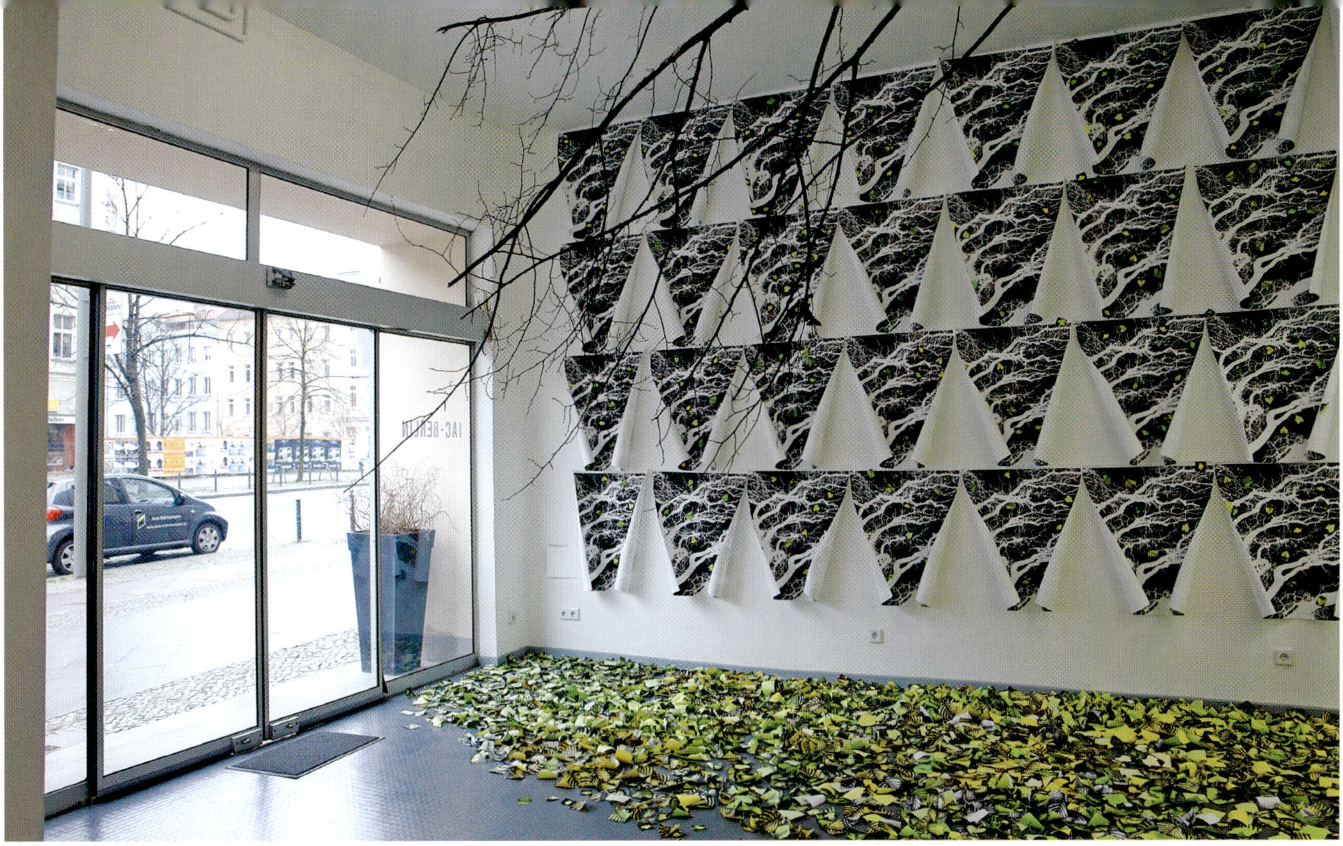

An earlier work from 2007, *Oturan Adam*, shows another aspect of Özmenoglu's approach, in which she combines screenprinted elements on thirty sheets of glass to create a monumental representation of a crouching male figure, hand to chin. Each sheet of glass bears the thick outline of a slice through a figure, as in a topographical map. Spaced out to create the sculpture, which is 120cm (47in.) in height, the 30 images combine to create the impression of a whole form, but one which shifts and changes according to the position of the viewer's eyes or the camera's lens. In this technique the various parts of the image are in a more permanent form than in the previously described installations, attaining something more akin to a conventional notion of sculpture. And yet the image of the man does not remain still, shifting as the viewer moves around, never fully resolving into bodily solidity. The feelings of deracination and alienation that are common in urban societies in a time of change are here captured for contemplation in an apposite manner.

Ardan Özmenoglu, by virtue of her age and geographical location, is an artist uniquely positioned to observe and comment on a world that is changing rapidly, in which the values of a traditional society are being questioned, and the orientation of a country with a long and important history is in transition.

www.ardanozmenoglu.net
(New technology, Large-scale printmaking and installation, The new generation)

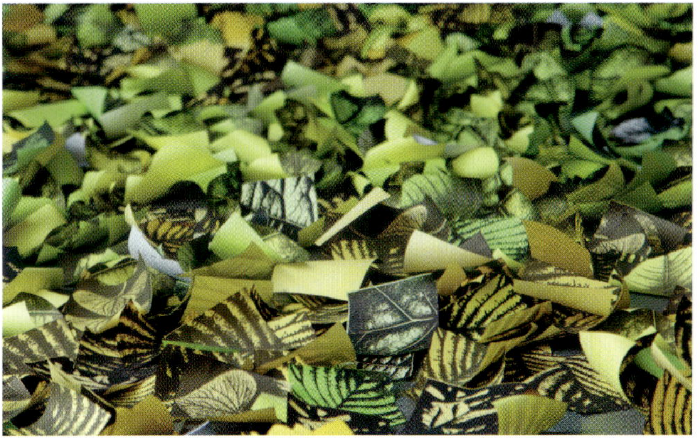

TOP **Ardan Özmenoglu,** *Out of Season (installation, IAC Gallery Berlin), 2008.* Screenprinting on Post-It Notes™, tree branch, 400 x 600cm. 157.5 x 236in

BOTTOM **Ardan Özmenoglu,**
Out of Season (detail) (installation, IAC Gallery Berlin), 2008. Screenprinting on Post-it Notes™.

AUKSĖ PETRULIENĖ

Born and educated in Kaunas in Lithuania, where she still lives and works, Auksė Petrulienė is accomplished in many areas of the visual arts, having trained in leatherwork, printmaking and the making of artist's books, in which she gained her master's degree in 2001. In many respects her work has always been experimental: the artist's book for her final degree was a very large-scale bound work with paintings on cotton sheeting that incorporated printed elements. Her solo exhibition at the Bleddfa Centre in Wales in 2003 comprised household cotton sheets painted with images exploring the theme of Mary Magdalene. It was initially installed in the orchard of the centre and subsequently within the barn and the church of St Mary Magdalene adjacent to it. She has also developed site-specific works for exhibition in botanical gardens. From 2004 onwards she has explored multimedia work, incorporating her images into performances by a jazz group, then as part of an audiovisual performance, until devising and leading Psilicone Theatre from 2005 onwards, a unique concept of performance that bridges many mediums, linking visual art to music, live image projection, and performance using silicone puppets and text.

In her description of the concept and approach of Psilicone Theatre, Petrulienė describes how 'Psilicone Theatre uses artistic silicone implants to make plastic corrections of the wrinkles of sadness on the face of the Lithuanian nation'. She states that her performances are focused on the social mission of printmaking in the contemporary world, and that this refers to the elements of social criticism running through all the pieces in the theatre's repertoire. In addition to mobilising a variety of techniques to comment on and criticise social and environmental problems the intention is also to point out possible solutions. She has a preference for making performances in spaces that are usually distant and distinct from the conventional spaces for encounters with the visual arts, such as the courtyards of blocks of apartments,

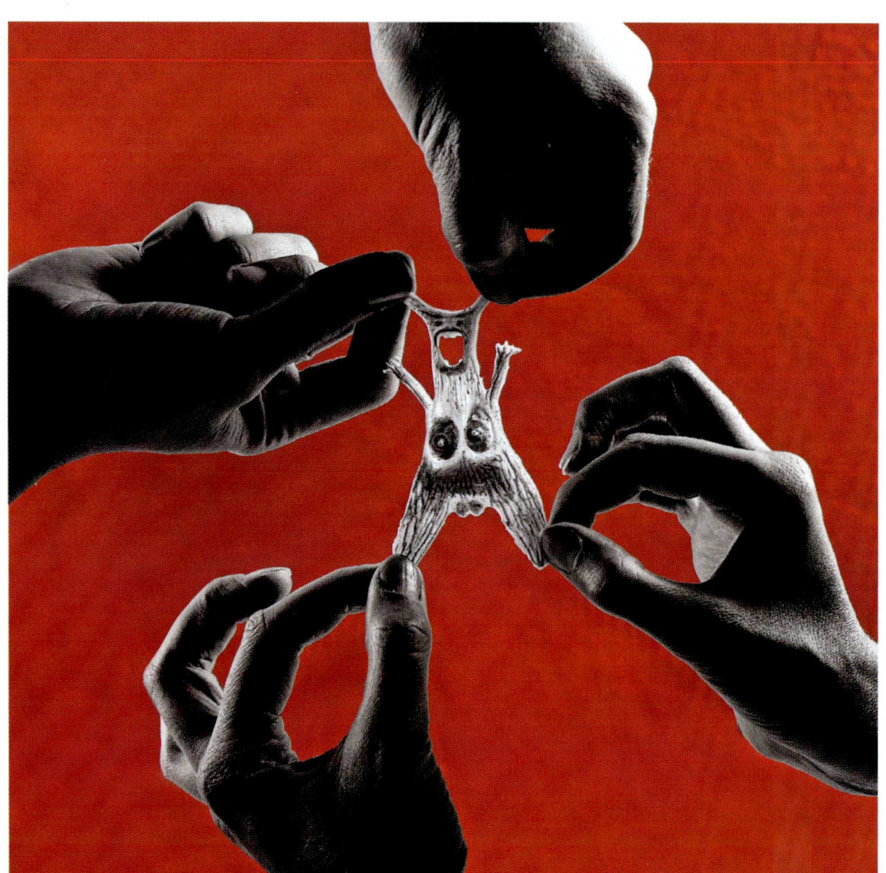

Auksė Petrulienė, *Silicone Puppet I, 2008.*
Digital print of silicone puppet, size variable.

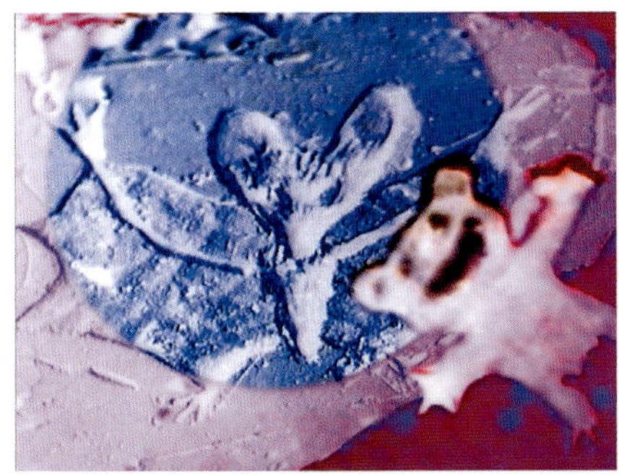
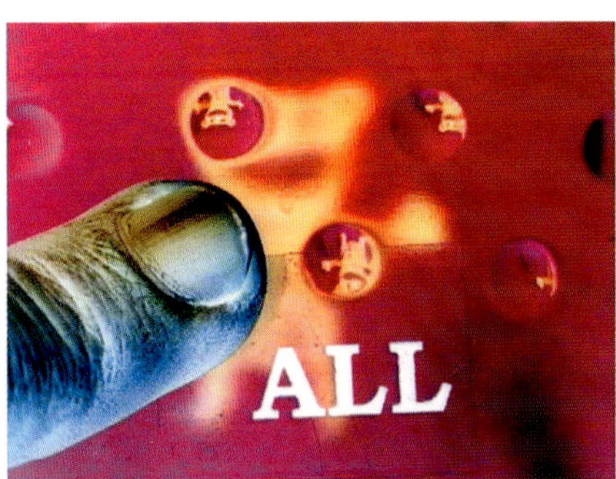

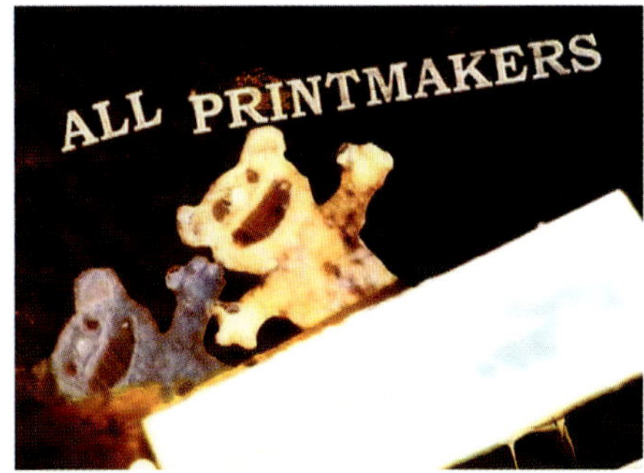

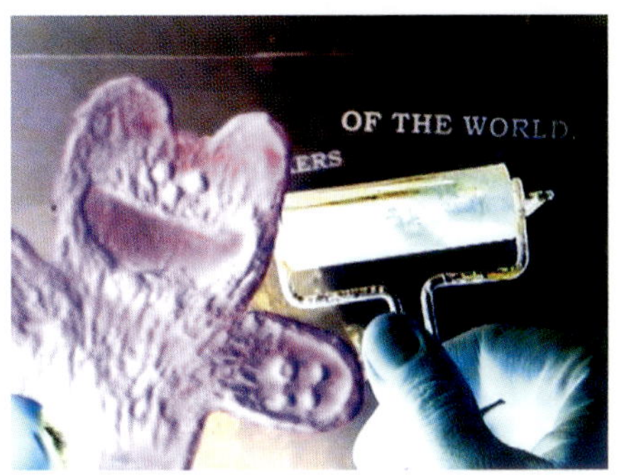

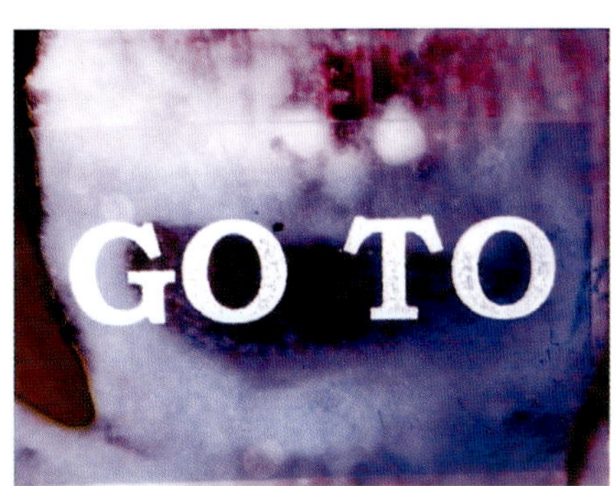

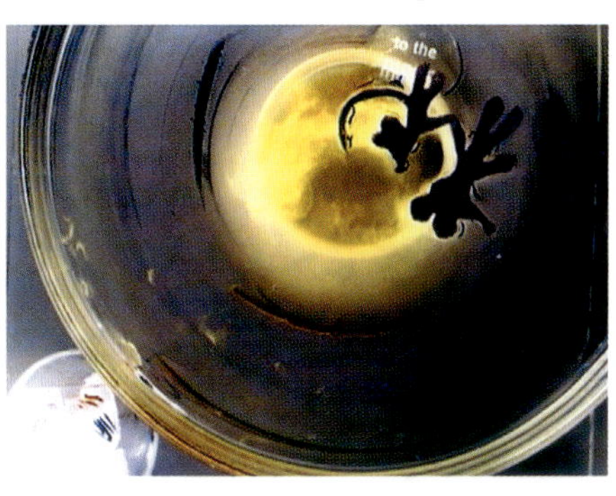
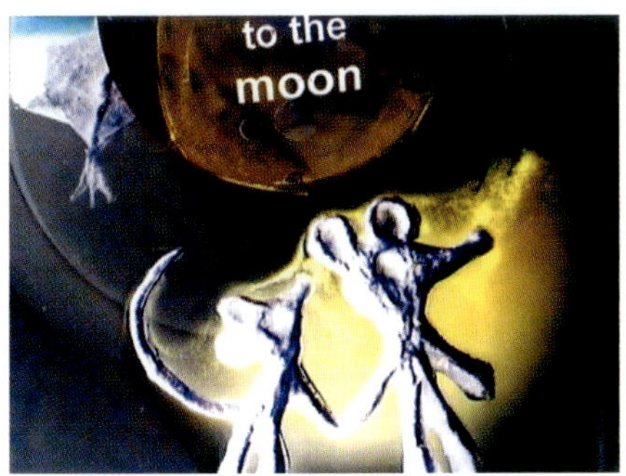

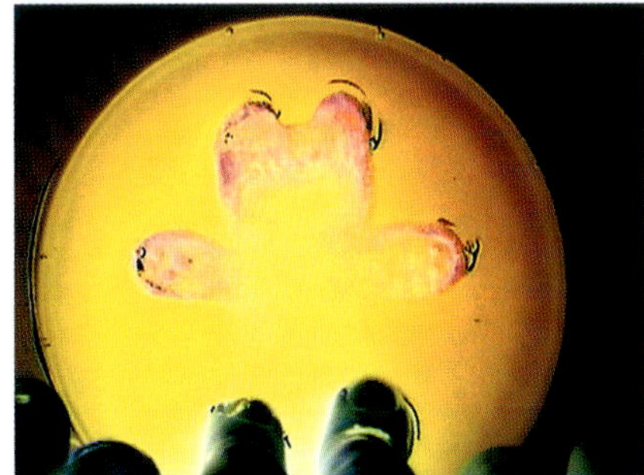
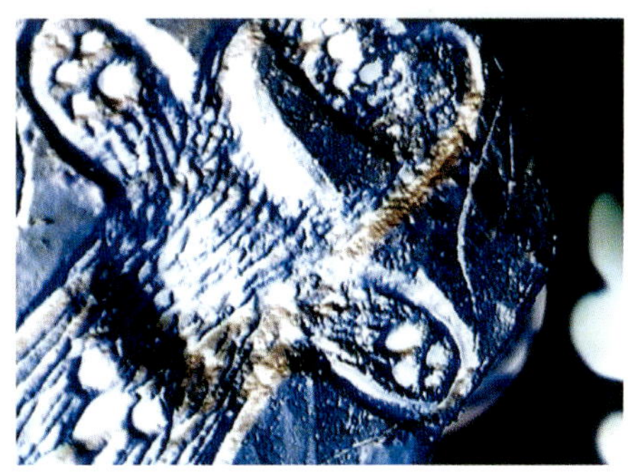

Auksė Petrulienė,
*Printmaking Moon Mission
(DVD stills montage), 2008.*
Size variable.

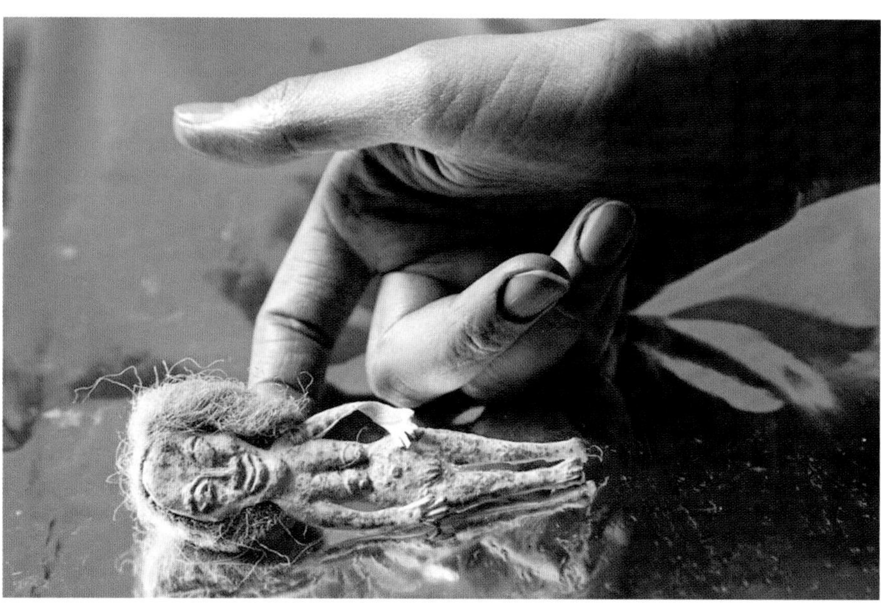

Auksė Petrulienė,
Silicone Puppet (Yoko Ono), 2008.
Digital print of silicone puppet,
size variable.

in playgrounds and in sports centres. Her preference is to work with social groups and with children and, as she writes, 'to meet unusual spectators and to know their needs and expectations of contemporary art'. She maintains that contemporary art can be used as an antidote to the problems that are threatening and damaging society. The unconventional territory that she has mapped out for her work is complemented by the choice of materials and forms that she uses within it. While many of the elements can be traced back to printmaking, their development in her hands takes them into new forms and directions.

Petrulienė begins with the creation of silicone puppets, cast from a plaster matrix, which become the characters in the dramas that she devises. The puppets can be stretched and manipulated and, if accidentally destroyed, can easily be recast in an identical form. Many of the fluids that make up the medium in which the puppets are immersed and the dramas enacted are drawn from printmaking, while others were originally cosmetics, household-cleaning fluids and the like. The varying viscosities and physical characteristics of these materials, as well as their colour and transparency, allow for a wide variety of visual effects and reactions. The scale at which the main part of the performance is created, essentially a normal tabletop, can be made as large as required through the use of an overhead projector and live-video filming with instant projection. This also allows for considerable flexibility in the choice of venues and for an enclosing, three-dimensional, projected environment. The performances are accompanied by live music – anything from solo guitar to woodwind quintet – and while they are tightly devised the nature of the materials used results in a fair degree of variation as individual pieces are repeated, so that each performance is essentially unique.

Among the pieces devised by Auksė Petrulienė for Psilicone Theatre are, *You Won't Beat Me*, in which a tough rabbit expresses environmental and social problems through a series of jokes; *Let Your Radiance Shine Through*, which marked the 20th anniversary of the Chernobyl catastrophe and the contentious problems of the Ingalina nuclear power station; The Jaws, an audiovisual performance realised in swimming pools and dedicated to George Maciunas, the Lithuanian founder of the Fluxus movement; *Here Comes Vilnius*, derived from national legends and prophetic visions to celebrate Vilnius's year as European Capital of Culture, in 2009; and most recently, Love Story Strangled and Shot, devised in conjunction with the multi-instrumentalist Tomas Dobrovolskis and based on the story of a notorious pre-war criminal, which examines the nature of desire, human nudity and social clothing. These performances incorporate an unconventional approach to dramas that deal with acute environmental and social problems, and take the contemporary visual arts to locations where they are seldom seen and where they would otherwise perhaps be unwelcome.

www.aukse.lt
(New technology, Large-scale printmaking and installation)

BODO KORSIG

Bodo Korsig was born in Germany and studied sculpture in Berlin, graduating in 1990; he lives and works in Trier in Germany and in New York. While he uses printmaking techniques, primarily woodcut, as a part of his practice, he is not in any conventional sense a printmaker, making the transition between sculpture, painting, print and drawing with ease. His work in recent years has been closely bound up with aspects of the scientific study of neuropsychology, and in particular, as he writes, 'the nature of human behaviour under extreme conditions such as fear, violence, pressure or death'. Korsig goes on to explain that, 'at the interface of biological determination and human awareness, I want to provoke a new perception of these processes through my art'. While this underlying philosophy makes specific demands on those who wish to attain a deeper understanding of the enigmatic work of this artist, the intrinsic quality of that work, the conjunction of phrases with seemingly abstract images, and the clean lines and shapes he creates as well as the mystery they convey, has in itself a direct visual fascination. The immediate concrete sensation of the work cannot be separated from questions about its abstract nature and meaning. This paradox places Korsig's work more closely with conceptual and abstract art than it does within any of the more recognisable and comfortable categories of printmaking. Such paradoxical attributes can be found in the printmaking of artists such as Jasper Johns (in particular his lead relief prints) and, in his etchings, Richard Serra; both men have explored the inherent formalism of the medium, as well as the limits to which it can be stretched, within their work, producing monumental images as a result.

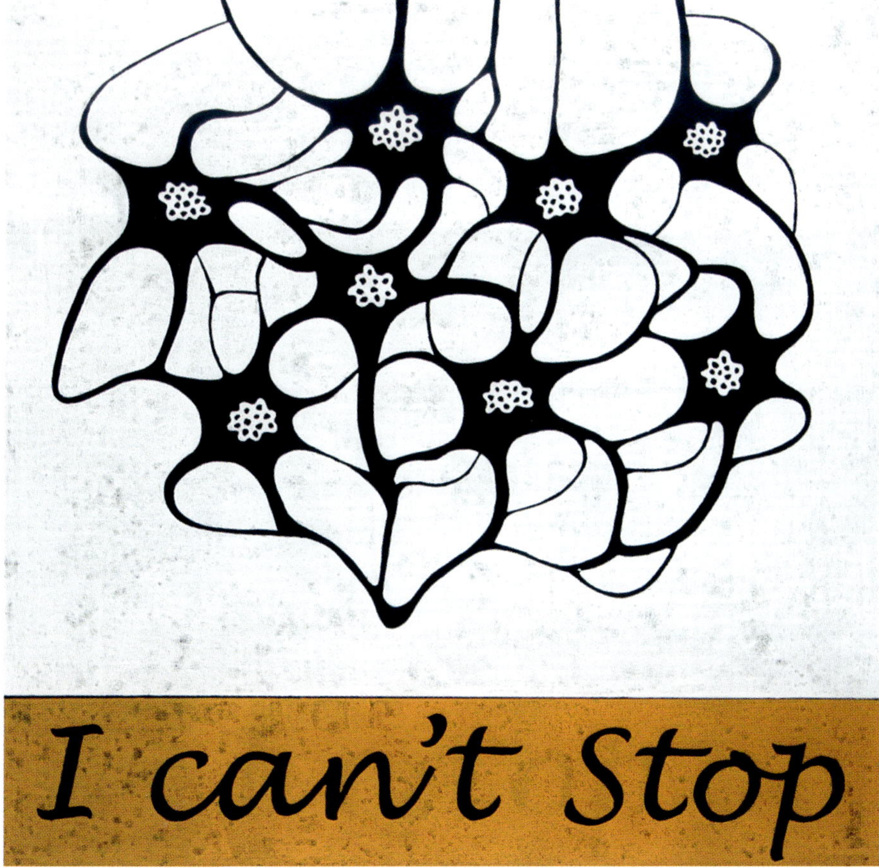

Bodo Korsig, *I Can't Stop, 2007.*
Woodcut on canvas, 90 x 90 x 10cm.
35.5 x 35.5 x 4in

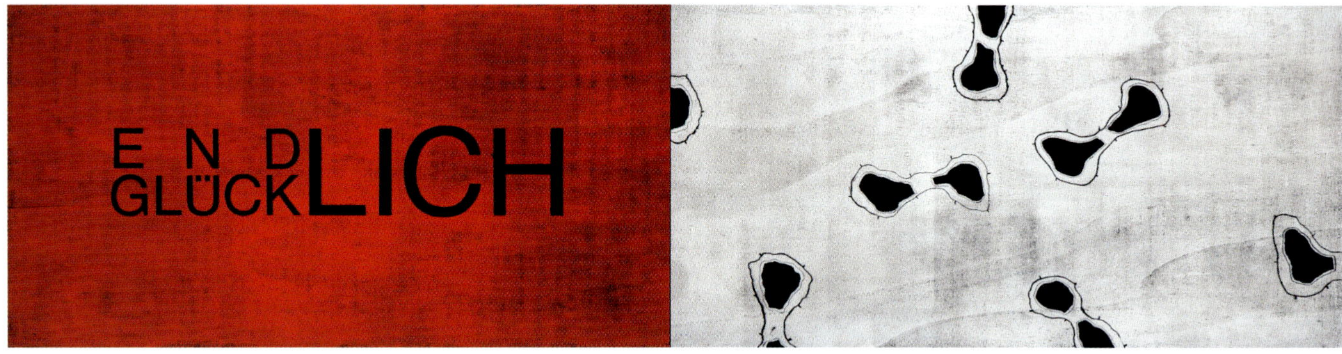

Bodo Korsig, *Endlich Glücklich, 2005.*
Woodcut on canvas, 65 x 170 x 10cm.
26 x 67 x 4in.

In 2006/7 a selection of Bodo Korsig's new work was shown at a number of galleries in Germany under the title *Where Can I Buy a New Brain?* This superficially amusing concept, not uncommonly uttered in a light-hearted way by those wishing to erase bad memories or gain new cognitive powers, does in fact go to the heart of the limits of science and philosophy, asking questions about the nature of personal identity and the difficulty of fully explaining the nature of consciousness and awareness. Just as none of the five senses can be experienced in isolation, each being connected to the others (as in, for example, the other sensory experiences – the sounds made by other people, the temperature or smell of the air, and so on – that can crowd in when looking at a painting in a gallery), so too do the mind and its constructs, the complex nature of a person's identity and their emotions all come into play when the artist creates or an observer considers work such as that made by Korsig.

Scale is an important factor in this artist's work, and the variation in size of his creations is a clue to the manner in which he approaches the problems that most deeply interest him. At its smallest his work can be held in the hand, delicate traceries of black resembling neural ganglia, cellular structures of primitive signs, and yet being none of these. They are produced using a very fine micrometric saw to cut into thin sheets of industrial pressed wood, are subsequently cast in aluminium, thereby destroying the original, and are then coated in varieties of black paint mixed by the artist. A similar technique, but using more conventional materials and tools, is used to create larger aluminium sculpture to be hung on or leaned against walls. The shadows produced by the ambient or display lighting add, literally and metaphorically, another dimension to these works. These extraordinary objects, as in the series, Hidden Mind, are exhibited in groups on white walls, speaking a language that is both arcane and indecipherable and yet curiously familiar. At the largest scale he produces very large woodcuts, sometimes using an industrial road roller to transfer the image from block to paper or canvas. His prints, usually made as unique examples rather than editions, range in size from 20 x 20cm (8 x 8in.) to 850 x 250cm (334 x 98in.).

Korsig's work deals with complex scientific matters, and also with the simplest and most complex of human emotions – love – which he refers to as a 'superpower', irrational and entirely rational at the same time, which causes the commission of often crazy and sometimes destructive acts, and which has been, and continues to be, at the centre of so much world culture and history. Science and art are not mutually exclusive, each operating within the full gamut of human sensations and experience. In Korsig's work they meet, interact and pose intriguing questions.

www.korsig.com http://bodo-korsig.bobdev.de
(Large-scale printmaking and installation, The third dimension, science)

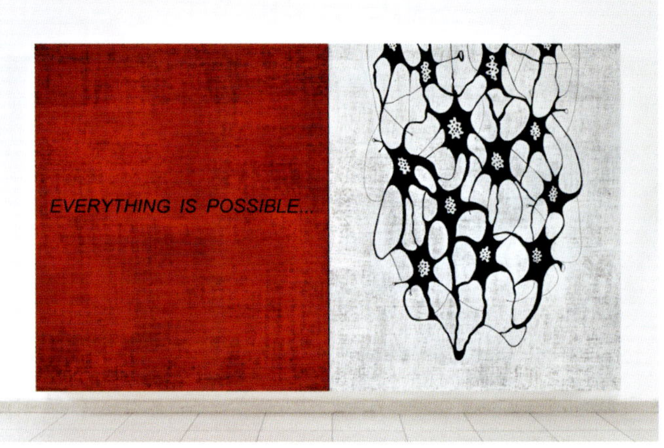

Bodo Korsig, *Everything is Possible, 2008.*
Woodcut on canvas, 350 x 250cm. 138 x 98.5in.

BRIAN JONES

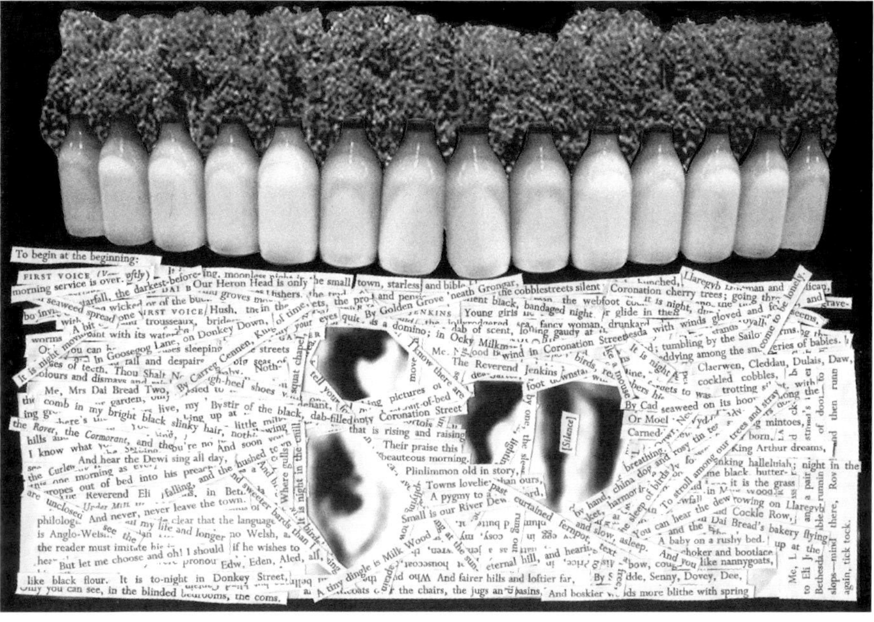

With roots in Liverpool (where he went to the same school as Paul McCartney and George Harrison, and to the same art college as John Lennon) and in North Wales, where he now lives and works, Brian Jones is an artist whose formative experiences lie in the counterculture of the late 1960s and '70s. He uses traditional printmaking technology, primarily screenprint, together with collage and painting, to create images that question, criticise or mock prevailing social and political values. He is a post-punk, new-pop artist, successor to the agitprop artists and commentators, and with a keen eye for the absurd, the ironic and the inherently unjust aspects of contemporary society. As he freely admits, while this mode of thinking and working might seem to some to be outmoded, a sad relic of a less enlightened past, the present circumstances of society make attitudes and opinions such as his even more necessary. While some might find his views extreme, they nonetheless hold up a mirror to the increasingly globalised society, and ask very necessary questions. His work is closely allied to the social and political commentaries in the work of Shepard Fairey in the USA, the inheritors of Situationism in Europe, and the work of many printmakers included on the Art of Democracy website. Political art, it can be argued, is needed more than ever in an age of spin and counter-spin and the ever-greater risks of deception and misdirection that come about through global 24-hour rolling news reporting.

His commercial work for social charities, and for pop and rock musicians and promoters, is fully documented on his website, and the evolution of his work can be traced through this medium. Witty and irreverent, angry and sarcastic by turns, his work is rooted in the political art of the 20th century but always with a twist that is appropriate to the current time. His 'subverts', such as *WasterCard* and *No Radiation*, play tricks with imagery derived from advertising and art history, while collages such as *Babylondon* belong in the long tradition of political collage such as in the work of John Heartfield. Among prints from recent years, *If You See Kay* is a subversion of an iconic Robert Indiana image, while *Blairman Mao* and *Idiot Son* offer defiant and highly critical images in the form of postage stamps, and the series *Madollars* shows the 'Queen of Pop' on a dollar bill. There are more – Jones is a prolific artist.

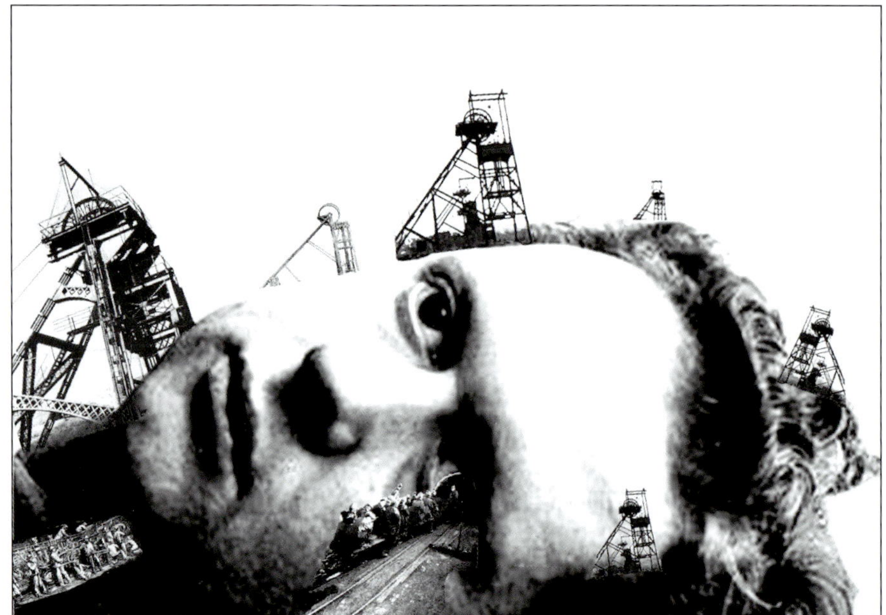

In the summer of 2009 Brian Jones was commissioned to design and produce screenprinted currency bills for use at the Green Fayre at the Workhouse in Llanfyllin. Visitors to the Fayre could exchange UK currency for the Dolydd notes and use them to purchase goods on sale at the event. So successful was this initiative that some of the traders are said to be considering using the Dolydd notes as part payment of their taxes to the local council. Substitute local currency is being used increasingly in Britain and elsewhere as a way of promoting tourism that also has practical local applications. Images of currency, as noted elsewhere in this book, are prevalent in other areas of contemporary printmaking.

In 2009 Brian Jones worked on two new projects involving printmaking, each taking a new and potentially controversial direction. A series of collages, produced in black and white, entitled *10 Ways to Kill Dylan Thomas*, is based on the celebrated 20th-century Welsh poet and writer, and the celebrity status that he has been accorded in the years following his premature death. The images take an ironic look at aspects of Welsh culture and tradition, and at the same time comment on the life of this writer, famous for his readings in the USA and with a voice familiar on British radio in the early 1950s. Wales remains a small country at the edge of Europe, but with a cultural pride that places it high in European terms, and Jones's collages, and the photopolymer prints produced from them, offer a provocative and timely consideration of the nature of celebrity and culture. *Mine Him Until Collapse* is a bitingly satirical view of the death of the Welsh coal-mining industry, while *Bury Him Under Milk Wood* not only alludes to the poet's most famous work, but also to the perilous condition of Welsh agriculture.

In a contextually connected but entirely different form, *In Memory of the Cow*, a cast bronze burger wrapped in screenprinted silk in a printed box, offers a satirical view of the fast-food industry. Brian Jones comments that it, 'juxtaposes the humble yet "iconic" burger with traditional materials and methods, sending "fast food" into the fires of Vulcan'.

www.artofbrianjones.com
(New uses for old technology, politics)

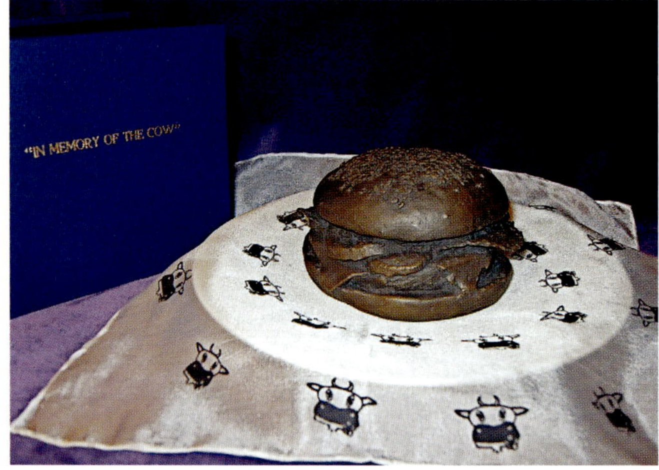

Brian Jones, *In Memory of the Cow, 2009.* Bronze, silkscreen on silk, clamshell box, (Burger 11.5cm. 4.5in (dia.) x 7.6cm. 3in. (h.))

CHIARA GIORGETTI

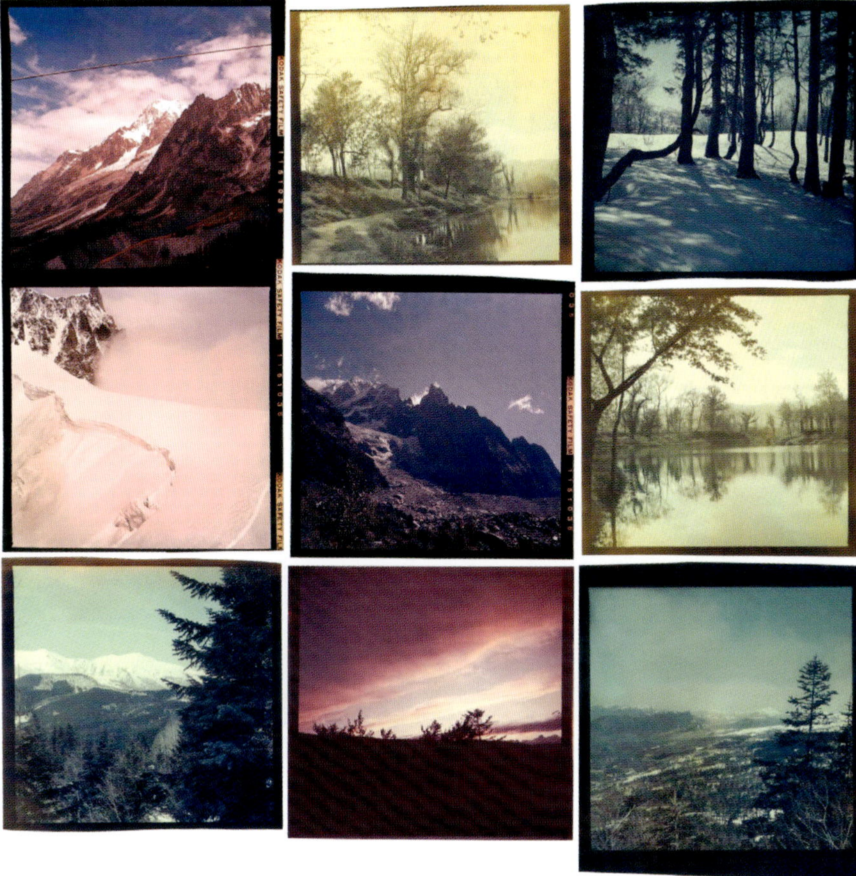

Chiara Giorgetti, *Nove immagini, 2009.*
Digital print on vinyl, 150 x 150cm. 59 x 59in.

As a rule, my work has always started with an image or a memory … I see my work as a way of dealing with the melancholy and absurdity of human existence.' This, from a statement about her approach to the making of images, is the key to the work of Chiara Giorgetti, who lives in Florence and works in Milan, one city the heart of the Italian Renaissance and the other the fashion capital of Italy.

Memory is the most mysterious of human faculties, the nature and functioning of which science has yet to unravel. It is at the core of our experience as individuals and participants in society, and our relationships are largely dependent on it. Some memories stay clearly fixed in our minds.

On the other hand, memory can play strange tricks, distorting the remembrance of the places we have visited and the people we have encountered, and in growing older we make mistakes in remembering these things in detail and proper sequence. We attempt to remember, and frequently fail – faces cannot be matched with names, and sequences of events can be difficult to recall with accuracy. So we keep diaries and notebooks, and make sketchbooks and photographs to help us to, as Wordsworth put it, 'recollect in tranquillity'.

Giorgetti's sensitivity to this central theme is quietly evident in her work since the turn of the millennium, implicit rather than explicit, subtle rather than audacious. Her concern is to explore human powerlessness in a technologically dominated

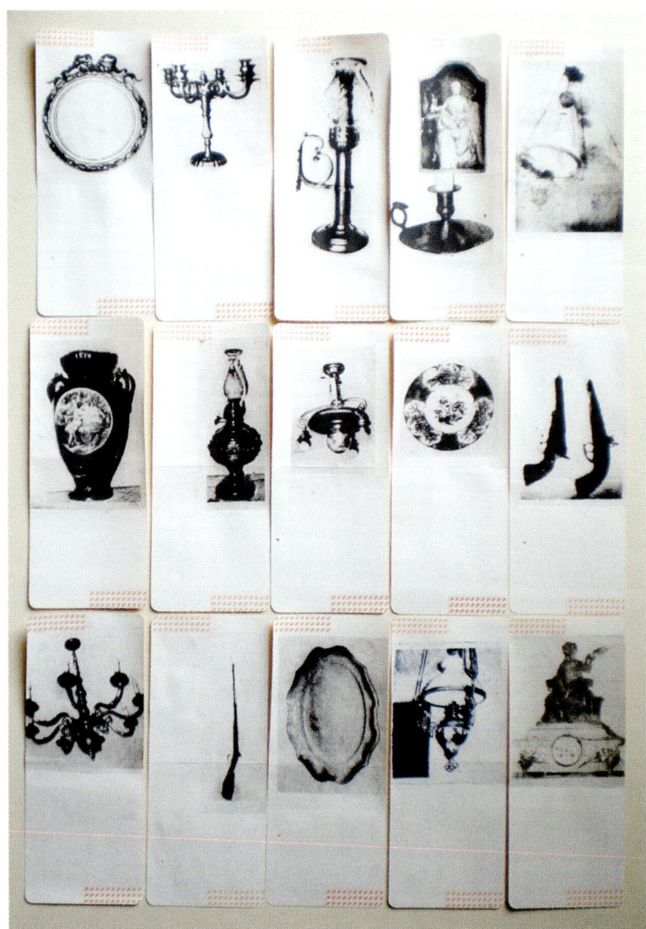

Chiara Giorgetti, *Gli oggetti di casa, 2008.*
Gum print on railway tickets, size variable.

environment, where the distance between individuals in a crowd is palpable, and where an existential aloneness (rather than loneliness) is a common element of daily life. It is from this point that she perceives melancholy and absurdity, and against which she places her images. She sets out, as she puts it, 'to present familiar but absurd images, decontextualised actors, a mise-en-scène in the manner of a stage that is waiting for the opening. Nothing is really authentic – it seems to be, but it's like a theatre.' In this way the elements that appear in her work – old images of athletes, photographs of mundane everyday objects, woods, leaves, natural and domestic locations, characters and images – seem both to be extremely familiar and at the same time to provoke a sense of estrangement. Some of the images that act as starting points are made by the artist herself, while others are appropriated from found objects or derived from photographs made by her father. It is from this basic vocabulary that her work begins.

In *Nove immagini* (Nine Images) (2009) Giorgetti begins with 6 x 6cm (2⅜ x 2⅜in.) colour slides taken by her father in the Alps and Apennines in the 1950s, and scans them into her computer complete with their original edges, striving to preserve the faded and oxidised colours, while at the same time removing defects caused by foxing, scratching and mould growth. Her father's recorded memories, which she shares at a remove, are thereby recaptured, renewed and enlarged in a set of nine as a digital print on vinyl. Those who see this work in reality or in reproduction can share in the artist's memories of her father's memories, recognising perhaps some parts of their own experience. With the series *Operazione sull'immagine* (Operation on an Image) (2008/9) Giorgetti takes the process a stage further, while following a similar principle. She begins with similar colour slides, but scans them into the computer before selecting parts to be output as black and white images on resin-coated paper, which she then annotates in pencil and gouache, making a hybrid print, creating a place of mystery similar to that which Dante describes as 'una selva oscuro' (a dark wood).

Between 1997 and 2009, Chiara Giorgetti made over 140 Polaroid® images in the various houses in which she has lived during that period. They have all the hallmarks of this now obsolete photographic medium and at the same time an inherent sense of the magic that came with making such images. Collected together and presented in a gallery, as a group and as individual images from her own repository of memories that the artist has chosen to share, they regain some of their original potency.

Other strands of her practice include printing, onto the backs of discarded railway tickets, gum images of household paraphernalia or images of athletes of the past taken from old newspapers, setting up a chain of resonances that captures the familiarity of household objects in the one case and the physical commitment of the athlete in the other. Once again, through this artist's images we are immersed in a world that is long gone.

www.printshow.it
(New uses for old technology, memory)

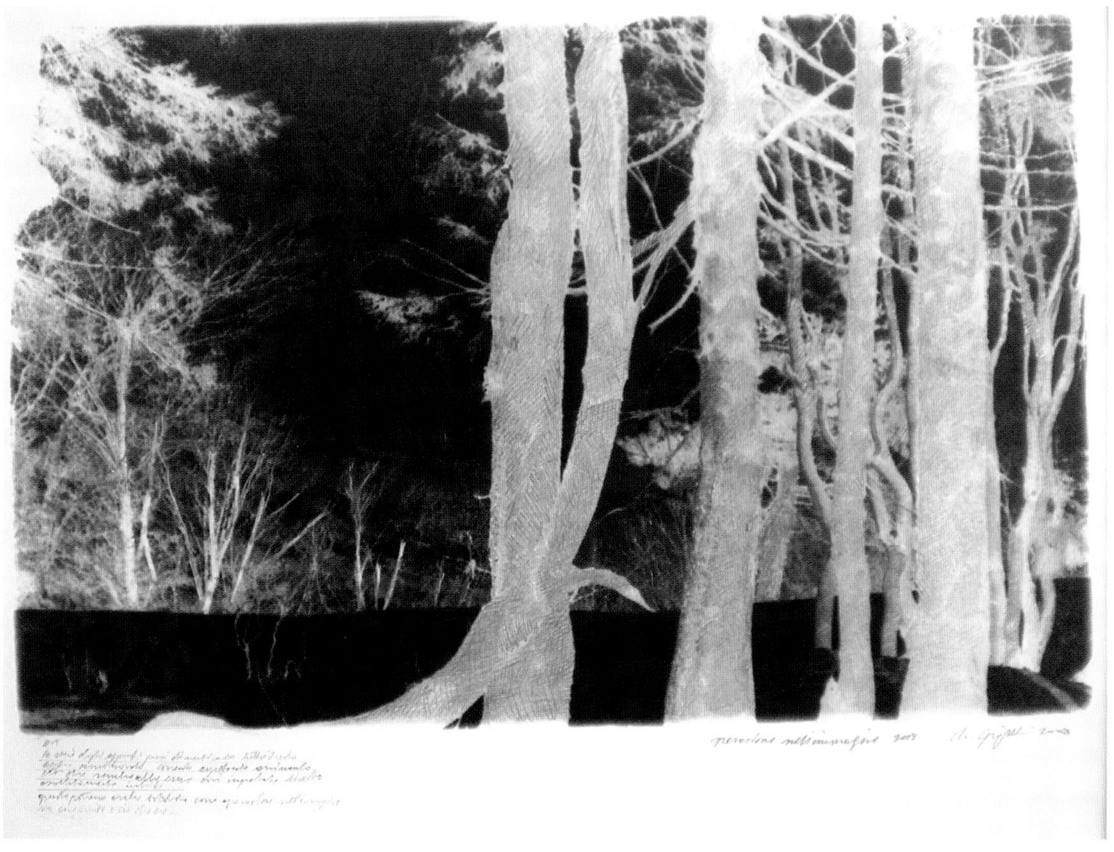

Chiara Giorgetti, *Operazione sull'immagine, 2008.* Black and white print from slide, pencil, gouache, 30 x 40cm. 12 x 16in.

CHRISTINA HALLSTRÖM

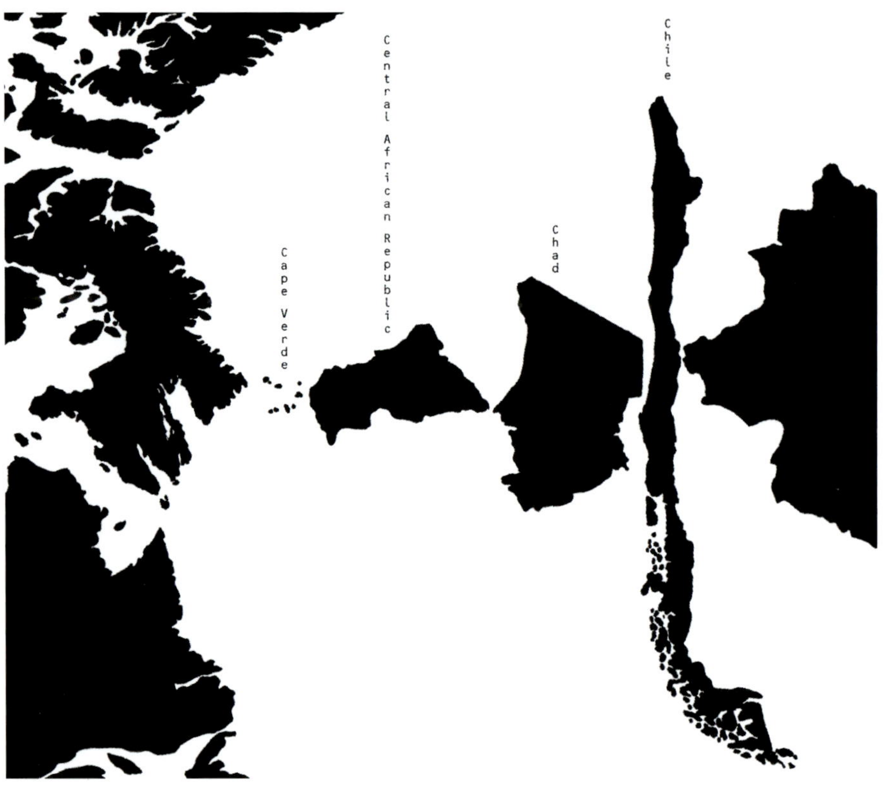

Christina Hallström, *Atlas (detail), 2007.* Ink on paper, giclée, 60 x 700cm (whole print).

Christina Hallström was born in Sweden but lives and works in Amsterdam, where she graduated in graphic design and visual communication from the Gerrit Rietveld Academie. Her work is involved with image making in video, film, photography and print. She collaborates frequently with musicians and dancers, and much of her work appears in the form of DVD files and printed images. Her work as a printmaker is in the extended and growing realm of digital imaging, where the matrix is a digital file rather than the more traditional intaglio or relief matrices. Her artistic motto, 'We exist insofar as we hang together', underlies the decision to base much of her recent output on a collaborative process. In various ways this is what printmakers have been doing for centuries, but in this artist's case the difference lies in her choice of technology and her global reach.

In 2007 she showed a major digital print, at the Tallinn Print Triennial, which that year was called *Political/Poetical*, at the Kumu Art Museum in Estonia. Given the title *Atlas*, this 750cm (295in.) long print depicted in silhouette 192 countries of the world that are members of the United Nations and four other states with some degree of international recognition. These states are centred on a horizontal line in alphabetical order, regardless of their size or status, with the scale adjusted to enable even the smallest to be visible, and with their names printed vertically above them. The alphabetical juxtaposition leads to politically curious neighbours, but above all reconfigures the atlas in a manner that questions the criteria by which the notion of a country can be defined. This print, and its deeper implications, provides a basis for the consideration of her work in other mediums.

Hallström describes *Noctilucia miliaris* as '… a film about how we relate to water … universally and spiritually connecting us as humans with everything alive on this planet …' It was filmed in late summer in the sea off the west coast of Sweden, where there is often an extensive growth in the algae which give the film its title. This noctilucent species lights up with the movement of any other form through the water; using this phenomenon, the artist collaborated with the dancer Lisa Larsdotter Petersson and the Estonian composer Märt-

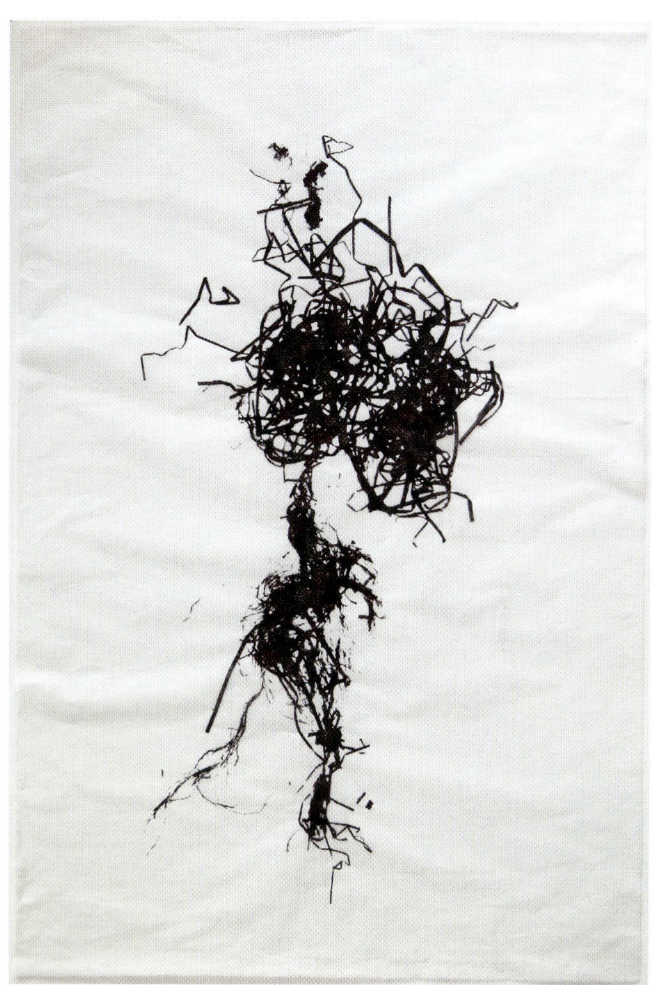

Christina Hallström, *Seaprint 02, 2009*.
Screenprint in Indian ink on Tengujo paper,
100 x 30cm. 39 x 12in.

Matis Lill to produce a film of the dancer swimming among these algae, recording her movements and their creation of noctilucence and incorporating original music by Lill in the post-production stage. The result is a lyrical evocation of light and movement, making the invisible visible. Related to this film is a series of stills produced as giclée prints. In *Seaprint*, a connected series of screenprinted images in Indian ink on Tengujo paper, the artist uses seaweed as the basis for prints which capture the calligraphic delicacy and fragility of seaweed taken out of its natural element. These prints have an inherent beauty but can also be seen as a comment on the threat to the world's oceans through pollution and global warming.

A journey to Ethiopia with the independent Dutch band The Ex proved to be a rich source of inspiration for Hallström. She made a film recording a concert given by the band in Addis Ababa that featured the Ethiopian jazz saxophonist Getatchew Mekuria and athletic local dancers. Dynamic camera movements complement the driving music, and together they capture a richly vital example of cultural fusion and world music. Before filming the concert the artist went outside the venue to see what was happening in the street. She was intrigued by the atmosphere of the evening and the coming dark, and filmed the scene, capturing the silhouettes of people coming and going over the hill outside the theatre. She notes that everyone was moving at a mellow pace, meeting and greeting, shaking hands, exchanging words, in a 'perfect flow of appearing and disappearing'. Seen in slow motion the film captures eloquently the rhythm and sense of place of this unremarkable event but, slowed down even more in the series of digital stills from the film, the effect is heightened. These images will in due course be screen printed, possibly as a filmstrip on fabric.

Christina Hallström operates at the edges of what can comfortably be termed 'printmaking', but her explorations of the potential of digital imaging, and the transference of such images into more conventional techniques, allow her the flexibility to approach her practice in ways that lead to idiosyncratic and sometimes unexpected results. By communicating the core of her work in the form of DVD recordings she is able to reach audiences in a way that framed prints do not always achieve. The themes she pursues are universal and democratic, and inform every aspect of her work.

www.cutproductions.net
(New technology, environment, memory)

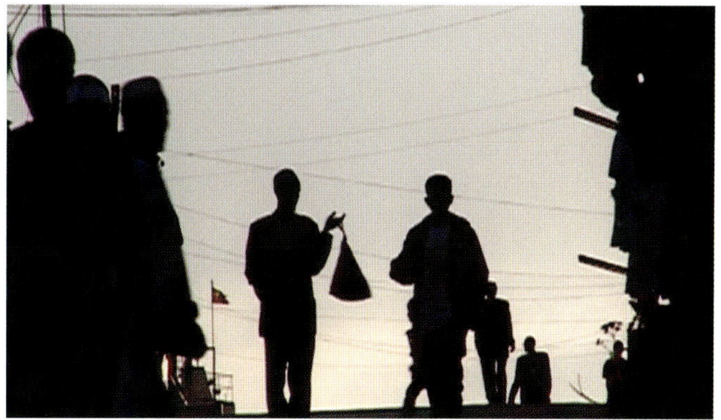

Christina Hallström, *Hill 13, 2007*.
Digital video still, size variable.

CURTIS WILLIAM READEL

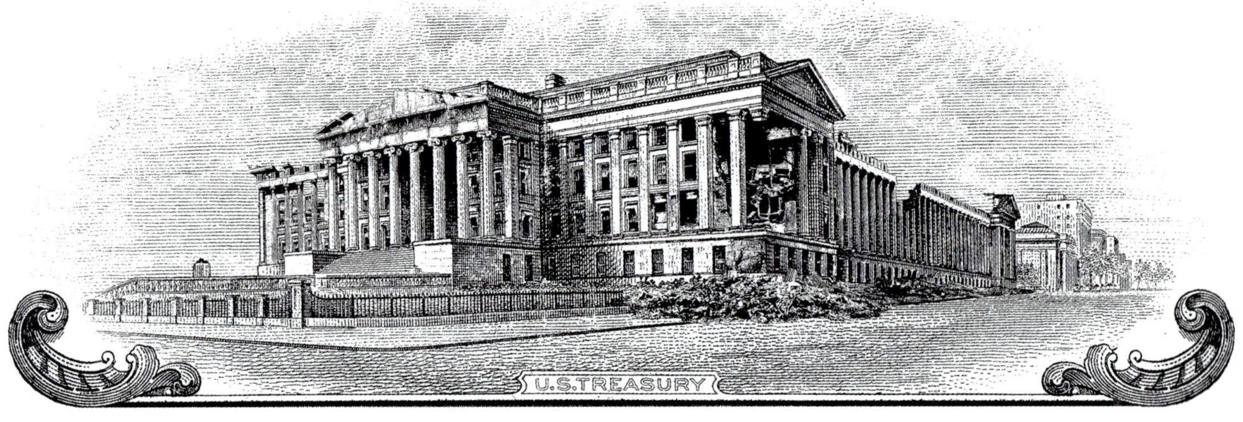

Curtis William Readel, *US Treasury in Ruins, 2009.*
Woodcut on Somerset Satin paper, 76.2 x 152.4cm. 30 x 60in.

Curtis William Readel gained his master's degree from Northern Illinois University in DeKalb in 2009. He is at the start of his career, but already has a good record of exhibitions in the United States and in Europe, including Estonia, where he won an award at the Tallinn Triennale in 2007. His work has for a number of years had a strong sense of social engagement, including eloquent life-size prints of homeless people printed on found cardboard cartons. But it is his work since 2006 that has provided this artist with the theme that he has since pursued with considerable success.

The design of currency notes, and the preparation of the engraving plates from which they are printed, has for many years been the preserve of artists highly skilled in the graphic arts. The results of their work are seldom looked at with a critical eye, being generally treated as a means to an end, a bill of exchange for goods and services. However, towards the latter part of the 20th century and increasingly since, artists have taken currency design and subverted it within their work as a way of making political or social comment. The Zero Dollar (1978–84) of the Brazilian conceptual artist Cildo Meireles, as well as currency-based works from 2008 by New York artist Laura Gilbert, derived from the familiar designs of US dollar bills, can be seen as responses to the crisis in capitalism and the world financial market.

Readel also uses US currency bills as the starting point for his work, but proceeds in a very different manner and in his idiosyncratic style. His motivation is, as with the other artists mentioned, social and political, expressing the sense of unease and despair that he experienced as a student in the dying years of the George W. Bush presidency. Some who see his work might regard it as being unpatriotic, but a more generous reading would see it as the work of a young American artist who observes the machinations of the financial world in his country and seeks a greater and more inclusive democracy. In this regard his work is closely related to the changes in administration in the United States towards the end of the first decade of the 21st century.

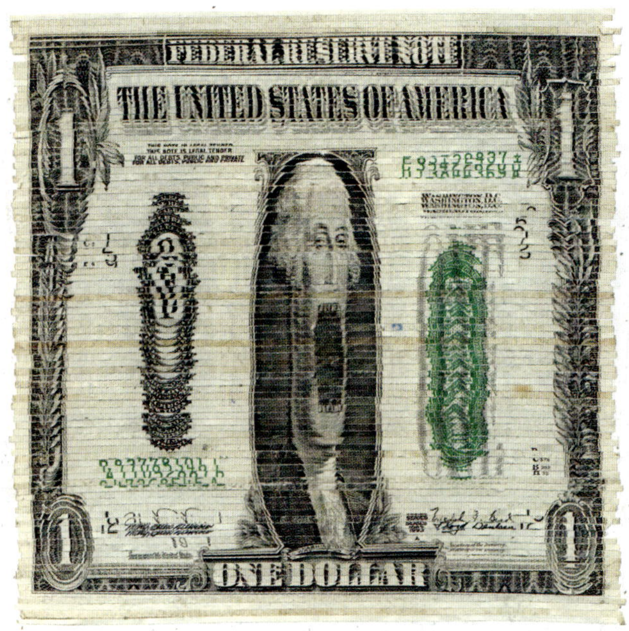

In his early work on the theme of currency Readel shredded dollar bills and then rearranged the strips from a number of bills to create collages in which elements of the design were exaggerated, stretched or compressed. For example, in *Stairway to Heaven* the reverse of the $5 bills are shredded and duplicated to extend the steps leading to the Lincoln Memorial, creating an image not dissimilar to an Aztec pyramid. These reconfigured images of the familiar produce a disorienting effect that summed up with an eloquent simplicity the growing sense of uncertainty about the future. In another early series, *Dead White Guys from US History*, screenprinted images of the portraits in cartouche of former presidents that appear on the reverse of dollar bills are reinvented with skulls beneath the hair and beards. Revered images of historical figures are offered in a different form as a potent memento mori, with a series title that can perhaps be read as being prescient of the first black president. Another work from the early phase is the small woodcut print *He Favors Our Corruption'*, in which the mysterious image of the pyramid surmounted by an all-seeing eye is subverted, with the regular courses of stone replaced by a pile of skulls – a bitter comment on the consequences of war and the legacy of imperialism.

Curtis Readel's work for his graduation exhibition extended his theme in both scale and approach and included a series of three woodcut prints, subsequently exhibited in the Packer Schopf Gallery under the title *Damn Nation*. These large prints, impressive in the skill of their execution, were derived from the images of iconic Washington, DC buildings that appear on $10, $20 and $50 bills – The White House, the Capitol and the US Treasury – here depicted in ruins. In appropriating these images the artist comments on the deterioration of public morality, the rise of corruption and the fragility of empires with the premonition of their eventual destruction. The publicity for the exhibition notes that, 'Reflecting issues of self-indulgence, corruption, and societal downfall, these metaphors signify that nothing is permanent.' Readel also worked in conjunction with the sculptor, Evan D'Orazio, to produce a bronze bust of George Washington, his head a skull, with the title *Genius Seculi* (The Guardian Spirit of the Century), which complements the decay shown in his prints. This artist's work, based on his deep concerns about the future, reflects an uncertain and changing world.

www.curtiswilliamreadel.com
(New uses for old technology, politics, The new generation)

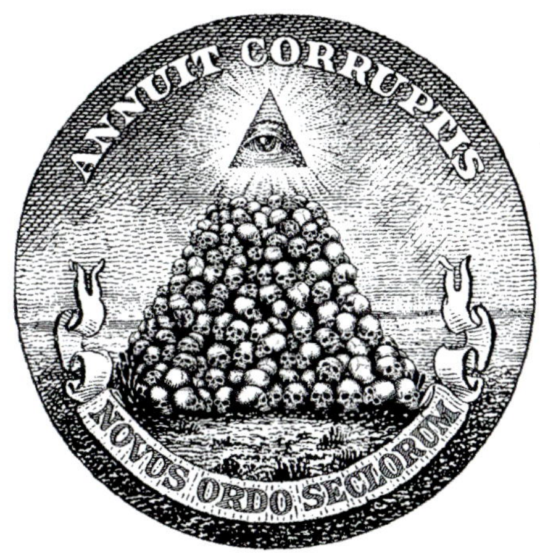

Curtis William Readel, *He Favors Our Corruption, 2008.*
Woodcut, 76.2 x 76.2cm. 30 x 30in.

DIANE VICTOR

Two things become apparent when first encountering the idiosyncratic work of Diane Victor: the extreme confidence with which she approaches the technical problems of making prints and drawings, and the uncompromising, even obsessive manner in which she approaches the contentious themes and subjects with which she chooses to work. Brought up on a farm in a deeply rural area of South Africa, Victor's close attachment to the land and peoples of that country lies at the core of her working practice in printmaking, and particularly in drawing, which remains the main motive force in her work. She studied at the University of Witwatersrand in Johannesburg, graduating in printmaking in 1986. Since then she has worked as an artist and has taught part-time at a number of institutions in the country. Her work, which has a powerful psychological and physical presence, and does not shirk from addressing the cruelty and violence that is still a prevalent factor in her country, has been exhibited to acclaim in South Africa and beyond.

Diane Victor is working on an ongoing series of small etchings, numbering 30 at the end of 2008, with the title *Disasters of Peace*. Inspired by the seminal series of etchings that Goya made during the Peninsular War of 1808–14, 'The Disasters of War', she intends that this series should alert people to the ongoing violence in a country that is still struggling to create a peaceful 'Rainbow Nation'. The images are of incidents and events, as reported by local media in the country, that show the extent to which social and criminal violence still runs deeply through South African society. As with all her work, these images are uncompromising in the clarity with which they show violence, and characterised not only by a fine control of line and tone but also by the scraps of phrases that border the prints, adding sardonic comments to the images. In one of the etchings, *Mad Bob*, the President of neighbouring Zimbabwe is shown stomping across the land, playing a toy tin drum, while in one corner the figure of Bob the Builder, the children's TV character, is changed into Bob the Bulldozer, and the word

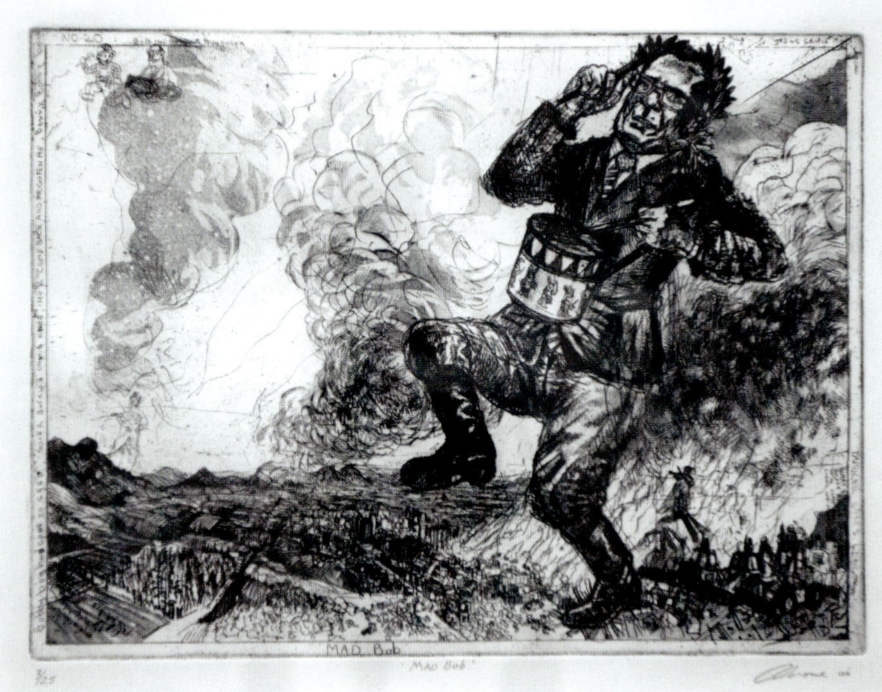

Diane Victor, *Mad Bob (from the Disasters of Peace series), 2006.* Etching, 28 x 32cm. 11 x 12.5in. Photo: John Hodgkiss.

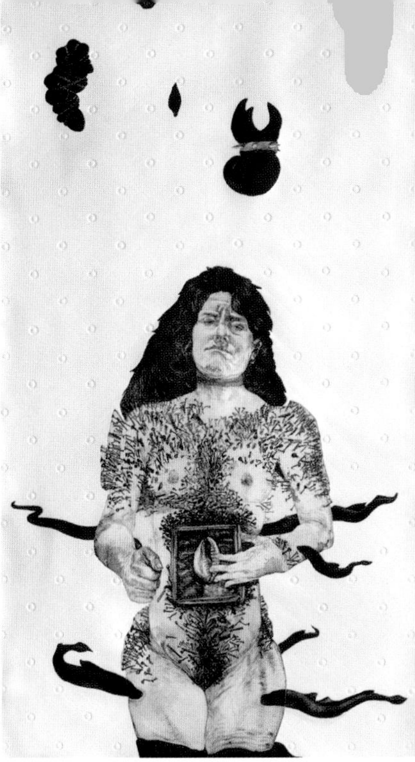

'marry' in the first verse of the folk song 'Bobby Shaftoe' is changed to 'frighten': satire, anger and black humour meet in these works, not dispelling the horrors they portray but sharpening them to powerful effect.

In her drawings, many of which are large-scale, the artist often uses her body as a reference, short-circuiting the need for a model but also closing the gap between the object and subject, and obviating the ambiguity of the artist's gaze on the model, which is so common in the canon of Western art. Some of these drawings are autobiographical, referring to the artist's experience during her travels in France and Austria, and many of them can be read on a number of levels. In 2004 she exhibited a major series of large drawings, *The Eight Marys*, in the Cathedral of St John the Divine in New York: her presence in each of the figures is clear.

This practice continues in some of Victor's prints, adding a further layer for interpretation. Two large prints made in 2004, in a complex blend of etching, aquatint, mezzotint and blind embossing, highlight the skill that Victor has developed in the making of powerful images. In one, *Learning Posture*, the powerful body of a black man is constrained in a ludicrous fashion by a tightly laced corset; the body has the rich density of mezzotint while the corset and other trappings are created in blind embossing. In the corner an ornamental grille, through a garden can be glimpsed, serves to symbolise the constraint of the figure, which itself symbolises unequivocally a lack of freedom. In the accompanying print, *Practising Poise*, a naked

standing woman stares out from a background embossed with the regularity of wallpaper. Images of primeval sharks nibble at the woman's body, which is studded with nails, as in African fetish figures. The woman holds a picture of a shell, exposing its open cleft. As with the man, the woman has yet to find her freedom.

Diane Victor once confessed to being, 'not a very vocal person' – that she, 'wouldn't be able to draw if drawings had voices'. When engaged on a new body of work she prefers to withdraw to her rural home, avoiding social interaction, the better to concentrate on the work. Nevertheless, her work speaks with a powerful and passionate eloquence of the troubled context and history of the country in which she lives. She is, for certain, a committed and engaged artist, albeit one who has said of herself, 'I do not intend to improve society but only to make people think slightly.'

www.art.co.za/dianevictor
(Post-colonialism, Politics, Memory)

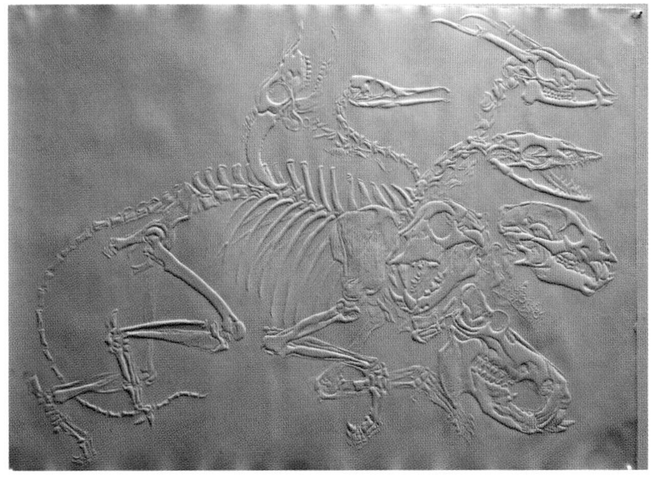

Diane Victor, *Beast of the Apocalypse, 2008.* Blind embossing on Hahnemühle paper, 84 x 120cm. 33 x 47in.

EGLĖ KUCKAITĖ

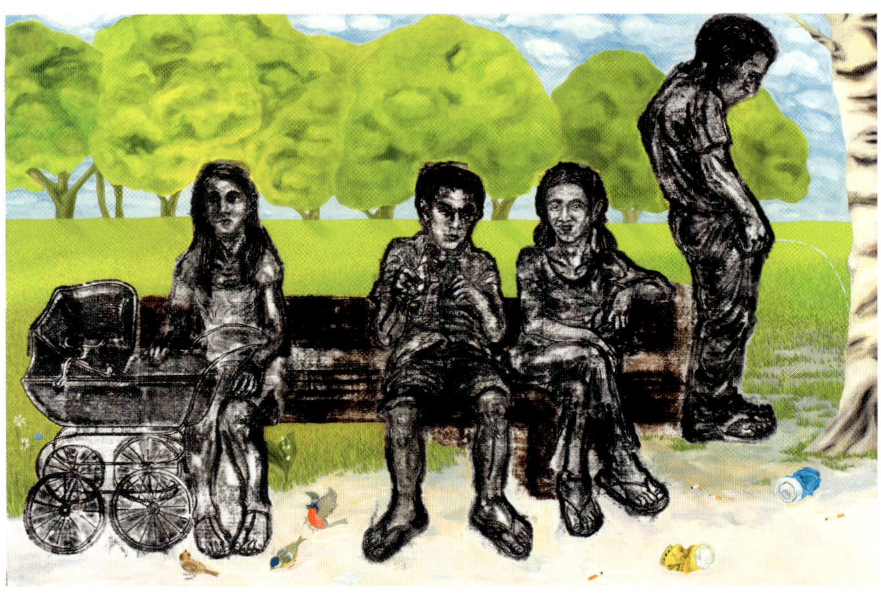

Eglė Kuckaitė, *Pranciška, 2008.*
Monoprint, oil paint on canvas,
157 x 235cm. 62 x 92.5in.

Lithuania is a small country in northern Europe, on the edge of the Baltic, with traditions that reach back into the country's historic forests of myth and legend. The constitution of the still-young Republic of Lithuania enshrines in its preamble, among other rights, 'the innate right of the human being and Nation to live and create freely in the land of their fathers and forefathers…' This determination has helped to foster the development of one of the most interesting and idiosyncratic arts communities in Europe. Eglė Kuckaitė graduated from the Academy of Fine Arts in Vilnius in 1995, and has since developed her practice in printmaking and other mediums, notably in book illustration, including work she did for a volume of folk tales.

This aspect of her work provides a clue to her activities as a printmaker, linking her acutely contemporary approach to ancient traditions and beliefs, through which her work has acquired a quiet strength.

Kuckaitė has exhibited widely and with success throughout Lithuania and internationally, and has been the recipient of a number of awards, including the prestigious Grand Prix at the International Triennial of Graphic Arts in Prague in 2007. This competition is unique, being between artists who have already been the recipient of major awards in other competitions. This artist's inclusion in the competition was the result of her being awarded the Grand Prix at the Tallinn Print Triennial in Estonia in 2004. For that exhibition she created a 500cm (197in.) square wall installation printed from rubber stamps, based on her own meticulous small drawings. Using the same technique for the Prague competition she created *Switching to the Light Mode*, in which Kafka and Čiurlionis, major cultural figures from the Czech Republic and Lithuania respectively, sit opposite each other winding wool – an essentially domestic activity that requires concentration and cooperation from both

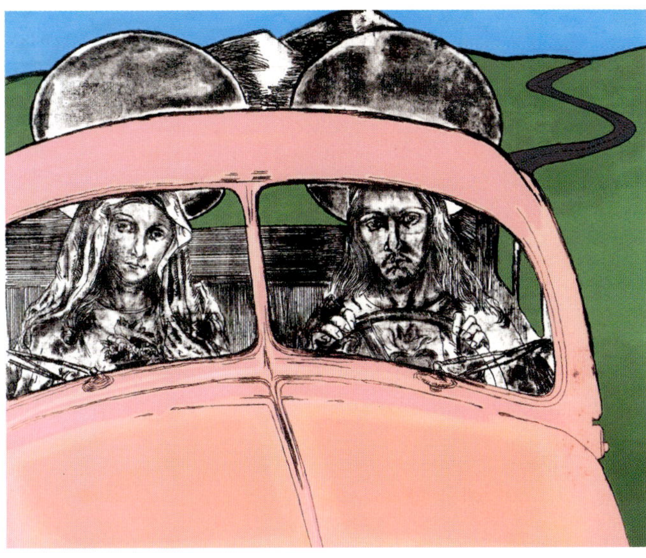

participants. Of this work the artist has said, 'A distance – a respectful distance – is required for this act. In the symbolic language of the twining of threads I am talking about the individuality of the personalities mentioned, the exclusivity of the act.' The work created a powerful and profound link between two creative geniuses in European culture. The comment of the Prague jury was, 'The conceptual complexity of Kuckaitė's work, combined with her unique and personal stamped images, links the worlds of the Czech Republic and Lithuania, and extends to all humanity. The simplicity of her fresh approach to the concept of transfer impressed the jury, whose vote was unanimous.'

While the scale of her wall installations is large, this artist also works in etchings, often at a small and intimate scale, with a plate size as small as 4 x 8cm (1.5 x 3in.) usually portraying, appropriately, intimate scenes that are almost calligraphic in the brevity and concision of the line, and which do not seek to disguise the marks used to make them. There are embraces and kisses, often between nude couples with delicately drawn hair or otherwise bald, as well as streetscapes of Vilnius, and Eglė, the grass-snake goddess of Lithuanian legend. The critic Julė Šiurkutė has commented that the artist 'seems more impressed by the Oriental way of structuring a view, where the image of the thing, its history, function and archetype, become inconsequential, opening instead huge vistas of longing, sadness or philosophy.'

In a more recent cycle of work, Eglė Kuckaitė has turned to a different theme, the business of growing up, with all the confusion and angst that entails. In these larger works, produced with monoprint and oil on canvas, the artist explores aspects of the experience of growing up. At first sight the technique seems crude, even unsophisticated, but with a deeper consideration it is seen to be totally appropriate to the subject matter. In one, *Pranciška*, which was also the title of the exhibition in Tallinn for which the series was originally made, there is a simply painted park scene with trees, a park bench, a few flowers and a number of brightly painted birds, cigarette butts and drinks cans. In this painted setting there are four teenage figures, rendered in monochromatic monoprint: a girl with a pram, another girl smoking, a boy drinking, and another boy urinating against a tree – just a normal day in the park, pregnant with the future. In another work in the same series, *The Heart is the Flame*, archetypal representations of Jesus and the Virgin Mary drive across an empty landscape in an old pink Volkswagen Beetle; their haloes stand up behind their heads like discs, or Sisyphean boulders pursuing them down the hill. The predominant religion of Lithuania, Catholicism, is held up, not to ridicule, but to question. This artist observes, records and moves on.

www.graphic.lt/en/artists/egle-kuckaite-en
(Large-scale printmaking and installation,
New uses for old technology)

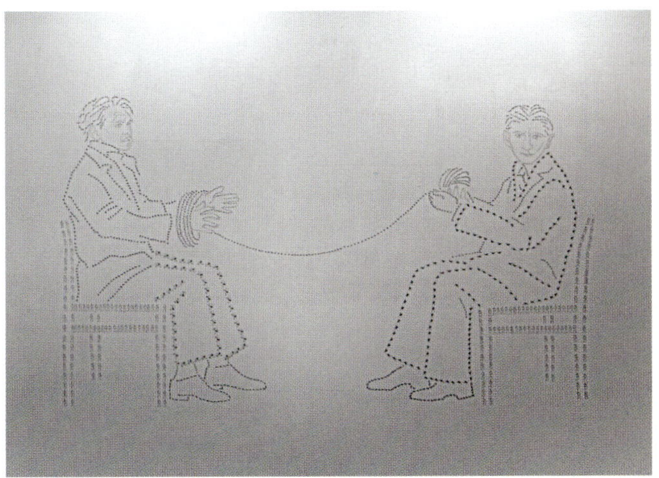

Eglė Kuckaitė, *Switching to the Light Mode
(installation at the Old Town Hall, Prague), 2007.*
Wall installation, rubber stamps, ink,
500 x 700cm. 197 x 276in.

GAIA PERSICO

The roots of Gaia Persico's practice lie in drawing and travelling, a combination familiar from the sketchbooks of travellers and artists across many centuries. In the case of this artist, however, the combination is predicated very much on 21st-century technology and on global mobility. Born in Rome, she studied for her master's degree at the Wimbledon School of Art in London, where she now lives. In addition to exhibiting widely she has curated exhibitions, and has won a number of awards. As well as pursuing her practice as an artist, she also works as a member of the cabin crew with a major long-haul airline, wherein lies the raison d'être and primary inspiration for her work.

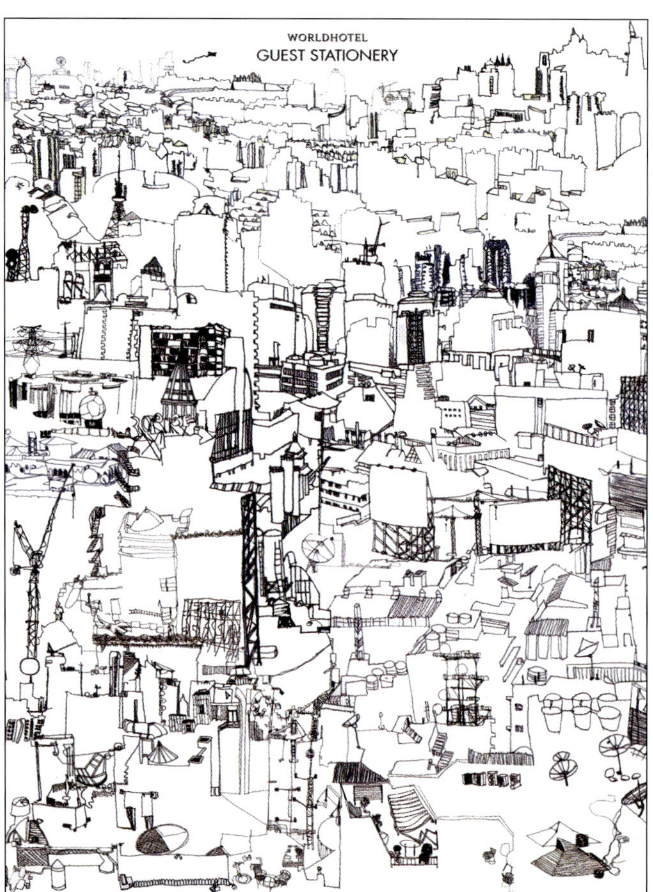

Gaia Persico, *World Hotel, 2008/09*. Inkjet print, 31.4 x 23.2cm. 12 x 9in. Commissioned for Blueprint magazine no.273.

She comments, as do many for whom frequent travel is a fact of life, on the sense of dislocation that comes from arriving in yet another city somewhere in the world for just a short stay. The international chains of hotels at which flight crew generally stay may have their own identities, but this is replicated in all the hotels in each chain, as a result of which waking in a hotel room in a strange city carries with it a comforting sense of familiarity that is only dispelled on drawing back the curtains. Travelling should ideally be about knowing where you are and how you relate to the place in which you find yourself: in many cases contemporary travel seems to work against that proposition so that one experience blurs into another.

The strategy that Persico has developed in recent years is to find the means for recording her presence in a location, to discover a way of saying, 'I was there'. One aspect of this work is seen in the drawings she makes in each hotel where she stays, always on the available hotel stationery and usually with the ballpoint pens provided in the rooms. She observes the view from the window and records it in simple lines on the hotel note or letter paper, the printed logo and address being integral to the drawings. A combination of such images was produced in 2008/09 in the form of an inkjet print entitled *Worldhotel*. The other aspect of this ongoing project involves using her laptop computer and the Photoshop® program to make a record of the view from her hotel-room window, making the drawing and later adding colour, using her finger directly on the laptop's touchpad. She comments that drawing with the aid of a mouse, or even a tablet and stylus, would give her too much control for her purposes, and that the lack of precision is indeed part of the ethos of her work. Once back at her home in London she refines the images and reproduces them on a conventional inkjet printer, using thin white card that has previously been printed on the back with the details of the location in the style of traditional postcards. These postcard prints are then carried with her the next time her roster takes her (or sometimes they are taken by a colleague) to the destination where the original drawing was made, so that they can be stamped and sent by conventional mail back to her partner in London. On arrival they bear the postmarks and other evidence of being sent through the international mail system, whereupon they form part of a growing archive. These small prints are evidence of her travel, but, more than that, are connected to her themes:

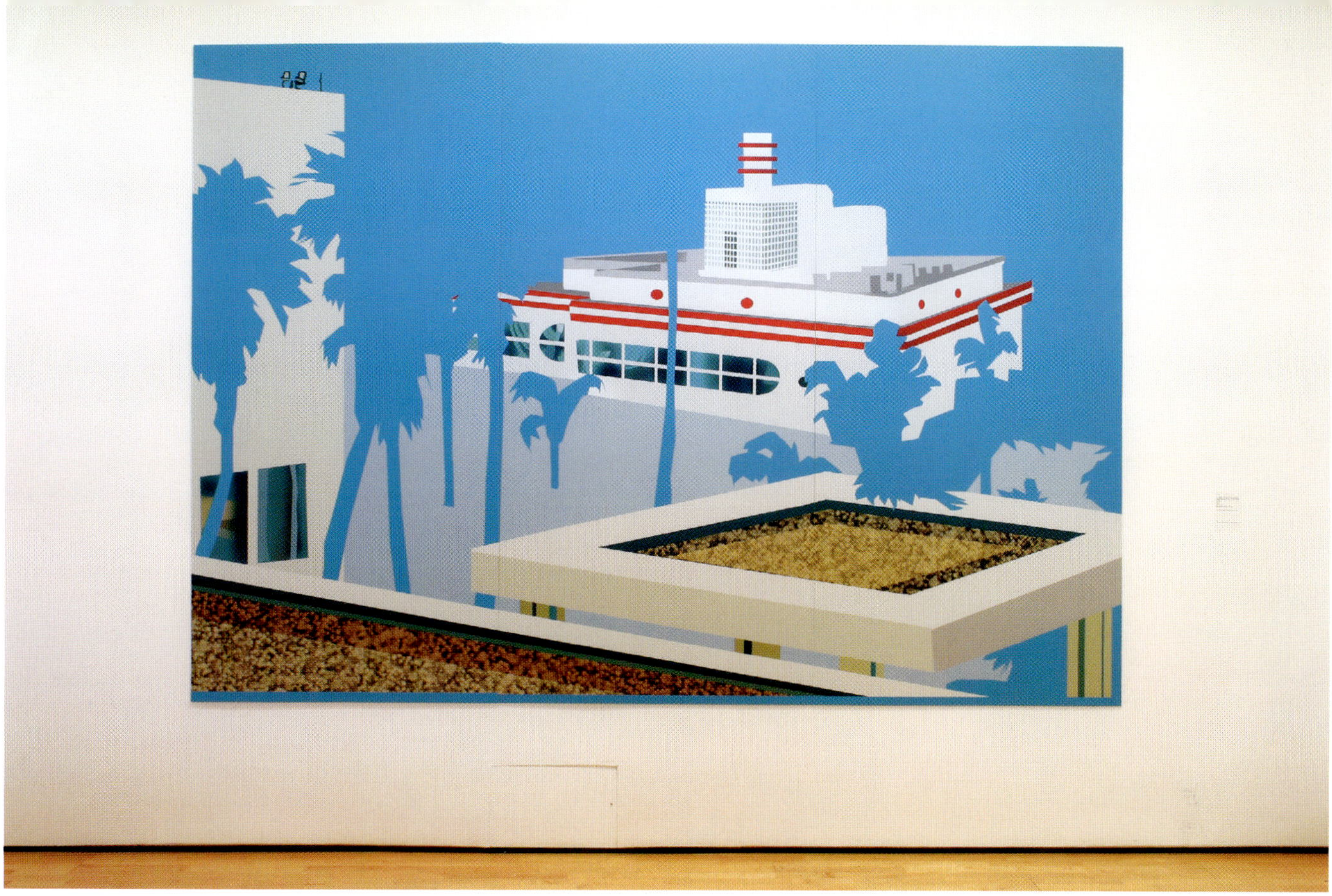

Gaia Persico, *Crowne Plaza Hotel, Los Angeles, USA, Room 4075, Fri 20 July 2007, 12.58, 2009.* Inkjet print on canvas, 233 x 330cm. 92 x 130in.

the need to capture something of the essence of travelling, the effects of long-distance travel, and the unsettling effect of crossing time zones only to arrive in yet another generic hotel in yet another destination, for yet another short stay during which very little can be discerned of the life and culture of that place. In short it is about the deracination that frequent travel can induce.

Some of the digital images of the postcards are subsequently used as the basis for large-scale inkjet prints – by which means they function very much in the same way as paintings – and for animations on DVD discs, to be shown on the small screens of DVD players or as wall-sized projections. These animations record movements of elements and changes in colour in the views that were originally recorded. These changes are can be very subtle, requiring well-focused concentration on the part of the viewer: in this way the meditative quality of time is incorporated into the image. In 2008/09 Gaia Persico began creating sculpture – a garden shed, a traditional fisherman's hut from Sardinia, a reed boat – that incorporates a DVD animation, adding yet another dimension to her work. Travel, as the old cliché puts it, broadens the mind.

www.gaiapersico.com
(New technology, The third dimension, Memory)

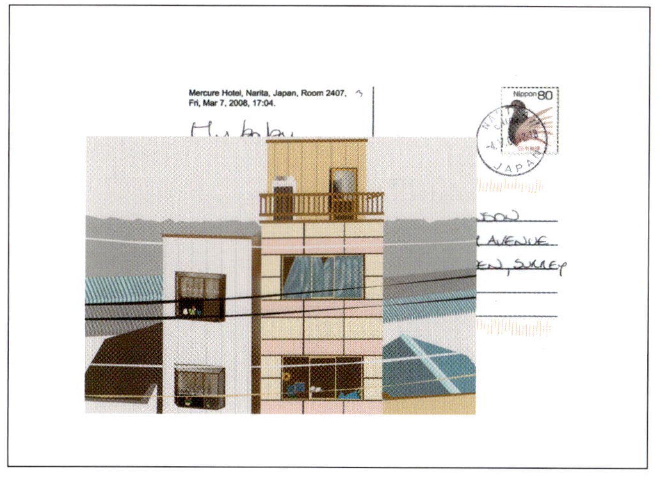

Gaia Persico, *Wish You Were Here (detail of Narita), 2005– (ongoing series).* Digital print on postcard, 10.6 x 15.9cm. 4 x 6in.

GERALDINE BERKEMEIER

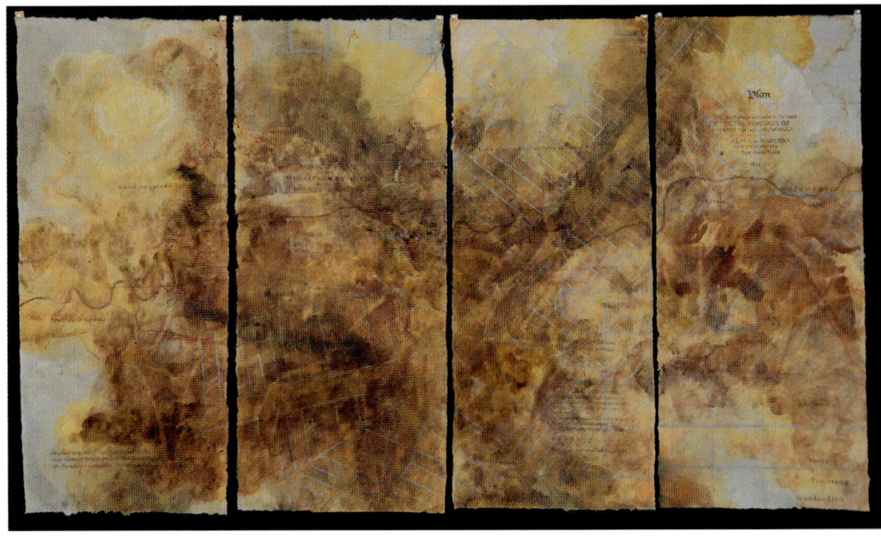

Geraldine Berkemeier, *Southbound, 2009.* Monotype, transfer and wash, 80 x 133cm. 31.5 x 44.5in.

The work of this artist, who lives and teaches in Sydney, is concerned with notions of land ownership, the impact of colonial exploitation, and the nature of the land itself. Geraldine Berkemeier spoke at the IMPACT 5 conference in Tallinn, Estonia, in 2007 about the problems faced by Australian artists based in cities, in particular those who are not of indigenous descent, in positioning themselves in a culture that is more than 40,000 years old, one that is 'non-materialistic in respect and harmony with the land', and 'carries with it significant cultural information, transcends the culture that produced it to speak universally, is celebratory, optimistic and joyful'. The rise to prominence of Aboriginal art, its considerably increased collectability and investment potential over the past 40 years, has produced a situation in which there are undoubtedly some conflicts, giving rise to accusations of exploitation and cultural dilution. This aspect of the cultural context has an influence on those artists of European origin, as they seek ways in which to enter into a deeper and more relevant relationship between their art and the country in which they live.

At the time of the conference Berkemeier had recently completed an exhibition project with Gary Shinfield, '*Sink or Swim*', which explored the question of asylum seekers reaching Australia from across the Pacific. In this respect Australia presents a paradox, in that during the 200 years since the First Fleet landed white European settlers on the shores of Botany Bay, a multicultural nation has developed, predominantly in the major cites on the coastal fringe of the continent, while the vast open spaces of the interior remain much as they always were, albeit with some notable exceptions that involve exploitation and environmental degradation. That the government of the country sought the means for discouraging a further wave of immigration was the subject of their joint exhibition, which toured several galleries in the country in 2006–08.

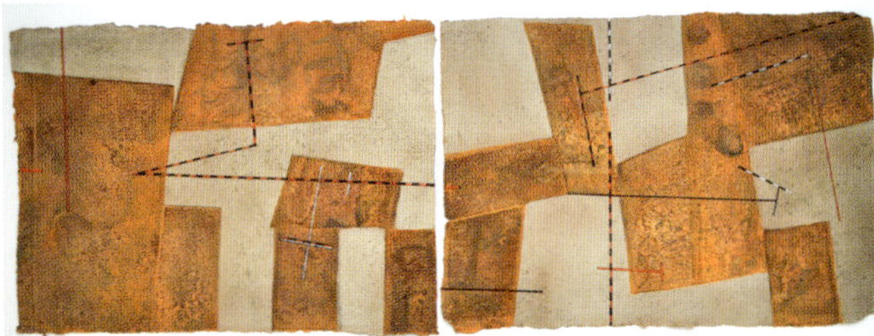

Geraldine Berkemeier, *Earthbound II, 2009.*
Relief print and drawn line on stained
handmade paper with embossing,
43 x 120cm. 17 x 47in.

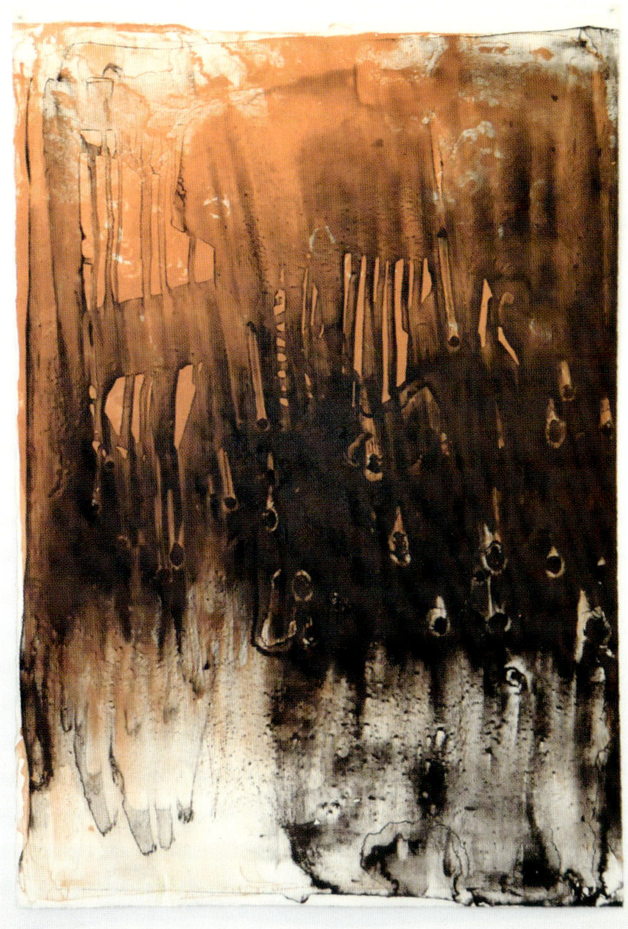

The question of exploitation also forms part of the context for her 2009 exhibition at the Regional Art Gallery in Goulburn, situated between Sydney and Canberra, and described as Australia's 'first inland city'. Goulburn is in New South Wales, which the British laid claim to in 1788, but before that the Goulburn area formed part of the traditional lands of the Gandangara people. Not far away is Marulan, first established as a private village in the 1820s and then as the old town of Marulan in 1835, which, as one of the oldest townships in New South Wales, is on the State Heritage Register. In recent years it has been bypassed by the Hume Highway and has become the site of a new quarry development. Prior to the destruction that such a massive excavation would entail there was an archaeological dig and, probably for the first time in Australia, it was decided to involve an 'artist in residence' to work with the archaeologists. Geraldine Berkemeier worked on the site during late 2007/08, developing the project that resulted in the Goulburn exhibition *Digging Marulan*.

She describes the exhibition installation, which includes sculpture as well as prints in various techniques (including relief and staining with some embossing on thick handmade paper), as addressing 'the archaeological process of sifting through layers of dirt and subsequent selection and rejection of artefacts and evidence often necessary in distilling information acquired through this process'. This scientific process is in some respects not so very different from the process of selection and classification of imagery and information that an artist goes through in the creation of a new work. In the case of archaeology a further layer of exploration is involved – namely, the seeking of information to better understand the history of the site through analysis of the layers of evidence of human habitation. Berkemeier devised her *Sifter* sculptures as semi-autonomous means of selecting for further study, or rejecting for re-interment, components of the soil passed through them. The natural colours of the soil at the site became the basis for the prints, providing pigment to be incorporated into them – establishing a direct link between the site and her interpretation of it.

In *Southbound*, using monotype, transfer and wash, she overlays a reproduction of the 1857 Plan for Farm Sales with washes of earth colours. In this work the palimpsest of the past reveals itself through the words on the old plan, some in English, others in English interpretations of Aboriginal place names. A large drypoint print, *Walking the Site*, reveals the traces of the artist's exploration, while other series of prints, entitled *Stain* and *Scrape*, as well as *Connect*, *Isolate* and *Earthbound*, provide a reflective interpretation of Geraldine Berkemeier's varying responses to her involvement with the past exploitation of this historic site, and its layers of fading memory.

www.gberkemeier.com.au
(Postcolonialism, Environment, Memory)

GUNTARS SIETIŅŠ

The invention of mezzotint is credited to Ludwig von Siegen, who in 1642 used it in a portrait print of The Landgravine of Hesse-Kassel. Von Siegen passed the technique on to Prince Rupert of the Rhine, Commander of the Royalist forces in the English Civil War, who taught the technique to Sir Peter Lely, renowned for the portraits he painted during that period. Thereafter mezzotint was used mainly as a method of making reproductions of paintings, but by the beginning of the 20th century had faded into obscurity. In recent years the technique has been revived and is now used by a growing number of artists, for whom the possibilities of printing in dense velvety blacks have proved irresistible. This density is a result of the technique that, through the treatment of metal plates (usually copper) with a rocker or roulette, produces a consistent surface of fine deep pits that can hold a lot of ink. Burnishing or scraping the prepared plate can create areas of tone or pure white, with a high degree of subtlety. Alternatively, in the 'light to dark'

method, the image is created by the skilful use of rockers and roulettes of different sizes, leaving the original surface of the plate as areas to be printed white.

Guntars Sietiņš, who was born in Latvia and is Associate Professor of Printmaking at the Latvian Academy of Art in Riga, has created a masterly body of work in this difficult technique, exhibits internationally, and is the recipient of a number of awards in international competitions. He also works in book and magazine design, and the design of currency notes and coins. Mezzotint offers an artist a rich resource for the creation of images that require a full tonal range from deepest black (sometimes in the case of this artist tinged with other colours) to clearest white. As for a philosopher or theologian, the full spectrum from darkness to light allows for deeply introspective works. The elemental primacy of black – the darkness, the chaos, from which light is created – is common to many world religions, leading to commonly held beliefs in the dualities of black and white, darkness and light, and many

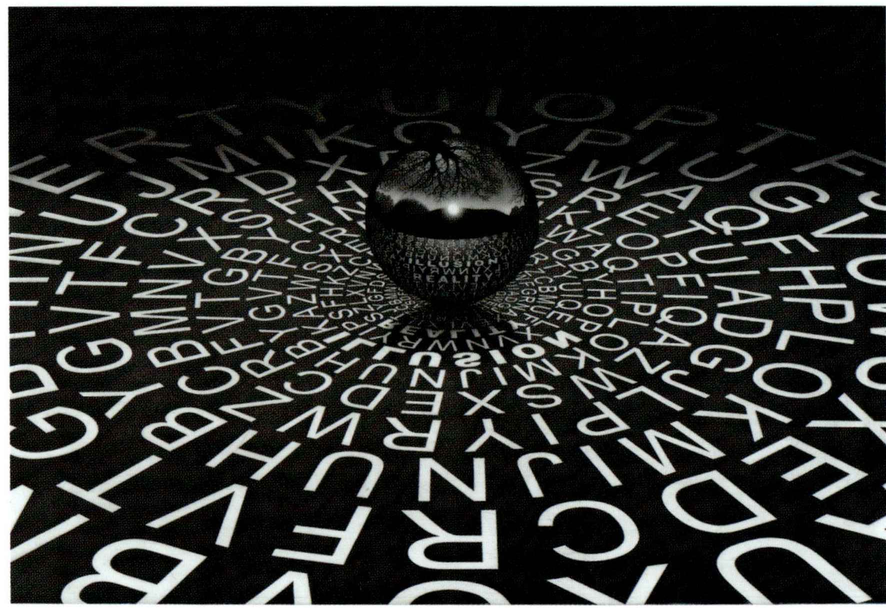

Guntars Sietiņš,
Characters 7: Illusion – Reality, 2008.
Mezzotint and aquatint,
60 x 90cm. 23.5 x 35.5in.

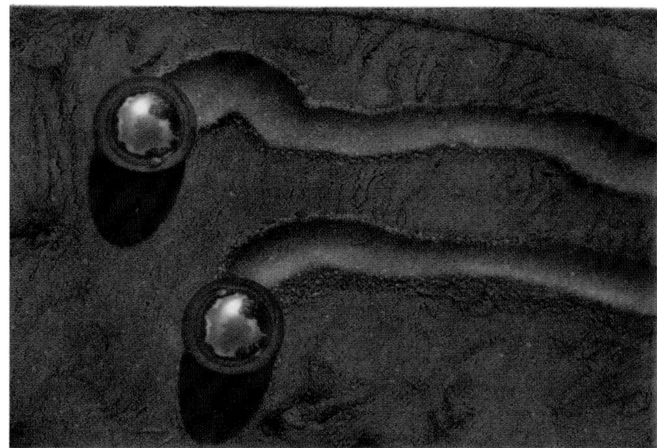

other such pairs of opposites. The challenge of manipulating a plate to explore images that depend on this rich spectrum of tones is one of precision, and the clarity of the images in mezzotint prints is one of characteristics that accounts for their growing popularity. To hold the imagination beyond first sight, however, requires more than mere technical skill: the image has to convey depths of meaning.

An early Sietiņš mezzotint, *State of Peace* (1987), shows the classical form of Ouroboros, the serpent swallowing its own tail, which symbolises the continuing cycle or the eternal return. In this image the artist has bound the serpent with twisted wire and depicts it mounted on a stone against a light background. In a series of prints from the final years of the 20th century the artist makes use of highly polished metal balls that he commissioned in 1994 for use as spherical mirrors. This motif has continued in his work up to the present, offering not only the element of perfect form that comes with a circle, but also the potential for including distorted reflections of reality. A series of prints that followed, entitled *Levitation*, made use of the spheres in photographic compositions that provided the starting point for the prints. The image of Ouroboros recurs in a different form in *Balance III* (1995), but in this image the serpent form balances on sand against the darkness, while balancing a metal sphere in which can be seen the reflection of a clump of trees. A celebrated drawing by M.C. Escher shows the

artist's hand holding a reflective sphere reflecting both him and the room in which he sits. Significantly, in the case of the Sietiņš print, and the *Characters* series of mezzotints with aquatint that followed later, from 2007 onwards, neither the artist nor the observer is reflected. The presence of the artist is clear from the existence of the work, but is not part of the manifest images: it as if he has chosen to hide within them. Instead the observer can regard the images for what they imply and for what they are – mysterious objects that reflect the surface upon which they are placed and the surrounding setting. In *Characters 5/ Light*, the sphere is placed in a lofty room on a tiled floor with a word in reversed letters, reflecting the room, together with the word 'light'. In *Characters 7/Illusion-Reality*, the sphere is placed on concentric circles of jumbled letters: the reflection is of a landscape, together with some of the letters, from which emerge the words 'Illusion' and 'Reality', a potent image for the work of this artist.

www.stoneandpress.com/prints/Guntars-Sietins/
(New uses for old technology)

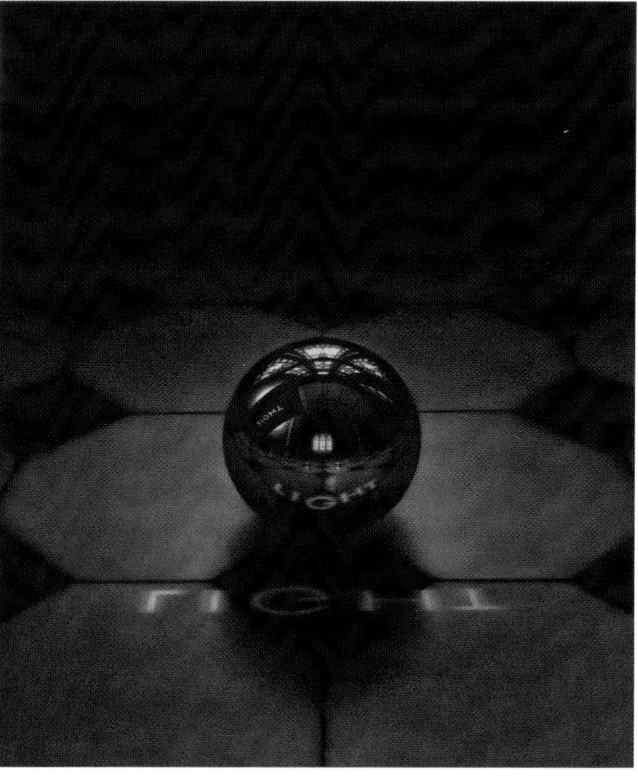

HELENA HORÁLKOVÁ

There is a long tradition in Central Europe of satire and social comment, whether in the form of theatre – for example, the Cricot2 Theatre of Tadeusz Kantor and the Black Theatre of Prague – or cabaret, which still survives in the region, albeit in a form adapted to 21st-century audiences. In addition there is an equally long tradition in the folk arts, including woodcut illustration, in which dark humour often plays a part. The centuries-long dominance of the region by one empire or another, and more recently the dark shadow of Communism, created an atmosphere in which protest could only be made in a symbolic manner, or as an 'underground' art form. In other parts of Europe, affected by different cultural imperatives, these traditions waned under pressure from increasing globalisation, although they do persist in changed forms in folk music and storytelling. In the 18th and 19th centuries satire was a more prominent part of the visual arts in, for example, France, with the powerful prints of Daumier being a prime example; and Great Britain, in particular through the acerbic caricatures of Gillray and Rowlandson, and the morally eloquent prints of Hogarth in series such as *The Rake's Progress.*

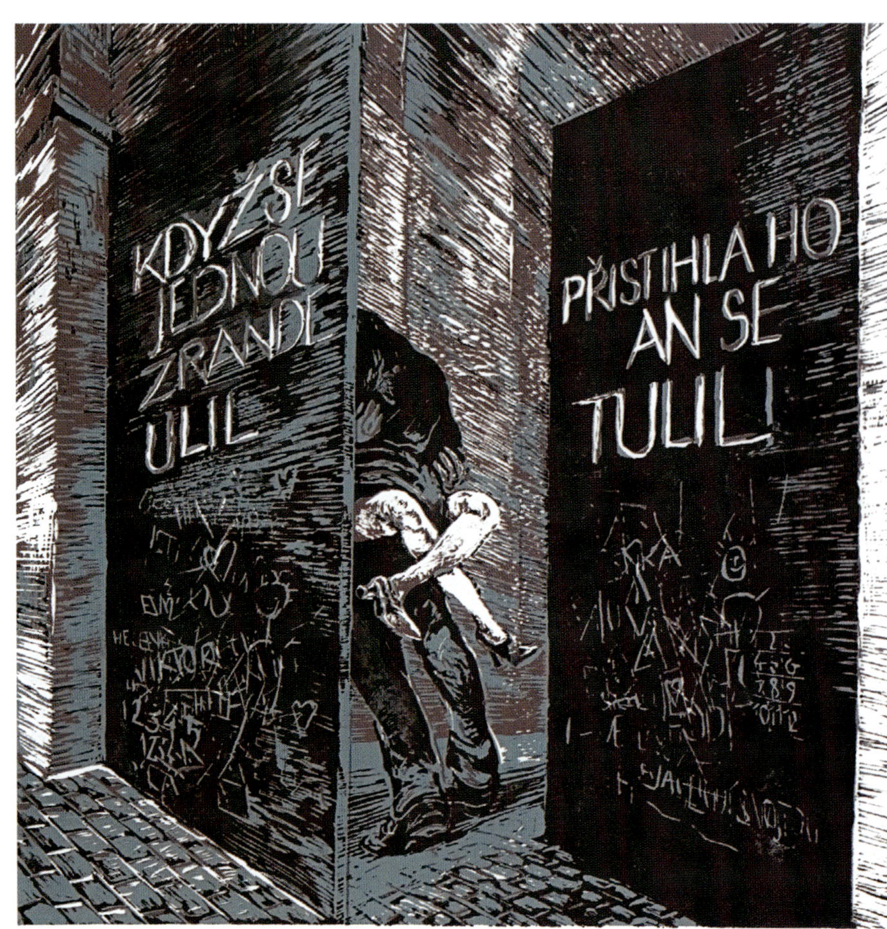

Helena Horálková, Byla panna, měla pána *(There was a maiden, she had a lad) No.6, 2006.* Linocut, 41 x 29.3cm. 16 x 12in.

Helena Horálková lives in Prague, and studied illustration there and in Berlin. She has a long record of solo and group exhibitions, and has been the recipient of a number of awards in her native country. Her early work in printmaking was mainly in etching and aquatint, in a style owing something to German Expressionism, and more lately to Symbolism, with images possessing something of the swirling lines and visionary power of William Blake. But it is in the medium of linocut that she has found a unique ability to create images that belong in the traditions but also have a continuing relevance, even in a world that has been changed by technology beyond anything her predecessors could have imagined. In relation to her work in intaglio prints she describes herself as being something of an alchemist, repeating the same experiment over and over, seeking an image nobler than the one that preceded it. She is also on record as saying, 'The deeply etched zinc plates are the mirror image of the scratches and scars that I suffered on the road through the labyrinth of the world.' This description is apt, and can been seen in her work from the 1980s onwards. It can be traced even more deeply in the two recent portfolios of linocuts.

The first of these portfolios, *Byla panna, měla pána* (translated approximately as 'There was a maiden, she had a lad') with 14 linocuts and an edition of 12, was made in 2006. It is based on an old urban song from Prague. The tale told is of a young woman who falls in love with a man who doesn't treat her well; when she discovers him being unfaithful to her she writes a letter rejecting him, and when he receives it he replies that if she doesn't meet him he will kill himself. This he does, and when the remains are brought to her she rejects him once

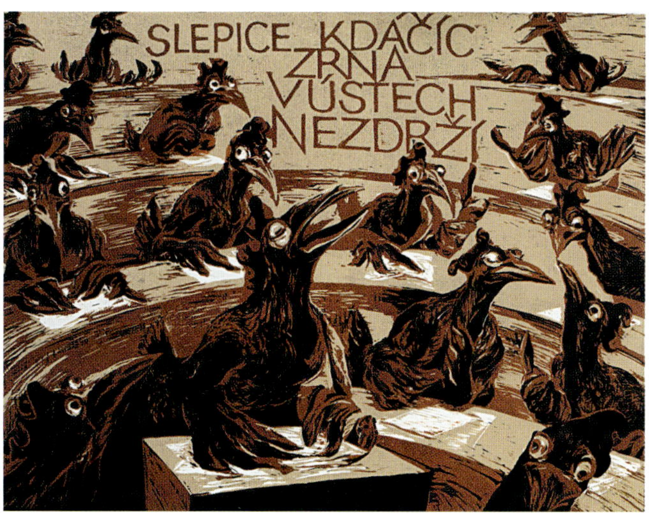

Helena Horálková, Slepice kdáčíc zrna v ústech nezdrž1
(A cackling hen cannot keep the grain in her mouth) (From Wise Sayings of the Slavonic People), 2008. Linocut, 29.7 x 41cm. 12 x 16in.

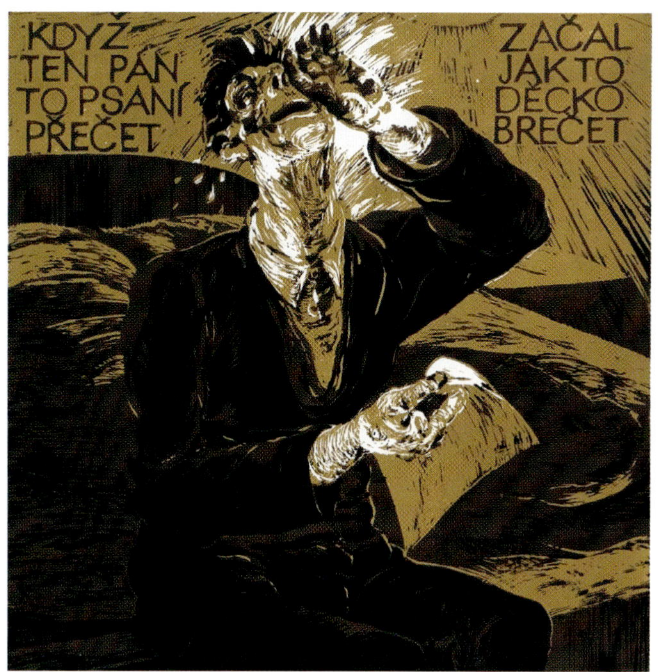

Helena Horálková, Byla panna, měla pána *(There was a maiden, she had a lad) No.9, 2006.* Linocut, 41 x 29.3cm. 16 x 12in.

again. The harsh humour of the song contains the elements of desire, betrayal and rejection, and is as relevant now as it was when it was first performed. The portfolio's palette of colours is limited, mostly to two or three colours for each print. The drawing style relates strongly to Expressionism and is entirely appropriate for the style and provenance of the song, while the dark humour and melodramatic nature of the words is echoed in the dynamic composition of each of the prints.

The second portfolio, *Wise Sayings of the Slavonic Nation*, comprises 12 linocut prints in an edition of 12. The text comes from the writing of František Ladislav Čelakovsky, and is a set of 12 aphorisms, many with a rustic and often coarse origin, but which nonetheless contain more than a little relevance for the present day. The prints are, as with the previous portfolio, produced in a similarly restricted palette of colours, and in much the same Expressionist style, but with a sharper, more pronounced sense of humour, entirely appropriate to the sayings. These include, 'Tongue-tied man and lazy cat are both bound to be hungry', and 'What is meant to hang will never drown, even if water runs over the gallows'.

Helena Horálková writes that she 'decided deliberately to turn away from relevant topics and have some fun', and 'I'll never be cool, I'm too naïve and besides I like the craft.' These sentiments are clearly apparent in these two portfolios, which are a triumphant assertion of the power of the traditional approach, provided that the artist has a clear contemporary view.

http://horalkova.wu.cz (New uses for old technology)

IGOR BENCA

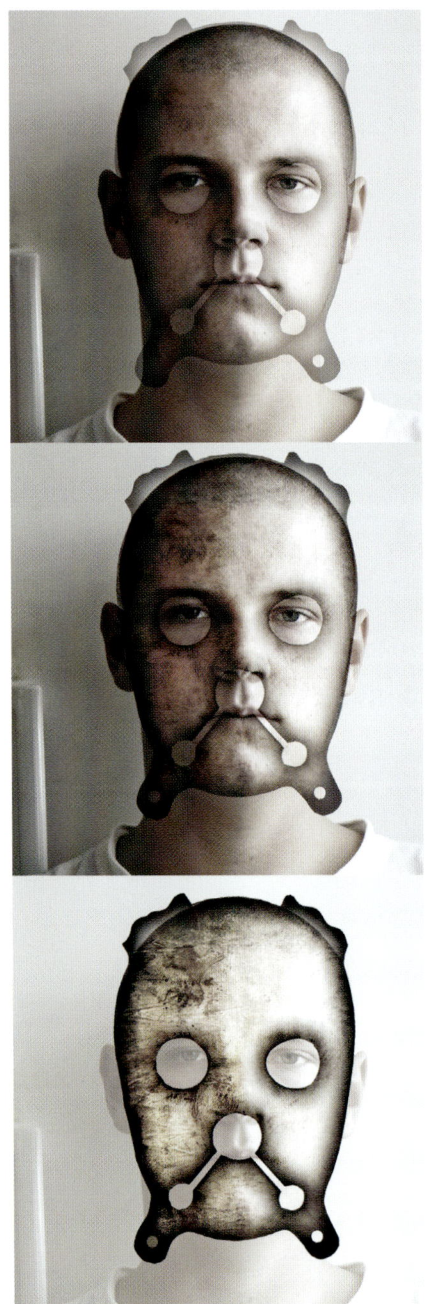

Igor Benca, *My Son – Faces – My Art Place 2, 2009.*
Digital and monoprint, 319 x 105cm. 126 x 41in.

The work of Igor Benca, more acutely than that of many artists, relates directly to the historical circumstances through which he has lived and within which he has developed his art. He studied throughout the 1980s in Bratislava, a city at that time in Czechoslovakia, and in addition to his work as an artist and designer since 1991 he has worked as a teacher, currently in the Art Academy in Banská Bystrica in what is now Slovakia. His academic training was therefore during the period in Czechoslovakia when the communist system in Europe was coming to an end. His working life began under that system, and continued through the Velvet Revolution of 1989 and the subsequent 'Velvet Divorce' of January 1993, when Slovakia and the Czech Republic became independent entities. It is not surprising that the work of this innovative artist has reflected those changes through the way it has evolved.

As a student Benca achieved a high level of skill in intaglio printmaking and the associated drawing skills essential to that traditional technique. These skills continue to provide the basis for his subsequent work in printmaking, his painting, and his work in a variety of aspects of graphics in Slovakia. The range of techniques he uses has increased, with digital, monoprint and combined techniques having been added to his work in etching and mezzotint. In the same manner he has widened the scope of his work, which now encompasses designs for postage stamps, as well as Ex Libris prints, which generally have a maximum dimension of 12cm (4¾in.), and his recent large-scale prints, in which the maximum dimension is over 3 metres (118in). The flexibility of this approach has given Benca's work a distinctiveness and individuality that is notable, even in a medium such as printmaking, where the term 'individual technique' is frequently encountered.

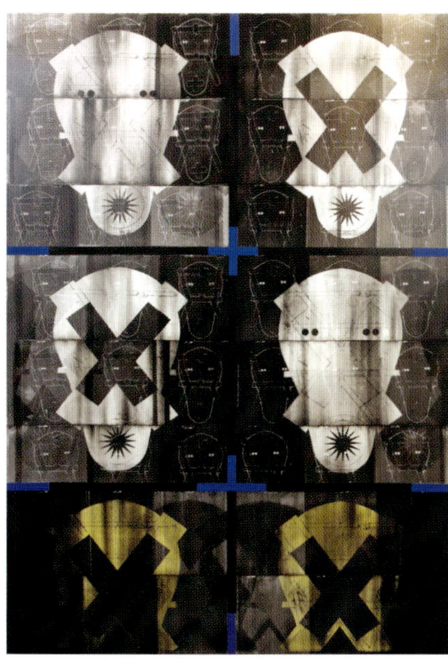

Igor Benca, *Night Sight 03, 2006.*
Combined print, 150 x 100.5cm.
59 x 39.5in.

The precise draughtsmanship and skilful technique essential to designing images as small as postage stamps and Ex Libris prints is as important as clear conceptual and imaginative ability. Throughout his extensive small-format work this artist has excelled in the creation of images that have an organic quality of line and shape that relates to the particular styles of Art Nouveau that developed in Central Europe, and a refined control of sumptuous colour. The Slovakian writer and critic Eva Trojanova, in her essay on Benca, has described these works as having the delicacy in line and shape of jewellery. She has also commented on the effectiveness of his decision to break away from the rigid rectangular format that Ex Libris prints have traditionally adopted, to create shapes that are more dynamic. The inspiration for such work contains elements that relate equally to biological forms and to machine forms containing elements of the idealistic design aesthetics of the 1930s. Decisions such as these allow the artist to explore in a dynamic and original way the essentially individual purpose of such small-format works.

The aspect of machine forms that is a distinctive element in Benca's small-format work becomes even more apparent in his large-scale work. In 1993 he made *On the Way to Heaven 01*, a print which marks a point of departure for much of the large work that has followed. This work is devoid of the richness of colour and complexity to be found in his smaller work, and like subsequent work relies on the presence of signs and symbols. Through this work comes a clear sense that the artist is using a personal language that expresses his unease with the increasingly technological society in which we live, and his concern at the distancing of human feelings that comes through our reliance on technology, with the price we pay being a loss of contact with the natural world.

A digital photograph made in 2003 has the title *Pokémon 00*, and this provided a further progenitor from which much of his subsequent work has evolved. The Pokémon figure that originated in Japan in 1996 became an international success, first as a computer game and subsequently across a wide range of merchandise. Its name is derived from the Japanese for 'pocket monster', and the global Pokémon phenomenon is an apt symbol for the profound effect that such creations can have on international consciousness. Benca took the essence of the character and turned it into a mask form, which appears in many guises in his work, singly or repeated in grid form across his large-scale prints, sometimes in conjunction with other elements derived from machinery. In two recent prints, 'My Son – Faces – My Art Place I and II', sequences of digital photographs have mask forms superimposed on them, becoming progressively more mechanised from top to bottom: the human face is shown being taken over by impersonal technological artefacts. The view is dystopian, but not without the possibility of salvation.

www.artbohemia.cz/Benca-igor
(New uses for old technology, New technology, Science)

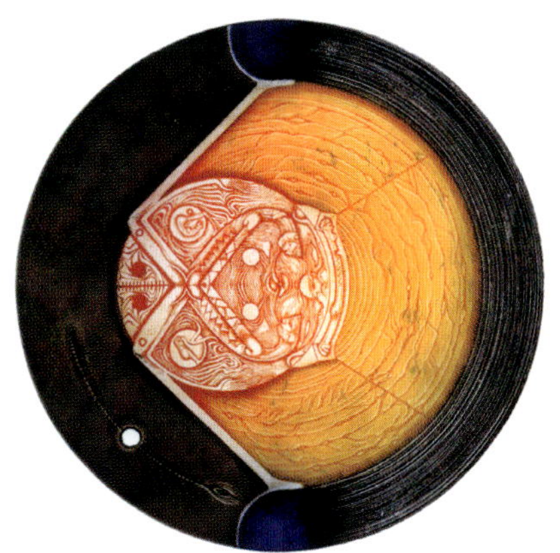

Igor Benca,
Sensors 06, 1999.
Etching and
mezzotint,
16.5 x 16.5cm.
6.5 x 6.5in.

JAN DAVIS

The work of Jan Davis is derived from, and relates to, the Australian landscapes in which she lives and works. Born in the state of Victoria, she followed her studies in Melbourne with a master's degree from Southern Cross University, where she now teaches. SCU is on the Gold Coast, south of Brisbane, the campus occupying a large area of land of which the Widjabal People of the Bundjalung Nation are the traditional custodians. The acknowledgement of custodians is a means for establishing that the land has a long and valued history that goes much further back than just over 200 years of British colonialism and Australian nationhood. It is also reflective of one of the central motivations in Davis's work – the search for an understanding of the landscape and her place within it: a study of place and belonging. Speaking at the IMPACT 5 conference in Tallinn, Estonia in 2007, she referred to a text by the artist Geoff Levitus, in which he 'described his profound disappointment at not being able to "fit" into the subtropical landscape in which he dwelt'. As a result of this he subsequently left his rural home to return to work in the city.

The landscape, and in particular the idea of genius loci, has long been a potent source of inspiration for artists and writers, which by extension offers a metaphorical context for understanding how we as human beings relate to each other, and more particularly to the environment in which we live. Jan Davis, who lives near the place where Levitus lived, based her initial approach to the landscape on the making of a garden (and on gardening as a form of meditation), with all the traditions and rituals that entails, as a way of deepening

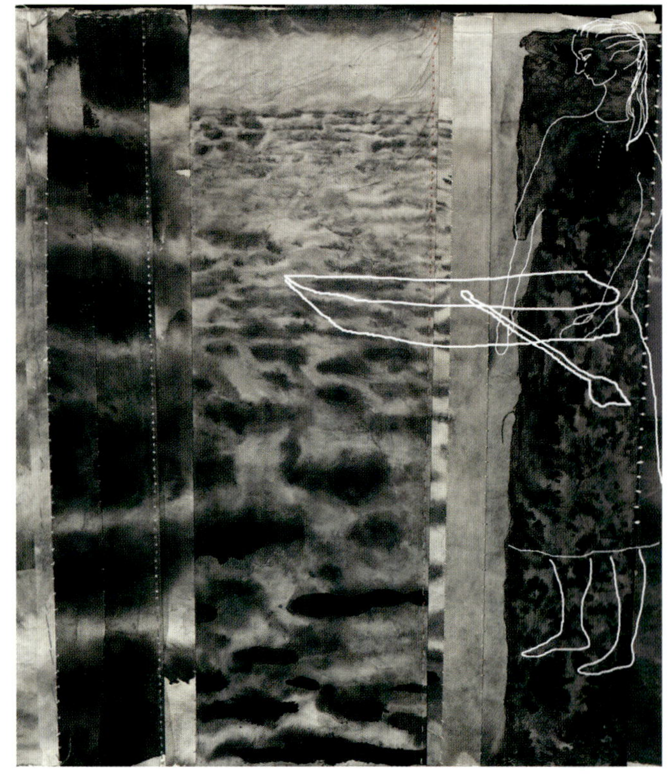

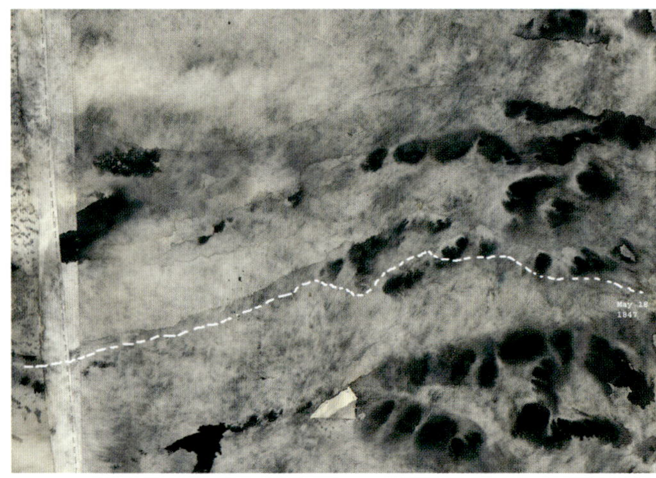

TOP **Jan Davis,** *Lohan Tuka Dreams, 2009.* Digital print on rice paper, 50 x 63cm. 20 x 25in.

BOTTOM **Jan Davis,** *May 18, 1847, 2009.* Digital print on rice paper, 73 x 62cm. 29 x 24.5in.

her engagement with the place in which she had chosen to live. In all of her work she searches for an understanding of the meaning of the land, through drawings – sometimes collaged or stitched together – prints and photographs, as well as videos, manipulating these works as a series of revelations. In writing about her environment she has said, 'although I know in a logical sense that I remain in a constant spatial relationship with my surroundings, in another sense the hills and valleys that embrace the house appear to morph and change throughout the day, throughout the year, providing dramatic and varied spatial shift, the experience of which could be said to be so different as to be experiencing another space.' This relationship with the ancient land, and the drawings that provide the basis for her work, comprise 'a rumination on my sense of dwelling in a particular place'.

The major project she is working on for her doctorate, which has the working title SEE/SAW: an investigation of place and belonging, is based on a deep study of East Gippsland, the location for stories that emerge from 19th-century diaries, and also stories told within her own family, which go back to the 1850 settlement of the land which remains her mother's home. She describes two 'key anchors' for both the stories and the project. One relates to the myth of a white woman held captive by Aboriginal tribes, which has never been verified despite three 19th-century expeditions over a 20-year period to find the woman, known to the indigenous peoples as Lohan-Tuka. The myth persists in accounts and letters from these expeditions, in a text by an indigenous author, in a diary and in a novel exploring the theme. As Davis writes, 'The story became a justification for extreme brutality towards indigenous people'. The second anchor comes from the family accounts relating to two tracts of land in the location from which the mythical stories of the abducted white woman emerged. These accounts, with all their dramatic detail, provide examples of the stories and myths of the immigrants about a land held sacred by

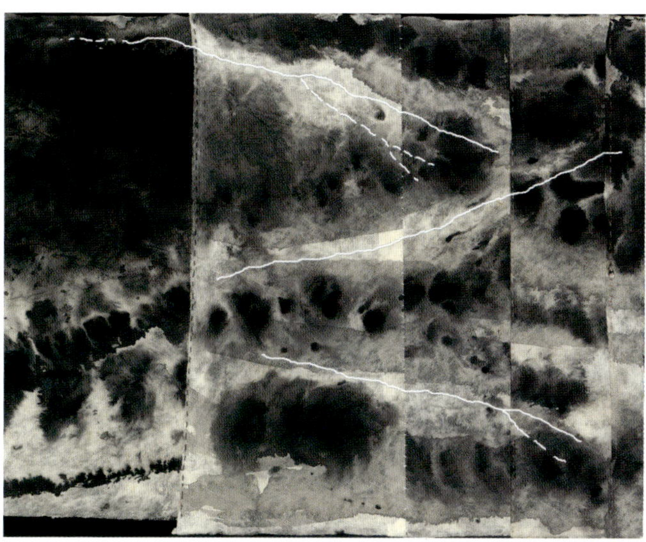

Jan Davis, *In Search of Lohan Tuka, 2009.*
Digital print on rice paper, 70.2 x 55.5cm. 27.5 x 22in.

Aboriginal peoples, for whom the history of the place stretches back into the Dreamtime. The struggles of the incomers to settle this land and make a living relate to a far shorter history, and the stories 'provide examples of frontier settler myths and function as stories to enable occupation of the place.'

Jan Davis's work on this project, as with others she has worked on, shifts between drawing and printmaking, using whichever means are appropriate in her pursuit of the poetics of place. She works with ink and wash on paper to create representations of maps and journeys through landscape, cutting them and stitching them together before photographing or scanning them into her computer, for reworking and output as large digital prints. This lengthy process enables a powerful meditation on the nature of landscape and who owns it, capturing something of the essence of the spirit of place.

http://visualartsnetwork.net.au/artists/artists_gallery/
(Postcolonialism, Environment)

JANET CURLEY CANNON

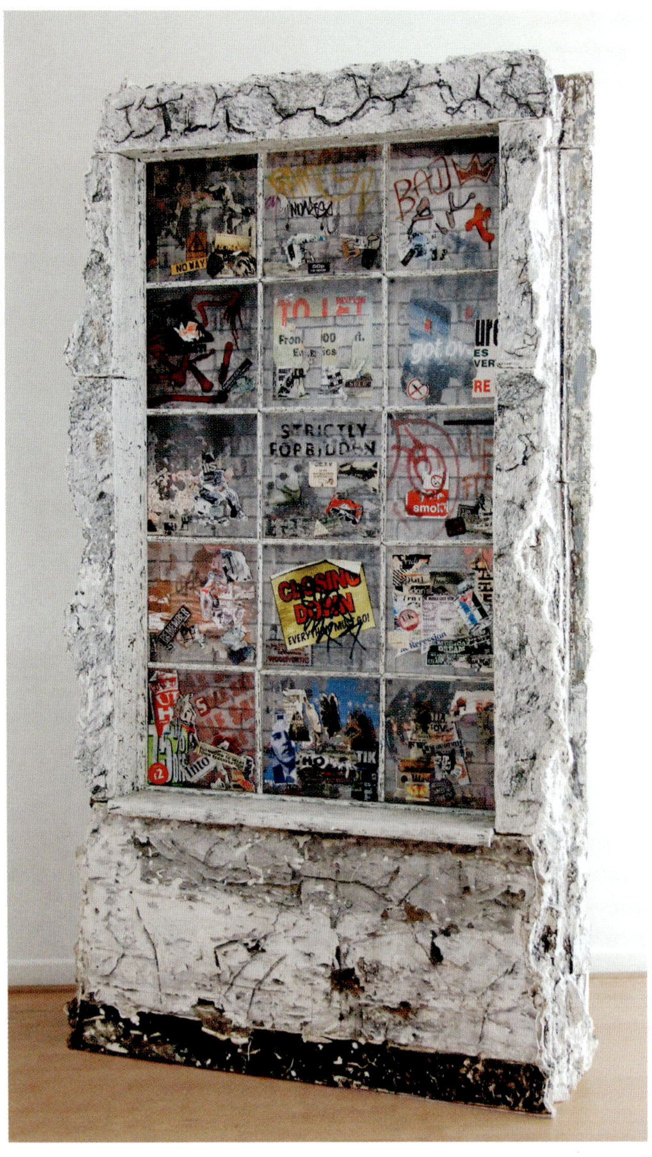

Janet Curley Cannon, *Daylight Robbery – East Side, 2009.*
Digital print, mixed media, 230 x 120 x 40cm. 90.5 x 47 x 16in.

The urban environment has for centuries been a source of subject matter and inspiration for artists. Beneath the surface of even the glossiest new building there is a rich layering of the past. We respond to the traces of others' lives and in turn leave our own traces, laying down another stratum of transient existence. Janet Curley Cannon was born in Seattle on the northwest coast of the USA, where she graduated in Art History, and the city remains a strong influence on her work: she describes it as being her muse, the place where her interest in architectural patterns began. She moved to the UK and worked for many years in the IT industry before returning to her studies, graduating from Camberwell College in 2005 with a master's degree in printmaking. She now lives near Bracknell, a 1960s new town to the west of London, where she has a studio in a former shop unit in the town centre. Bracknell is changing, and the signs of decay are increasing as the continuing growth in the southeast of England brings about shifts in population. As with many other towns and cities regeneration projects are attempting to breathe new life into a decayed urban environment.

Janet Curley Cannon works within this context and writes of her work, 'I am interested in recording the traces of modern life we leave behind – the painted layers or forgotten marks slowly decomposing on surfaces and structures, and the accumulation of printed material left to disintegrate in the public domain.' She makes use of a wide range of media, both digital and traditional, often in combination and increasingly in experimental form, that takes her work into the third dimension, exploring new methods of printing on textured surfaces, or building collaged prints into such surfaces, and more recently using techniques for the wet transfer of digital prints onto fresco. In addition she works with digital animation and video as an extension of her printmaking, with the added elements of sound and duration providing further layers of complexity. A film lasting even one or two minutes can encapsulate a wide range of observations about the environment, provoking a closer consideration of what might at first sight seem to be a straightforward and unremarkable image. This eclectic approach to mediums, using them in ways that are sometimes unconventional, gives Cannon a vocabulary of means for addressing her concerns in observing, recording and interpreting the environment around her. However, for all that she is absorbed in the use of digital tools and techniques, she remains committed to using a sketchbook as the initial step in a process that is resulting in increasingly complex responses to the world around her.

Daylight Robbery is a major work, developed in 2008/09. This is printmaking taken into the third dimension on a large scale. The title is a common cliché for an unfair charge or 'rip-off', but its origin lies further back in British social history. It is believed to originate in the late 16th century when a tax was introduced on houses with more than six windows. The tax was even more socially divisive than other taxes: those unable to afford the tax, or unwilling to pay it, took the expedient step of bricking up windows, and in some cases painting a form of trompe l'œil window on the surface. Those willing and able to pay the tax then had an obvious way of flaunting their wealth, and some of the great houses from the period are noted for their excessive use of windows. In working from this curious

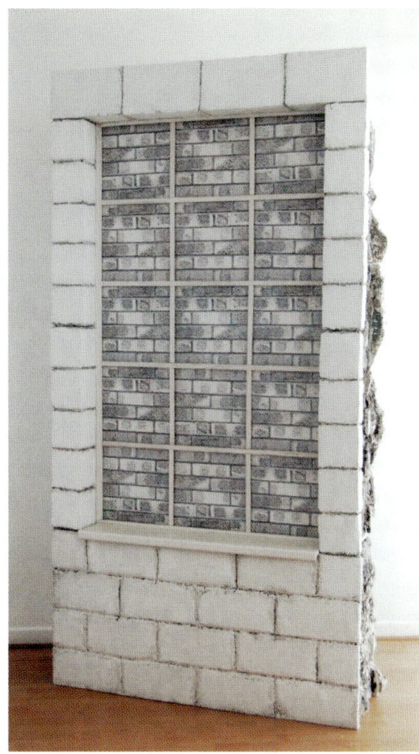

Janet Curley Cannon, *Daylight Robbery – West Side, 2009.* Digital print, mixed media, 230 x 120 x 40cm. 90.5 x 47 x 16in.

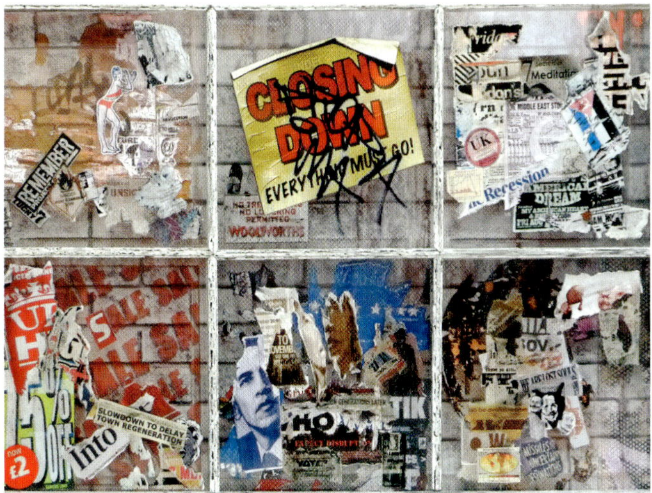

Janet Curley Cannon, *Daylight Robbery – East Side (detail), 2009.* Digital print, mixed media, 230 x 120 x 40cm. 90.5 x 47 x 16in. (whole piece).

historical basis Cannon is commenting on the crisis in the international financial situation that developed throughout the period she was making the work, which has led to businesses and houses being repossessed and their windows boarded or bricked up. *Daylight Robbery* has clear connections, not only to the historical context, but also to the growing divide between the 'haves' and the 'have-nots' in Western society.

The work uses a range of digital print techniques, other media including painting, and a range of building materials to create a prefabricated modular structure that can be moved from place to place in the back of a car. Fifteen window blocks are constructed in acrylic sheet, on the surfaces (there are four) of which digital prints are collaged before the blocks are assembled into a wood, foamed-plastic and plaster framework. One side of the 'windows' thus formed is left in clear and pristine condition to allude to the wealth that still remains, while the other is densely collaged with scraps of images that convey the despair of those adversely affected by the recession. It is a powerful work that repays close attention, and acts as a potent symbol of the times in which we live.

www.jcurleycannon.com
(New technology, The third dimension, Environment)

JELENA SREDANOVIĆ

n the 19th century Novi Sad, the second city of the Republic of Serbia, acquired the epithet 'the Serbian Athens' because of the influence its cultural and political life exerted on the region. Like so many cities in Central and south-eastern Europe, it is built on the River Danube, and today remains an important industrial centre and also the financial centre of the new republic. In addition to a long cultural history, Serbia has a vibrant contemporary arts culture that is not well-known outside the country. This is partly due to the tangled problems that developed among the various countries of the Former Republic of Yugoslavia, especially in the closing decade of the 20th century when the region erupted into violent internecine conflict. Novi Sad, like the capital Belgrade, suffered considerable damage during the NATO bombing campaign of 1999, which led to the destruction of the three bridges across the Danube. Since then considerable progress has been made in rebuilding the city, mirroring Serbia's growing ambition to join the European Union.

Jelena Sredanović was born in Novi Sad in 1982, and she still lives in the city. She graduated with a master's degree in graphic art from the Academy of Fine Arts, where she is currently following a postgraduate course. Her further studies have taken

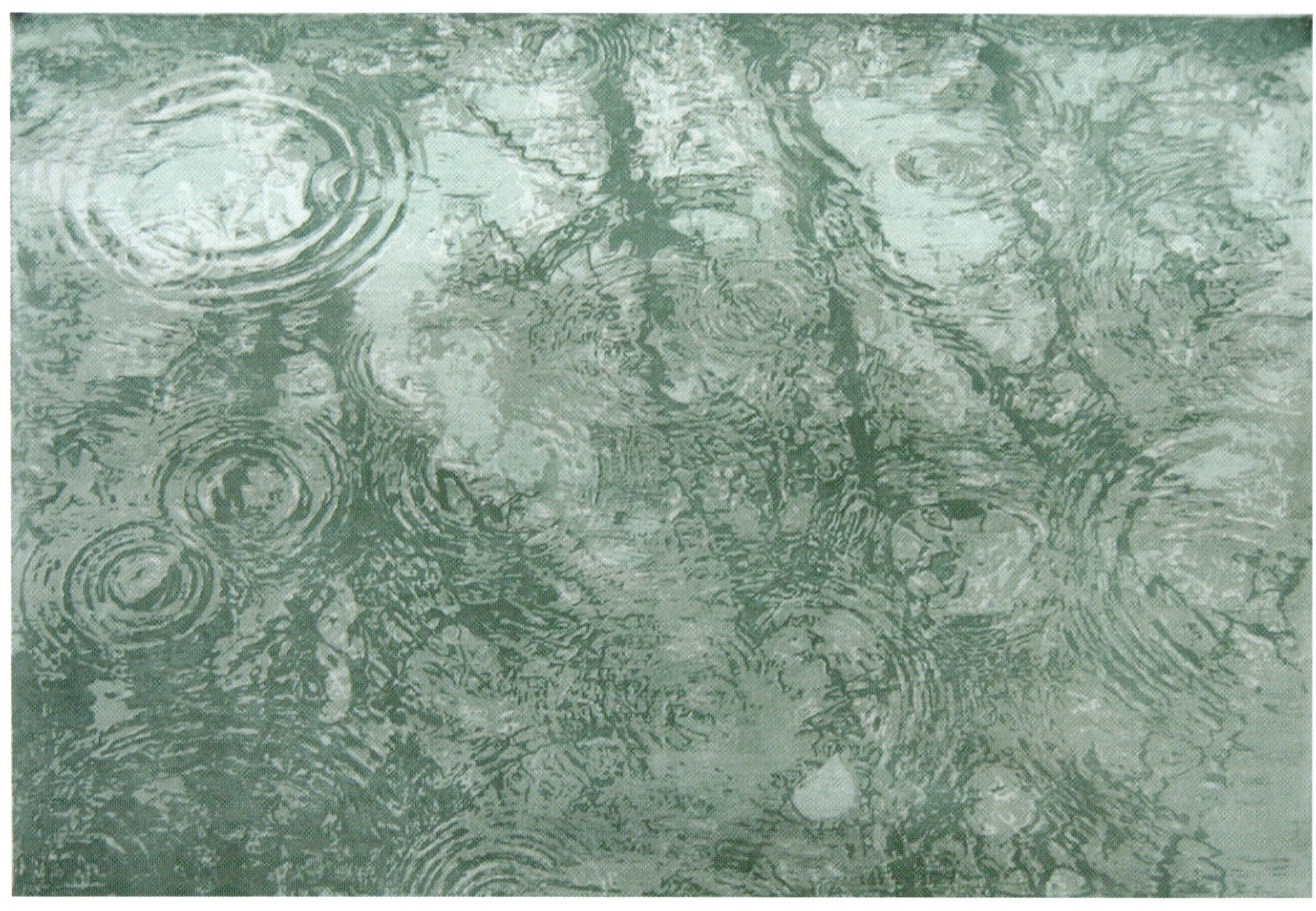

Jelena Sredanović, *Drops and Shadows, 2008.*
Woodcut, 68 x 99cm. 26.5 x 39in. (block)
on 69 x 100cm. 27 x 39in. (paper).

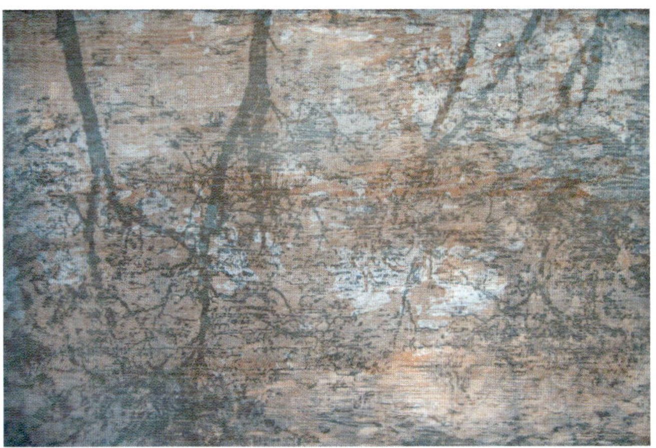

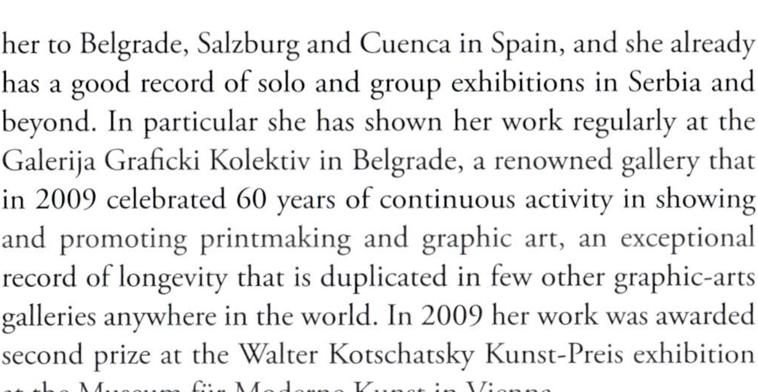

Jelena Sredanović, *Reversed Picture, 2007*. Woodcut, 68 x 99cm. 26.5 x 39in. (block) on 69 x 100cm. 27 x 39in. (paper).

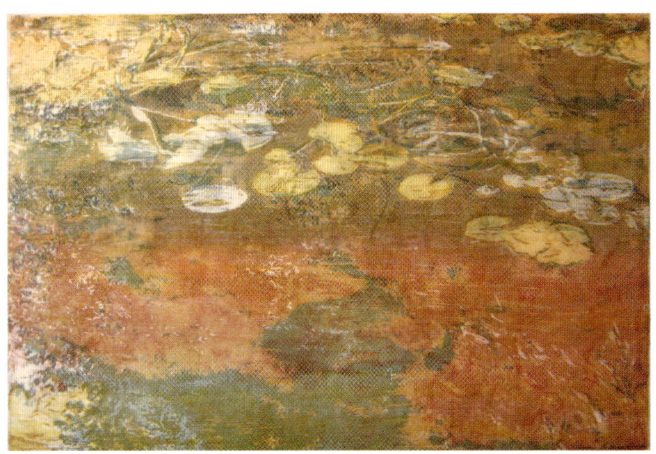

Jelena Sredanović, *Interaction, 2008*. Woodcut, 68 x 99cm. 26.5 x 39in. (block) on 69 x 100cm. 27 x 39in. (paper).

her to Belgrade, Salzburg and Cuenca in Spain, and she already has a good record of solo and group exhibitions in Serbia and beyond. In particular she has shown her work regularly at the Galerija Graficki Kolektiv in Belgrade, a renowned gallery that in 2009 celebrated 60 years of continuous activity in showing and promoting printmaking and graphic art, an exceptional record of longevity that is duplicated in few other graphic-arts galleries anywhere in the world. In 2009 her work was awarded second prize at the Walter Kotschatsky Kunst-Preis exhibition at the Museum für Moderne Kunst in Vienna.

Considering the times through which she has lived and in particular the violent period at the end of the century when she was in her late teens, one might have expected a young artist to have responded with work that reflected the trauma of those times. Instead, since the beginning of her postgraduate course in 2005, Sredanović has produced a body of work of great maturity and with a consistent sense of calm and order, derived from the recording of images of reflections on water. She writes, 'The reflections of trees on calm ponds, waves that curl and eddy in a way to cause the vibrating effect of light beams, shadows that spread out crosswise and overlap with circles of water, are the most frequent subjects of my prints. The reflections on the water form shapes that start to take on an autonomous life of their own.'

Her initial recording of reflections on water surfaces is meticulous, the result of an acute ability to concentrate on what is before her. Just as a fisherman learns to defocus his eyes in order to see movements beneath the water, so too does this artist have the ability to concentrate her visual sense on the infinitesimally thin water surface and to see in it the patterns of light and shade and the colours that together form the continually moving images before her. This ability is in itself a rare thing, as anyone who has tried to do the same will realise. Having collected a record of these experiences she then begins the process of transposing them into her work, firstly as drawings and then traced onto wooden sheets that will, after months of meticulous hand carving, become the blocks from which she pulls her prints.

What begins as a concentrated mental process becomes an intensely physical one throughout which the intensity of the mental image must be maintained. She appreciates the history and traditions of the woodcut technique, and the creation of a matrix, the natural surface of which imposes a distinct characteristic of its own that works in conjunction with the individual characteristics imposed on it by the artist in the search for the most appropriate combination of line, texture and colour. Only when this point is reached can Sredanović produce her prints, for which she uses translucent Japanese papers. For her this choice isn't only a matter of the tradition, but an essential part of her practice. She sees this process as being the creation of layers, in that she often conceives the image as being printed on two or three sheets of paper that are superimposed for presentation. The layering, and her careful control of multiple colour, sometimes requiring six separate plates, imbues her work with striking qualities, combining a high level of technical skill with a sensitivity that conveys a deep impression of the serenity of light on water.

www.artfacts.net/en/artist/jelena-sredanovic-227161/profile.html#top (New uses for old technology, The new generation)

JEOUNGEUN LIM

Framing prints behind glass for exhibition always presents a problem – that of reflection. To observe one's reflection in the glass, superimposed on the image behind, creates another layer through which the observer must look in order to find the image that the artist intended should be seen. Further than this any image is the result of the artist's intervention between the seen (or imagined) and the work that is presented for view. Illusion plays a major part in much contemporary art, the creation of perceptual conundrums and multiple potential interpretations of the effects of light. Jeoungeun Lim is aware of these paradoxes and, not wishing to compromise her work, incorporates them into her practice. The result is a range of work that defies the usual categorisation, presenting instead a hybrid form that offers a very different aspect of contemporary art.

Jeoungeun Lim was born in South Korea, and studied there and in the United States, being awarded master's degrees in both countries. She lives in Seoul, where she works and teaches, and has exhibited widely both in her own country and internationally. Her earlier work from the mid-1990s is closer to what many people would consider to be conventional printmaking, using traditional intaglio and relief techniques; but in that period she also produced works in printed fabric and computer print, as well as those that include three-dimensional elements. That her work has for many years featured a strongly experimental aspect, as well as the use of traditional techniques and approaches, is entirely consistent with the society in which she lives and works. South Korea has a deeply traditional culture, derived in large part from Confucianism, with a long and distinctive history, while at the same time being one of

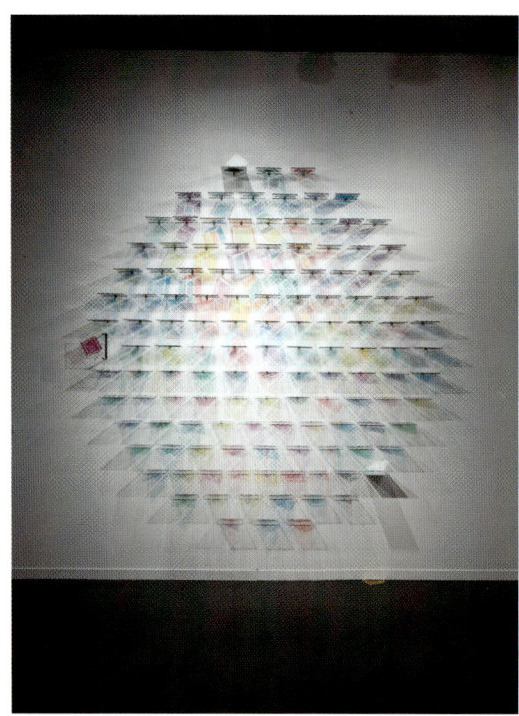

Jeoung Eun Lim, *Variation of a Cube (Installation), 2005.* Stencil and etching on glass, fitments, size variable.

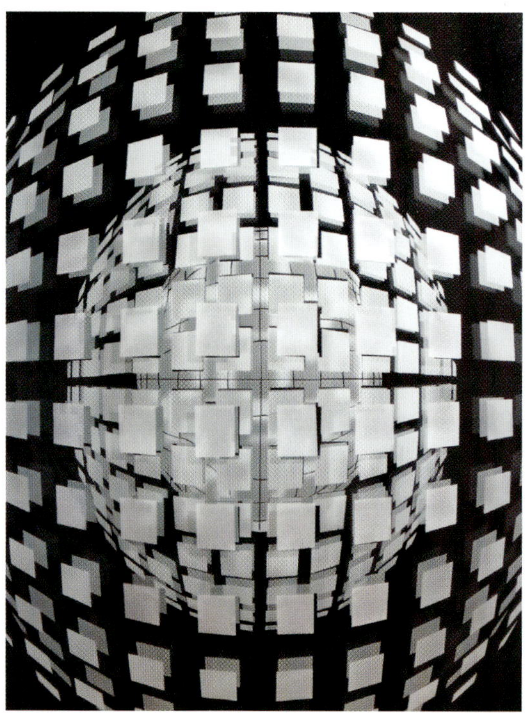

Jeoung Eun Lim, *Multiple Existence, 2004.* Sandblast on glass and mirror, 74 x 64cm. 29 x 25in.

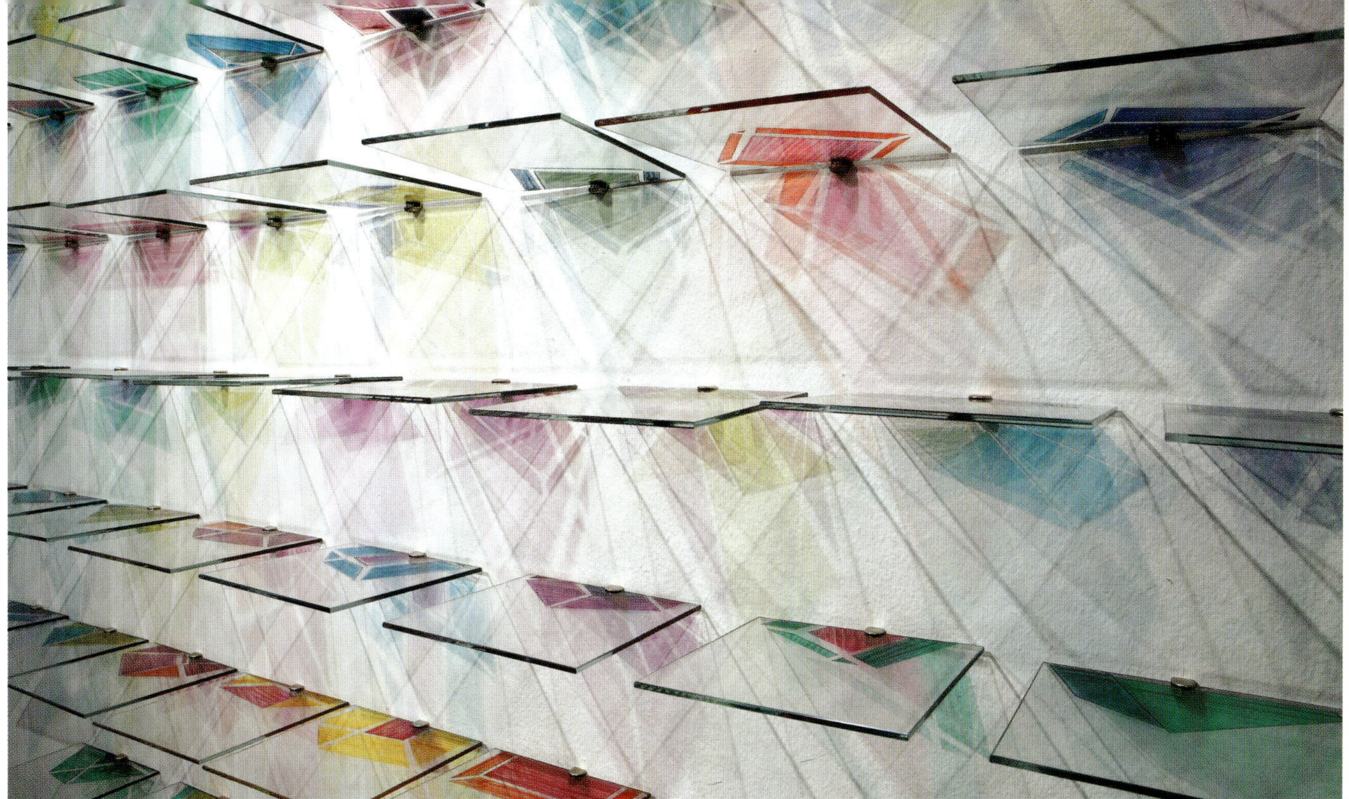

Jeoung Eun Lim, *Variation of a Cube (detail), 2005.* Stencil and etching on glass, fitments, size variable.

the major industrial cultures in which the development of high-technology products plays a primary role. The syncretic nature of contemporary Korean society does not represent a contradiction – there is a sense of complete fusion between what might otherwise seem to be disparate aspects that could not be reconciled with each other. It is not surprising therefore that the position of the contemporary visual arts, with printmaking pre-eminent among them, is a strong one, fusing the traditional and the modern aspects of the culture of this country. Lim's art both grows from this too-little-appreciated culture and typifies the balance between tradition and innovation.

A key work in this artist's development was *Alice in Wonderland* (2005). Occupying two walls of the Kwanhoon Gallery in Seoul, it comprised a large number of 20cm (8in) squares of glass, each attached with a proprietary fixing at right angles to the wall, and each bearing a symbol derived from, or inscribed within, a square. The symbols were taken from many sources, including traditional symbolic Korean and geometric Islamic designs. These were applied to the glass in a range of colours of differing translucencies, using stencil printing, with the consequent printed elements being baked in a kiln to fuse the colour with the glass. The strict grid formed by the installed elements related to formal mathematical order, which was subverted by the reflections and transmissions of coloured light caused by the precise positioning of spotlights. The perceptual tricks caused by this conjunction, which varied as observers walked past the work and observed it from different distances, added a level of mystery to what was in essence a

carefully structured exercise in geometry. Lim made a related work, 'Variations of Cube' (2008), for the Gallery SoSo, which comprised an installation of squares of glass and mirror, fixed to the wall as in the previous work to form a circular shape, with each element bearing a mixed-media printed image derived from geometric variations on a cube. As a result of precise illumination by spotlights the reflected and transmitted images cast a more formal overall pattern of coloured light onto the gallery wall.

Another aspect of this artist's output is found in a series of framed works, each 54cm (21¼in.) square and 5cm (2in.) deep. These works have a formal structure within the frame, incorporating digital images with Plexiglas geometric forms that add reflected and transmitted light. The size, in contrast to the installations, allows for a closer and more intimate consideration of the content of the digital images: their cumulative effect, as well as their relationship with the compositional grid, the cast shadows and the reflected light. One series within this format is *Identity* (2008), which encourages a close inspection of the works, and beyond which some mystery still remains. If the light is reduced in level, or if the spotlights are moved, the work takes on a shifted identity, relative to other identities, but individual, symbolic of the identities we take on in society.

www.gallerysoso.com/exhibit-en/11-LJ
E/exhibit-current-main.html
(New technology, Large-scale printmaking and installation, The third dimension)

JESÚS PASTOR

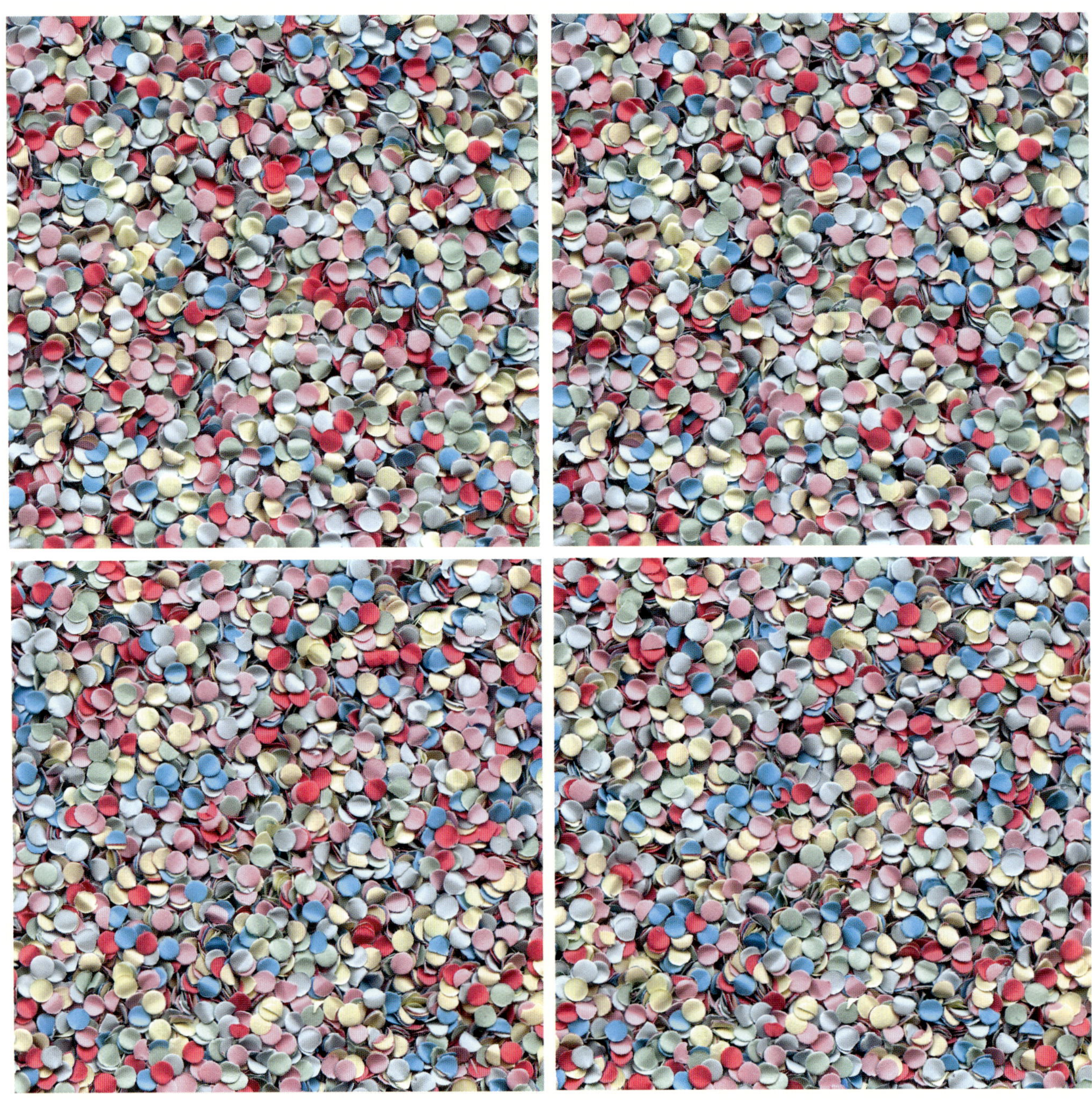

Jesús Pastor, *Pensando en Liebzitz, 2009*. Lambda print, dibond, methylacrylate, mounted in aluminium, 4 of 125 x 125cm. 49 x 49in.

Some artists working in printmaking mediums continue to follow that course throughout their careers, while others use printmaking as a starting point beyond which their work can lead in unexpected directions, sometimes a long way from what is generally considered as printmaking. Jesús Pastor is one such artist, and his recent work, while being derived from his work in the early 1980s, is now perhaps more accurately classifiable as either sculpture or photography or even installation. It continues, however, to pose questions about the reproducibility of images, and the means by which one form can be derived from another – in other words, to operate in a world that is parallel to that of printmaking.

Born in Bilbao, educated in philosophy and literature as well as fine arts, Pastor taught engraving at the University of Salamanca before taking up his present position as Professor of Drawing in the Fine Arts Faculty of the University of Vigo in Pontevedra. In the book accompanying his 2007 exhibition in Salamanca, there is a section in which Pastor lists a large number of quotations from literature and philosophy that he has found fascinating or relevant to the thinking behind his work over the years. He refers to these selected texts as being 'a bit like a small box of personal tools: they delimit a place, display or intuit a zone, in a sense they inform about the ground one should tread in relation to my works …' Among the authors of these texts are Derrida, Bataille, Mallarmé and Lewis Carroll. In referring to Carroll in particular he writes of the world created by the author in Alice in Wonderland, its paradoxical nature in the sense that whatever is most improbable becomes the most likely thing to happen next. He goes on to refer to the space of drawing, which like the world of Alice is not so much a physical space as 'a reflected realm'. Pastor's observations in regard to literature and philosophy are one of the keys to understanding both his work and the realm he has created in which his artistic consciousness has developed.

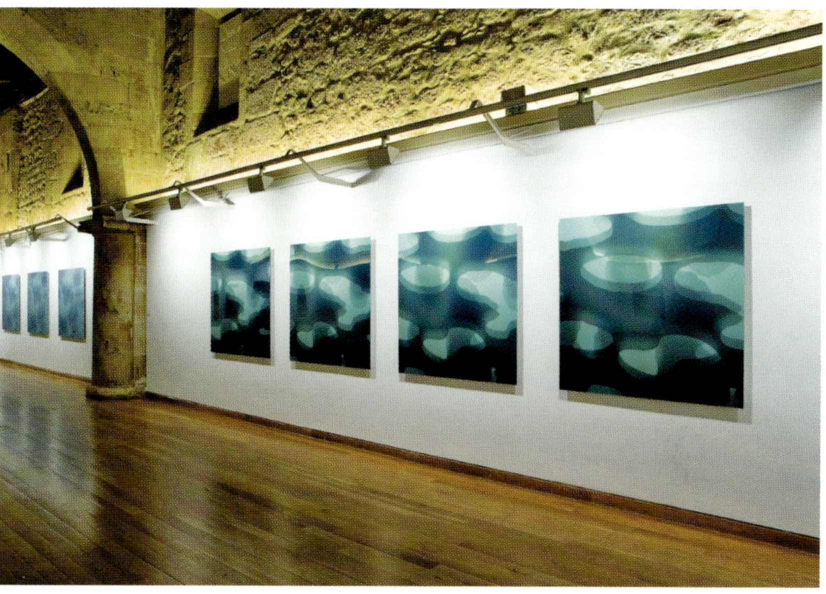

Jesús Pastor, *Sin título (montaje 1), 2007.* Photograph on aluminium and methylacrylate, size variable. Installation at Patio de Escuelas Menores, Universidad de Salamanca, Spain.

Even in the early 1980s, when his work could be more clearly understood as 'printmaking', Pastor was experimenting, in particular with the then-innovative technology of electrostatic reproduction, using a photocopier to register impressions of his hands and his face. He printed these out as works in their own right, but later used them as the starting points for more conventional prints in which he manipulated the images and added colour. Even at this stage he was working with ideas concerning the nature of reality and the passing of time. Later in that decade, following an intense period of drawing, his works became more abstract, using etched and engraved metal and images dealing with figure/ground relationships and textures. Through the 1990s his work involved materials such as etched marble, sometimes incorporating encaustic colours, pierced marble and aluminium, sometimes enamel, and at one point with cast aluminium providing the positive form for the negative holes in the marble, flowing outwards from them to establish a relationship echoing that of matrix and print. Each step was a logical development of that which preceded it, a gradual evolution that took time to mature.

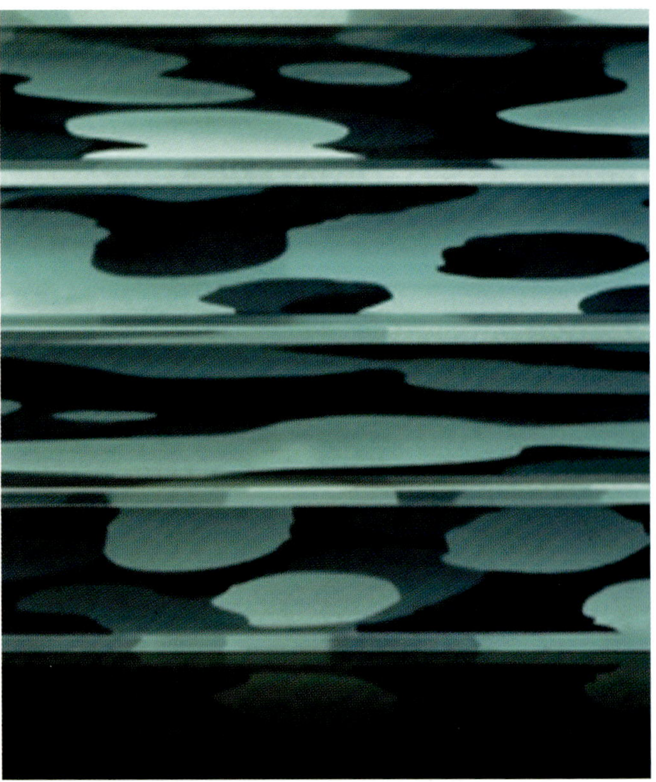

Two major exhibitions in the first decade of the 21st century brought a synthesis of much that had gone before. In *Latitudes* (2006), at the Circulo de Bellas Artes in Madrid, he showed a new body of work that included a circular installation of circular magnets, each carrying a large number of metal filings, coloured either deep blue or purple, creating a multitude of miniature spiky landscapes. Other works in cast aluminium that explored the paradoxes of figure and ground followed on from his earlier work in marble, and there were also wall-mounted works comprising four sheets of glass laminated together and bearing etched images. The light on these works created a vibrant green glow within the glass and cast traces of this colour on the wall beneath. Another major exhibition at the University of Salamanca followed in 2007, in the Patio de Escuelas Menores, a space that had in the past been used for photographic exhibitions. For this exhibition Pastor developed the themes explored in the Madrid show, to include works derived from drawings and reproduced as photographs on aluminium and Plexiglas. Subtly different from each other, these large photographs repaid careful viewing by creating a quiet impression of the passing of time, as the small differences between successive images revealed changes of an almost liquid quality. Laminated glass works occupied the corners of the exhibition space, which the artist himself had designed, to create a work in which all the constituent parts merged to create one impression.

http://c5coleccion.com/artistas/pastor/obras.htm
(New technology, Large-scale printmaking and installation, The third dimension)

JOAN HALL

St Louis, Missouri, is where Joan Hall lives and works, and is the Kenneth E. Hudson Professor at Washington University in that city. Like her birthplace in Ohio, the city of St Louis is a long way from the sea; nevertheless, it is the relationship of human beings to the sea that provides the foundation for her creative output. Her work is also about edges and limits – not only shorelines, but also the edges that separate healthy and diseased cells, or the edges of illusion. St Louis, close to the geographical centre of the United States, marks the edge beyond which 19th-century westwards expansion began, as commemorated by the Gateway Arch that rises high above the Missouri River: from the top of the arch the Old West, and the new, extend far into the distance.

Joan Hall is a keen sailor and keeps her boat on a nearby lake. But it is sailing on the ocean – the Atlantic or the Caribbean – that provides the leitmotif for much of her work. In the past she has incorporated images of nautical instruments and tackle into her work, as well as the shifting nature of the colour and translucency of water. Sailing provides a balance between the precision of navigation and the intuition through which a sailor senses the changes in wind and current and makes small adjustments to the sails; it is an activity through which the city-bound pressures of time become meaningless, encouraging meditative connection with the natural world, a timeless moving space in which creative thought can run free. There is, as John F. Kennedy remarked, an inextricable bond between human beings and the ocean; he went on to add that

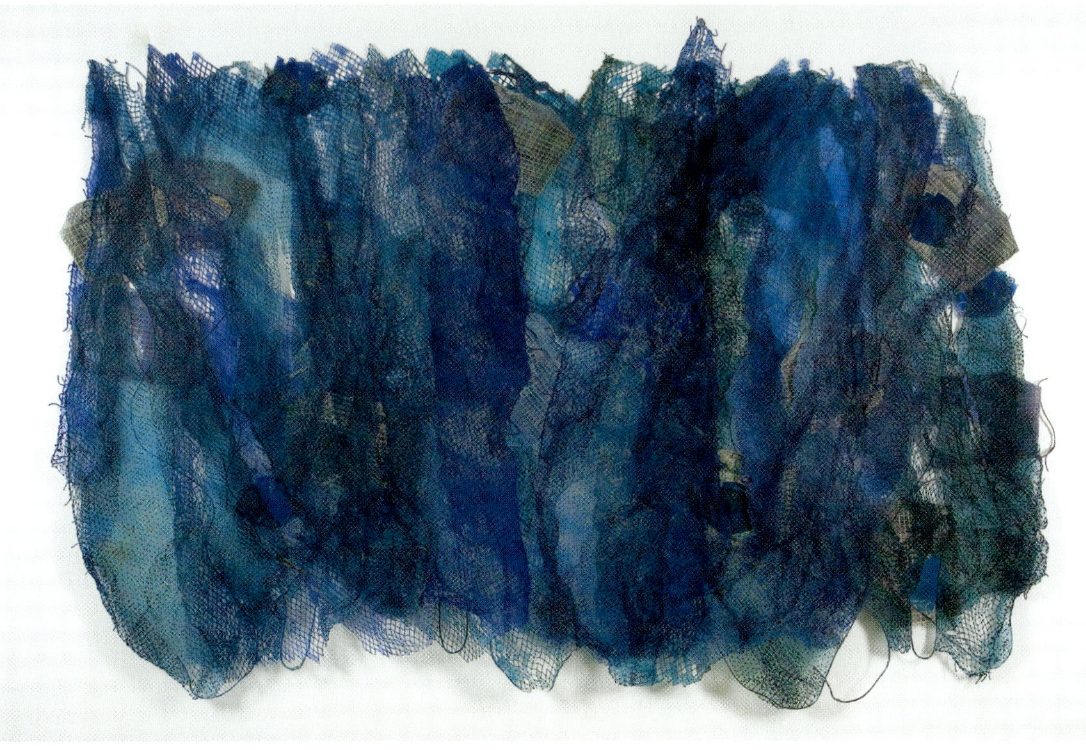

Joan Hall, *Would You Swim the Ocean for to Ease My Pain, 2006/07.*
Mixed-media print on paper and Mylar. 267 x 383.5cm. 105 x 151in.

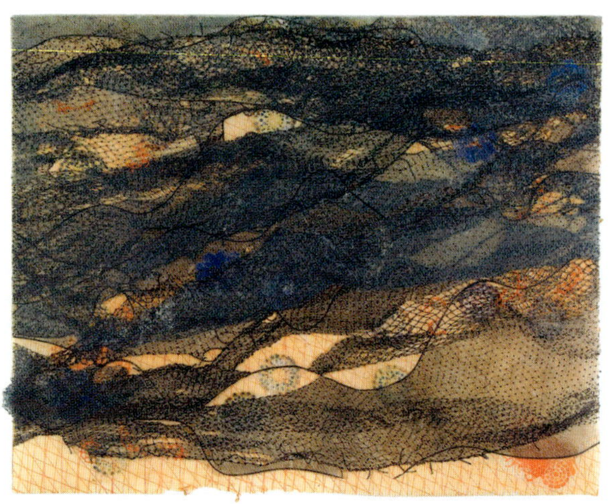

Joan Hall, *Catching a Miracle, 2006/07*.
Handmade paper with Kozo and Gampi fibres,
collagraph, relief, digital print and Solarplate™
etching, 147 x 180cm. 58 x 71in.

'all of us have the same proportion of salt in our blood as exists in the ocean … we have salt in our blood, sweat and tears … when we go back to the sea … we are going back from whence we came.'

Another crucial but connected strand in the work of Joan Hall, which has developed during the past few years, relates to the unprecedented problems caused to the oceanic ecosystem by the intervention of man and pollution. This concern is echoed in yet another aspect of her work, which is concerned with the mutations of healthy cells into cancerous cells, and the potential for cure that ancient plant lore might contain. Shifts and edges are the starting points for Joan Hall's work, which itself occupies the edges between printmaking, painting and sculpture, allowing those who see it a new series of spaces within which to find room for contemplation.

The artist's studio is in one of St Louis's former industrial buildings, giving her the space for the large presses and tables that her work requires and also, in the basement, room for the equally large tank in which she produces the handmade paper that is integral to her work. She has developed a technique by which she can single-handedly produce thick sheets of paper up to 2.4 x 3 metres (8 x 10ft). As a number of other printmakers and artists have found in the past three decades, making your own paper by hand allows for total artistic control throughout the creative process, integrating form and image with materials in an organic way that is not as easily achieved using manufactured paper.

While the subject matter varies, the basic process that Hall has developed provides her with flexibility of imagery and approach, which combines with the literal flexibility of materials that this requires. Having produced the paper she prints on it, usually with intaglio techniques such as collagraph, Solarplate™ or relief, with colour added through paper pulp or acrylic painting. The images include nets, cellular structures and other images, and the completed unique print is laminated onto a thin transparent Mylar® sheet, after which a long process begins of cutting out areas with scalpels. The resulting image is flexible, resembling a net, and is used as the basis for the construction of the final piece. This is formed in layers, incorporating other printed elements, thin sheets of paper, smaller forms in paper laminated onto Mylar®, images from plant or marine life, and, to mount the work for exhibition, pins bearing on their heads further paper and Mylar® forms. As a result of this process the works produced have, through their inherent flexibility, a variable size, often measured in metres (or feet), with some being destined for display in public spaces.

There is an eloquent poetry at the heart of all Joan Hall's work, through which the marine and cellular imagery, with its fragmentation and mutability, becomes not only illustrative but also symbolic. It invokes memory, recollection and reflection, with colours and shadows that change with the shifting light – works that seem to have emerged from the ocean.

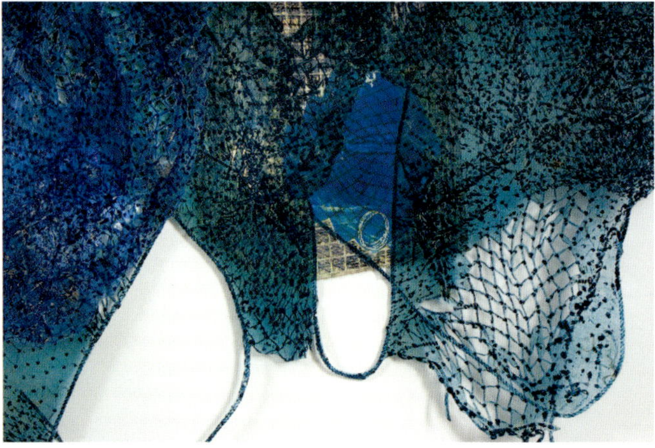

Joan Hall, *Would You Swim the Ocean for to Ease My Pain (detail), 2006/07*.
Mixed-media print on paper and Mylar. 266.7 x 383.5cm. 105 x 115in.
(whole piece).

*www.brunodavidgallery.com/artistDetail.cfm?id_*
artist=6&n=Joan+Hall
(Large-scale printmaking and installation,
The third dimension)

JOANNA PAVLOPOULOU

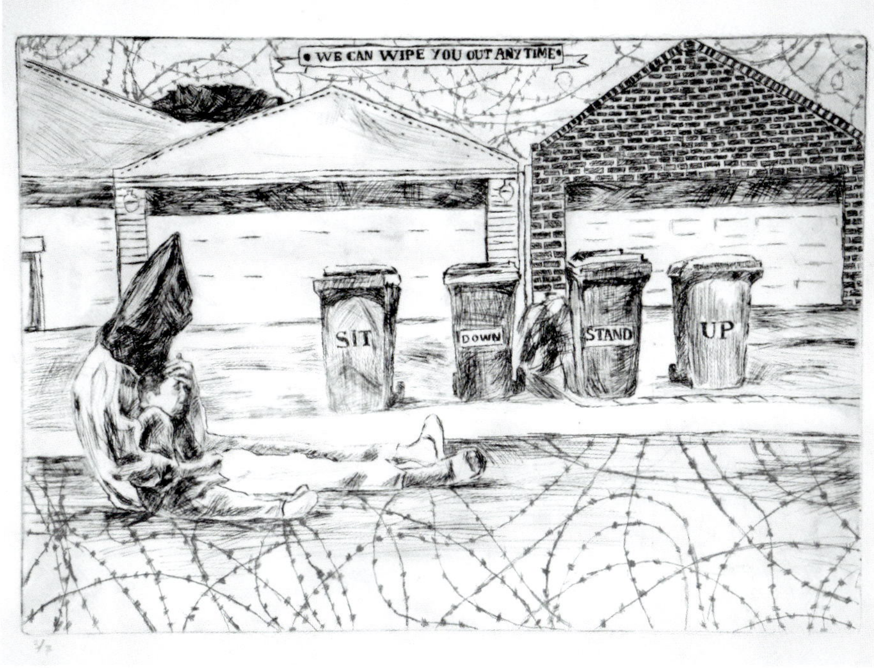

Joanna Pavlopoulou, *Untitled 11, 2009.* Drypoint on Plexiglas on paper, 35 x 50cm. 14 x 20in.

The people of Ancient Greece are renowned for their development of democracy – rule by the people – and opportunities for people to make their views known were highly valued. As history shows, however, that democratic ideal has sometimes been overshadowed as the society underwent extensive changes over the centuries. In late 2008 and early 2009, sparked by the shooting of a 15-year-old student by police, and fuelled by a growing discontent among younger members of Greek society, rioting broke out in a number of cities, among them Thessaloniki. The continuing unrest was met with considerable force and eventually fizzled out. But in October 2009 a snap election saw a complete change in government, as democracy once again had its way. Of course, the discontent in Greece has found its echo right across the developed world, and the common perception of a growing gap between the haves and the have-nots in many Western countries is backed up with reliable statistics. These things form part of the background to the work of Joanna Pavlopoulou, a student coming towards the end of her printmaking studies at the Aristotle University in Thessaloniki.

Her work is based on her observations of the world in which she lives. In particular it reflects contemporary social problems – the abuse, isolation, loss, pain and loneliness of the least fortunate – as well as the timeless subjects of life and mortality. In addition, it is to some extent about what she sees as the failure of the suburban way of life, and is critical of 'the so-called "American Dream"', as she puts it, and its promises of a better tomorrow. She writes of her prints, 'The dark atmosphere and a sense of "waiting" combined with political statements, or issues that have been torturing humanity since the beginning, may be confusing sometimes … The presence of children is mostly symbolic …'

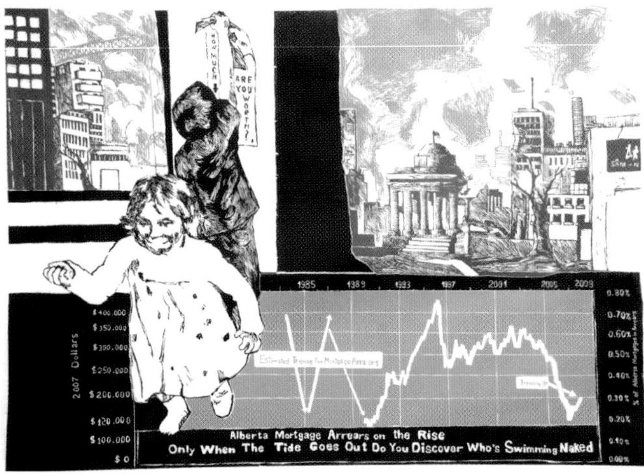

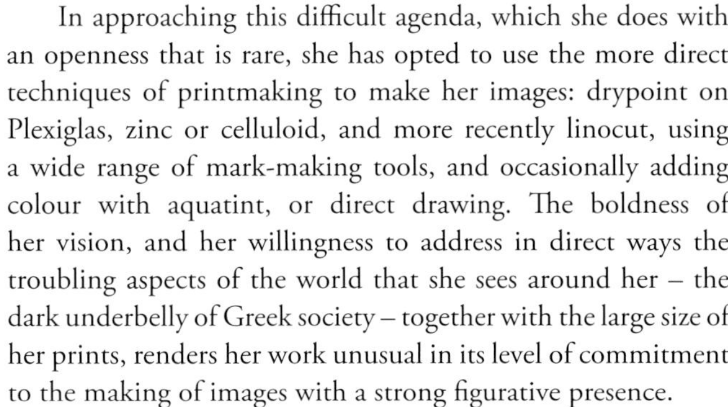

Joanna Pavlopoulou, *Crisis, 2009*. Linocut on paper, 66.5 x 90.5cm. 26 x 36in.

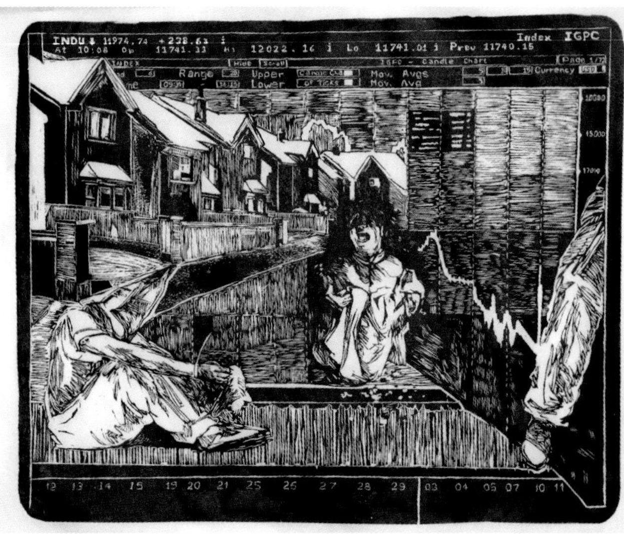

Joanna Pavlopoulou, *m.o.p. part 2, 2008*. Linocut, 45 x 53cm. 18 x 21in.

In approaching this difficult agenda, which she does with an openness that is rare, she has opted to use the more direct techniques of printmaking to make her images: drypoint on Plexiglas, zinc or celluloid, and more recently linocut, using a wide range of mark-making tools, and occasionally adding colour with aquatint, or direct drawing. The boldness of her vision, and her willingness to address in direct ways the troubling aspects of the world that she sees around her – the dark underbelly of Greek society – together with the large size of her prints, renders her work unusual in its level of commitment to the making of images with a strong figurative presence.

Pavlopoulou's work is continually evolving, and is still at an early stage. She has in recent months moved towards linocut for the making of the matrix – in order to explore ways of maintaining the same atmosphere within a different medium – and is making a conscious use of more colour, though not to the diminution of the 'dark' message in her work. She also plans to extend her work into mixed-media prints with lithography. The titles continue to be derived in part from song lyrics, as are the phrases included as a frequent feature of the work. She also continues to use children, a decision of which she writes, 'Children still have a leading role in the compositions, and the purpose of them being there has multiple explanations. Sometimes they appear to behave in an "adult" way, symbolising a destroyed childhood and early maturity.' Growing up as she did in a suburban area outside the centre of the city has also influenced the imagery in her work. She comments on the way in which the comparatively privileged existence of the suburbs remains desirable to many, but also leads to people growing more impersonal towards each other, and sometimes inhuman, fighting to maintain the fake peace and joy, but hiding the poison inside. She has referred to this as leading to something of a 'frontier town' mentality in the place where she grew up, and wonders if this has led her towards making prints in order to exorcise that experience.

A linocut print from 2008, *m.o.p. part 2*, combines an image of a suburban street with a sheet of newspaper from which a falling graph continues to fall. The presence of an adult, suggested by a trousered leg, intrudes into the image, in which two smaller figures – children perhaps – adopt postures familiar from images of Abu Ghraib hostages and the aftermath of disasters. *Crisis*, a linocut from 2009, combines elements of the adult world of city business centres and financial graphs with the tentative additional forms of two children – one appearing to run away while the other hides his eyes – a nuanced comment on the fallibility of the world financial system. These are unsettling images from an artist whose progress will be fascinating to watch.

http://inkteraction.ning.com/profile/JOANNA93
(Politics, The new generation)

JOSCELYN GARDNER

Joscelyn Gardner has, since her graduation in 1985, built up a body of work in printmaking and installation that has focused on her Creole identity from a postcolonial feminist perspective, addressing the history of slavery in the Caribbean and its relevance to contemporary society. She was born in Barbados into a family that had been resident on the island since the 17th century, and during her childhood lived in South Africa and South America as well as in the Caribbean, before studying printmaking and film in Canada. She subsequently taught part-time and worked in the arts in Barbados before returning to Canada to study for her MFA degree. She has exhibited internationally for many years and has represented Barbados in a number of major exhibitions, including the São Paulo Biennials in 1994 and 1996.

Slavery is a stain on the world that will not be erased until slavery itself ceases to exist. Despite the 200th-anniversary celebrations in 2007 of the abolition of slavery in the British Empire, and the 250th anniversary celebrations in 2009 of the birth of William Wilberforce, slavery in one or another form still exists in many parts of the world. To address the complex issues that underlie this uncomfortable truth, in which history, morality and politics collide, requires strategies that are clear and unambiguous. Gardner's MFA thesis in 2003 was, 'White Skin, Black Kin: Theorizing the Representation of Creole Identity'; this led to a major exhibition, *White Skin, Black Kin: Speaking the Unspeakable*, in the Barbados Museum in 2004, which included lithographs, installations with DVD film, and mixed-media exhibits. The exhibition sought to address the context in which plantation slavery had existed on the island, exploring not only the injustices of the lives of the slaves but also the lives of the plantation owners and their families, whose wealth was built on slave labour and exploitation.

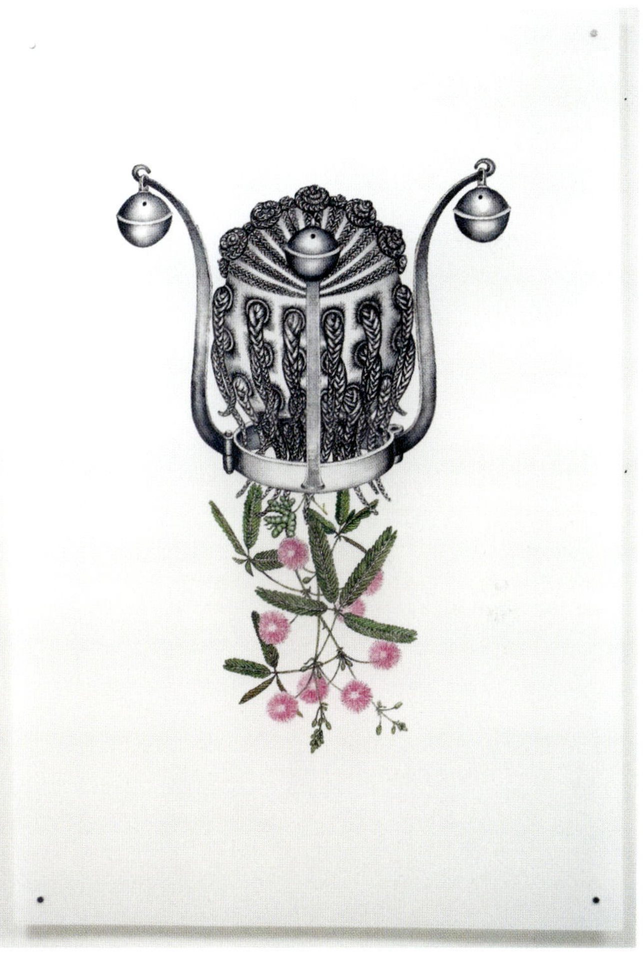

Joscelyn Gardner, *Mimosa pudica (Yabba), 2009.* Lithograph with added watercolour, 91.4 x 61cm. 36 x 24in.

Creole Portraits, a series of lithographic prints on frosted Mylar®, explored the complexities of the ways in which the hair of black women is distinctively styled through complex patterns of braiding – cornrows – extensions and dreadlocks. While these portraits have contemporary resonance, suggesting as they do the connection to contemporary fashions in hair (which have by the osmotic process of fashion 'crossed over' into the hairstyles of white women), they also contain contrasting elements that might escape a cursory glance. Interwoven with the braided and combed patterns of hair are shackles and manacles, the metallic symbols of enslavement and confinement; the marks of ownership. In the Barbados exhibition these images were also printed onto pillowcases, with the addition in white embroidery of the names of enslaved women. These, together with a wall text by Toni Morrison, were exhibited in the Prisoner's Cell that forms part of the historic building of the museum. Other parts of the exhibition included historic portraits of plantation owners and their families, artefacts from the museum's collection, and DVD film projections that explored the nature of life on the plantations through historical re-creation.

New images in the *Creole Portraits* series were subsequently shown in an exhibition at the Brooklyn Museum in New York in 2007. *Infinite Island: Contemporary Caribbean Art* explored aspects of the response of visual artists to the nature of Caribbean identity, both in the islands and in the communities of the Caribbean diaspora. Gardner's contribution was a series of portraits that took further than previously the inclusion of images of the hard metal objects of oppression and torture.

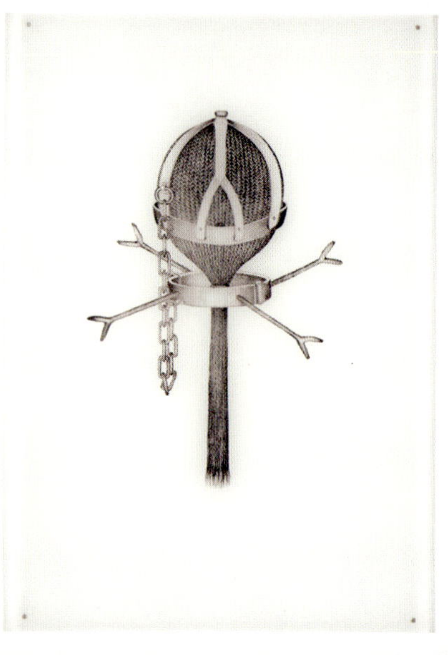

Joscelyn Gardner,
Old Moll (from Creole Prints II), 2007.
Lithograph 91.4 x 61cm. 36 x 24in.

These lithographs on Mylar®, each dedicated to a female slave on the Egypt plantation, were exhibited as if in the home of a gentleman collector of the 18th century, by incorporating printed vinyl columns. Wall texts listing the names of 70 of the Egypt women complemented the images. The whole effect was an even more potent statement about the violence of subjugation.

In her recent series of images, from 2009, the artist follows the theme but incorporates hand-coloured images of the plants from which slave women derived drugs to cause abortion as a form of resistance to their reproductive role in the slave economy. The injustices of slavery persist, despite the continuing efforts of international organisations and individual governments to eliminate them. The reasons for this are many, but include the unwillingness of society in general to accept the continued existence of such barbaric transactions, and then to work towards their elimination. The Irish writer and satirist Jonathan Swift wrote, 'For in reason, all government without the consent of the governed is the very definition of slavery.' Artists such as Joscelyn Gardner play a vital role in bringing the truths and experience of slavery to public attention.

www.joscelyngardner.com
(Politics, Postcolonialism, Memory)

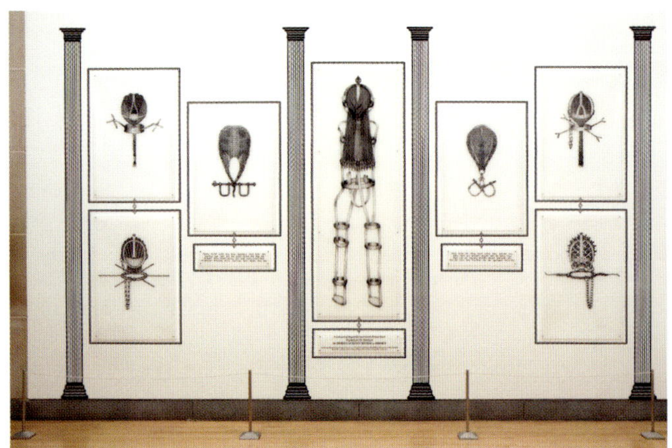

Joscelyn Gardner, *Creole Prints II (full installation), 2008.*
Lithographs and print on vinyl, 274 x 457cm. 108 x 180in.

KIKIE CRÊVECOEUR

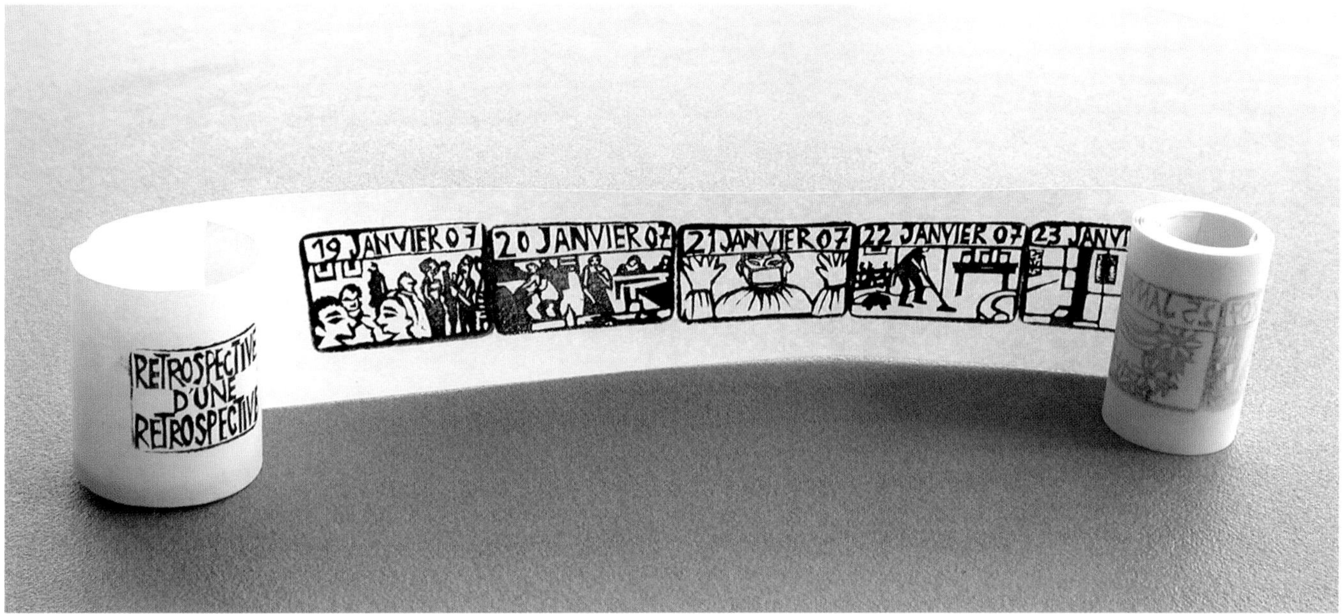

Kikie Crêvecoeur, *Retrospective d'une retrospective, 2008/09.* Rubber-stamp prints, size variable.

Kikie Crêvecoeur was born and educated in Belgium, and has a long record of international exhibitions and awards. Exhibiting a playfulness that comes as a relief from the serious intent of much contemporary printmaking, her work abounds with wordless stories, which are nevertheless eloquent, amusing and sharply observant of human foibles and gestures, as well as the natural world.

The lightness of approach and originality in some of her earlier work harks back to the activities children resort to in school to allay the boredom of lessons. To take a rubber eraser and to write a word or name in reverse, using wet ink, and then to press it onto paper was a common diversion for many of us, and perhaps one of the earliest experiences we have in printmaking – certainly up there with the potato cut. Crêvecoeur, however, continued to develop this simple approach in her work of the late 1980s to build up complex and skilful images, using an object intended for erasing 'print' to create memorable pictures that hold the attention.

Taking large pieces of rubber measuring around 6.5 x 5cm (2½ x 2in.) as a module, and cutting images or patterns into the surface, she then used them as matrices to print in black ink on white paper, in a grid whose final size might be 73 x 50cm (28 x 19in.). In some cases she added colour to the images after printing. The titles of these works are sometimes light-hearted, such as *The Public in front of a film during the interval*, which captures the full repertoire of bored expressions that might be expected during an intermission; or a comparable levity can be found in the images themselves, such as in *The Dance*, in which fragments of arms, bodies, faces and legs are printed in black on white in a sequence that recalls strip cartoons, or frames from a film.

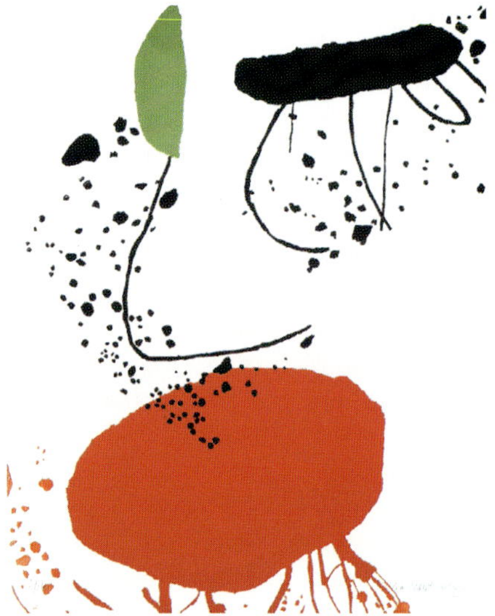

Crêvecoeur continued to use this technique in the early 1990s, but with different aims and results. The prints still relied on a grid of elements, but the results, often with added colour, were more abstract, setting up complex rhythms and resonances within a relatively small area. These interim works led on to the larger works she has made from the mid-1990s up to the present. While her attachment to prints made with erasers continues it now works in parallel to her work in linocut. By changing to a larger matrix, typically up to 47 x 37cm (18½ x 14½in.) the artist has given herself greater freedom in which to explore her language of gestures and tones. The imagery in many of these works is abstract, albeit with allusions to aspects of her earlier work. The combination of prints and the dialogues that are set up between them offer fascination over repeated viewings; there are tensions and resolutions – figurative in some instances, broadly gestural in others. Her work is reminiscent of the swirling harmonies and discords of jazz or blues, or the shifting rhythms of drumming in much ethnic music.

In the early part of the 21st century there was a pronounced change in her work. *In Tacet 1 à 4* (2000) and *Onymie 1 à 4* (2001), six linocuts in each are made to be displayed together, and in each set there is much more colour compared with earlier work, the areas of ink are larger – almost covering each print – and the smaller elements derived from earlier work are used as counterpoint. In works such as these the language is entirely abstract, but with similar resonances to previous pieces. Subsequent works have explored the use of black imagery derived from plant and tree forms to be seen around her studio, printed on colour backgrounds. This imagery appeared again in a major work from 2006, *Bribes et Échappées* (Snatches and Fragments), which comprises 39 black linocuts on white paper, to be shown in three rows of 13, the order being infinitely variable. Abstract and figurative at the same time, this work achieves a high level of skill in fusing form and meaning.

Kikie Crêvecoeur's recent work shows a return to prints made with erasers, in two series that gained her an award at the Biennial of Contemporary Print in Liège in 2009. One, *Retrospective d'une retrospective*, is printed on a long narrow roll of paper, with one image being made each day for four months, and the other, *Conte(s) à rebours* (Misunderstood Tales), comprising one image made each day for a year and printed on separate Post-It™ notes. She has also worked in conjunction with others, for example on the 2009 book of poems by Serge Meurant, Une Saison en éclats (A Shattered Season), for which she produced a masterly series of images.

www.cultureplus.be/Kikie%20CREVECOEUR.htm
(Large-scale printmaking and Installation, New uses for old technology)

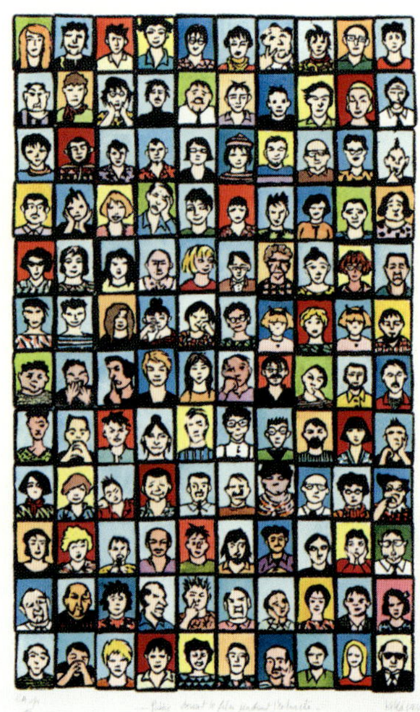

Kikie Crêvecoeur, *Public devant le film, 1986.*
Gum print with hand colouring,
73 x 50cm. 29 x 20in.

KLAVS WEISS

Klavs Weiss was born in Denmark, where he lives and works in a small village in western Jutland. He trained in ceramics, and is a self-taught printmaker who has exhibited widely and made performances in many countries. Together with Karen Havskov Jensen he runs the ET4U Gallery in the village where they live, which since 1999 has shown work by a wide range of international artists and performers. This project is aimed at encouraging an interest in and practice of the contemporary arts in a rural area affected by depopulation, and has led to many interesting outcomes.

It has long been accepted that printmaking is a visual-arts medium that depends to a large part on the artist's willingness and ability to collaborate with others in order to produce prints. In addition, the affordability of prints in comparison with the relatively high prices of paintings and sculpture make it accessible to a potentially wider range of people. The relationships established through this medium between artists and the public have a good social value from many points of view. Klavs Weiss takes the process of engagement with other people to a different level, at which performance and public interaction play a major role. The immediacy and accessibility of his printing performances contrasts with the inevitable distance between the work of a painter in a studio and the exhibition of the paintings in a gallery. To witness such a performance is to become involved with it, and the interested and engaged reactions of participants prove that contemporary art can relate to people in new ways, as celebration, thought provocation or social comment. Weiss's work has achieved all these during the time he has been making performances.

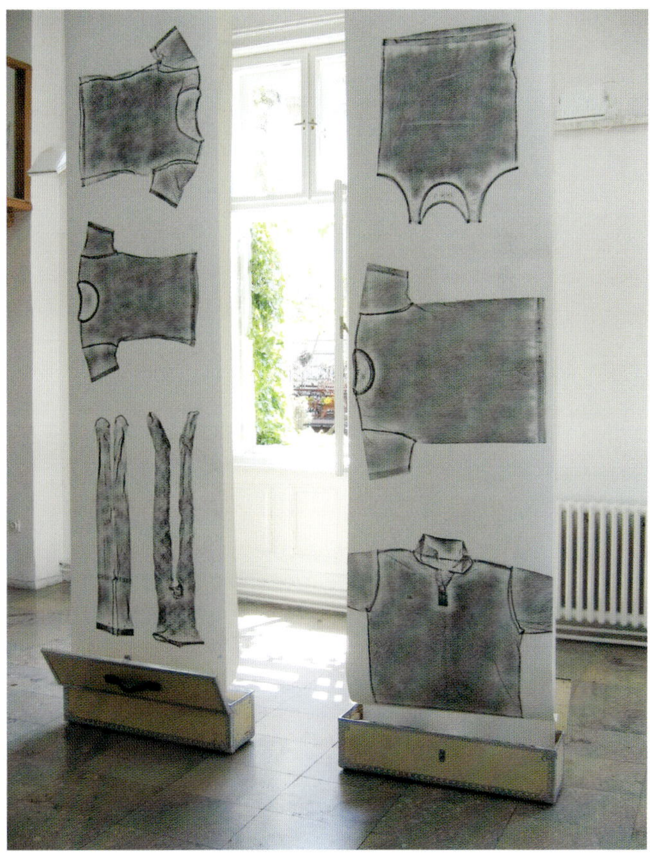

Klavs Weiss, *Miss Jovanović and Mr Petrović, 2004.*
Print on fabric, wooden and metal boxes, 1000cm. 394in. (length of each roll of fabric). Installation at Galerija Akademia, Belgrade, Serbia.

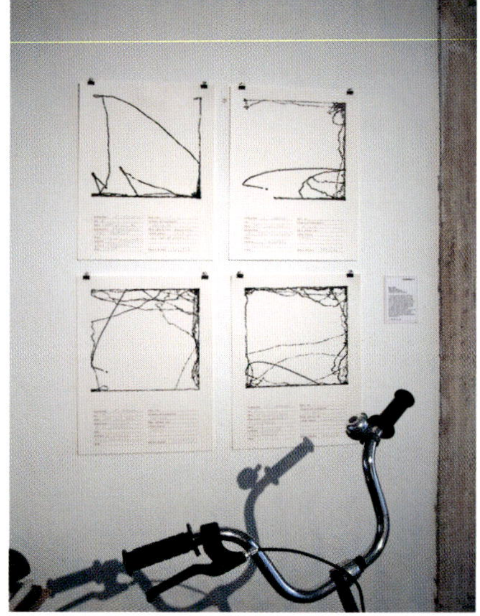

To give one example, in 2000 he presented a performance at the Gutenberg Pavilion in Mainz in Germany, as part of the birthday celebrations for the inventor of moveable type. He made 'printshoes', wooden soles bearing type letters on sole and heel, which were attached to the participants' normal shoes. Having stepped on an inking tray they could then walk, or otherwise move, across the surface of a large sheet of paper, and in so doing leave imprints of the letters. The performance was accompanied by live music, and the conjunctions of letters, and the density of the ink, produced the final result. Since then Weiss has made a series of what he calls *Ball Print* performances in a number of cities and locations, using varying means to produce the prints: a Renault van in rural Denmark, a hand-pulled go-kart in Trois-Rivières in the Canadian province of Quebec, and a bright green tricycle in Kraków in Poland. The common factor in all cases is the method of printing: a wooden tray in which a sheet of paper is placed in or on the vehicle, following which an inked iron ball is placed on the paper and the vehicle is driven or moved from point to point in the chosen location. As it moves the iron ball rolls across the paper, leaving a trace of its movement, which records the changes in direction and the unevenness of the surface in unpredictable ways. At the destination the route and distance are noted and a photographic record of the performance that can then be exhibited, together with the documentation, as a record of a journey.

Another aspect of his work is seen in the print installation he made for the Engramme festival in Quebec in 2004, and at FLUC in Belgrade in Serbia in 2005. This consists of two cases, each containing a 10-metre (32ft) roll of paper upon which are printed the impressions of all the clothing that a man and a woman would require for a long weekend holiday. The prints replicate every texture, fold and seam, recollecting the people who once wore the clothes, and giving an insight into their lives that mixes humanity with voyeurism. In Quebec the piece was titled *Mme Gagnon et M. Tremblay*, while in Belgrade it was titled, *Miss Jovanović and Mr Petrović*, in both cases these being common names in the cities where the work was shown.

In 2009, during his residency in Llanfyllin in Wales, Weiss made another performance with one of his 'printing vehicles'. These comprise a wooden wheeled framework with a large wooden wheel around the rim of which is fixed a rubber strip cut to produce a text: the vehicles are powered by a fan driven by rubber bands, or a balloon, or (as in Llanfyllin) by a firework. The text reads, 'This machine produces a line the length of which shows the power of a peaceful bomb'. The brevity of the performance, and the surprise engendered by the explosion of the firework, makes for an entertaining experience, and the resulting message is eloquent. Art can indeed move.

http://klavsweiss.dk
(New technology, The third dimension)

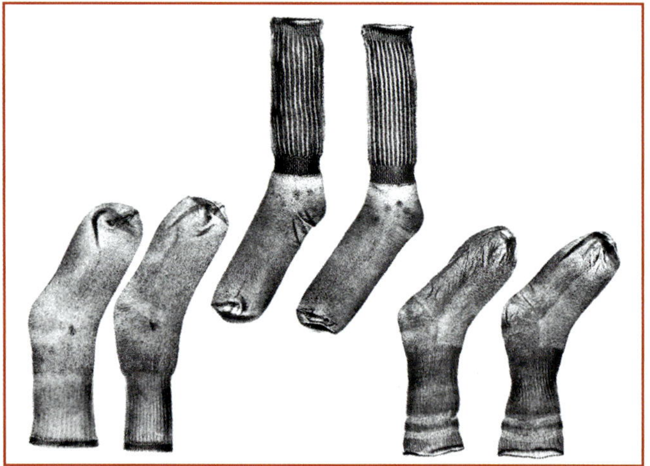

Klavs Weiss, *Miss Jovanović and Mr Petrović (detail, socks), 2004.*
Print on fabric, wooden and metal boxes, 1000cm. 394in. (length of each roll of fabric). Installation at Galerija Akademia, Belgrade, Serbia.

KONSTANTINOS KISSAS

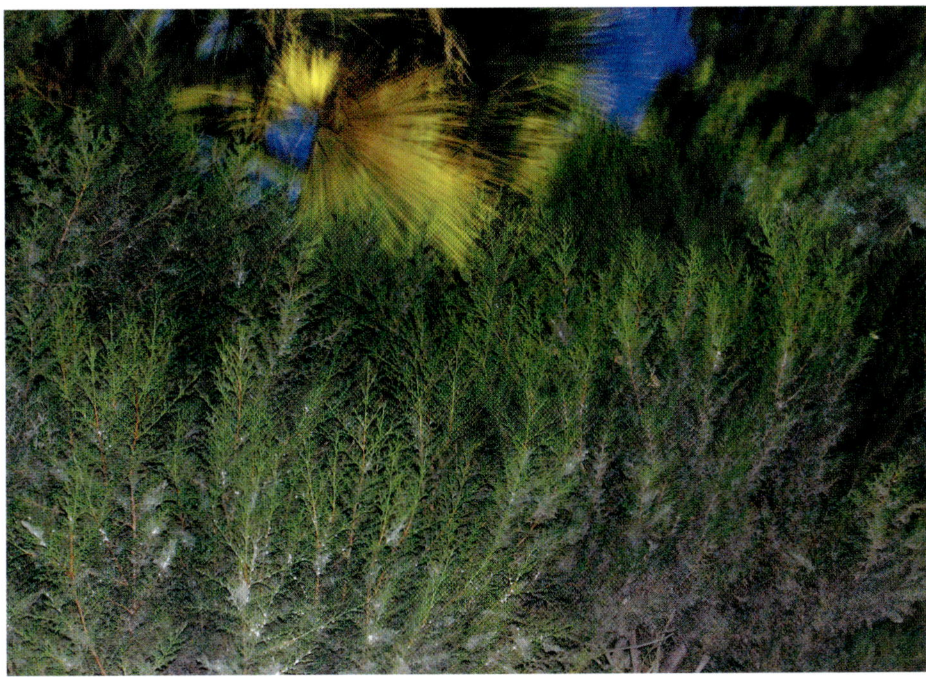

Konstantinos Kissas, *Untitled, (from Night-time series), 2006–08.* Digital print on matt archival paper, 87 x 110cm. 34 x 43in.

'The word "photography" comes from the Greek $\phi\hat{\omega}\varsigma$ (phos) "light" + $\gamma\rho\alpha\phi\acute{\iota}\varsigma$ (graphis) "stylus", "paintbrush" or $\gamma\rho\alpha\phi\acute{\eta}$ (graphê) "representation by means of lines" or "drawing", together meaning "drawing with light."' (Wikipedia, 2009) This definition is helpful in formulating a more inclusive definition of printmaking, positioning photography much closer to traditional printmaking techniques than purists would like. The argument about the necessity of a matrix can be settled when the digital file, stored on a card or computer hard drive, is seen as being the matrix, from which images may either be printed, or transmitted in electronic form, or replicated within a digital photo frame. There has, however, to be something beyond the images that can be produced by anyone using even the simplest digital camera if the results are to be seen to be acceptable within the extended canon of printmaking. In fact, this criterion is no different to that applied to printmaking in traditional techniques – there are as many poorly conceived etchings, lithographs and screenprints as there are poorly conceived photographs: the use alone of a traditional technique does not imbue a print with a special aura.

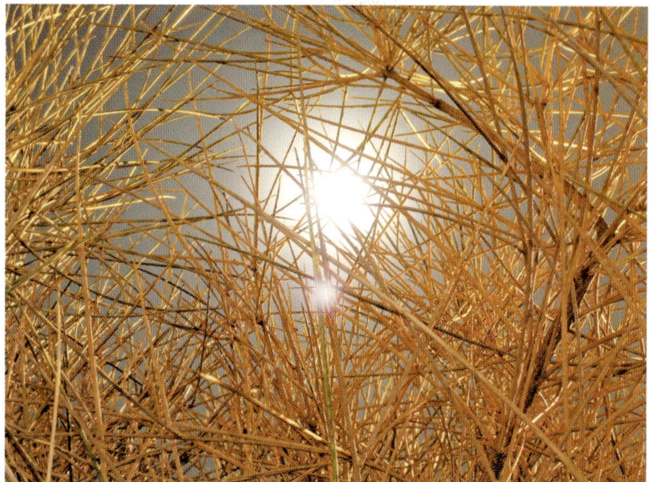

Konstantinos Kissas, *Untitled, (from Night-time series), 2006–08.*
Digital print on matt archival paper, 87 x 110cm. 34 x 43in.

Konstantinos Kissas was born in northern Greece in the ancient city of Thessaloniki, where he lives and works. He received his higher education in Athens and in France at the École des Beaux-Arts in Saint-Étienne, and has shown his work internationally in group and solo exhibitions, including a major solo exhibition in Thessaloniki in 2009. In an introduction to the catalogue of that exhibition Kissas writes, 'According to one of the Orpheus myths regarding the origin of the universe, the female goddess of Night is the mother of all beings, the creator of Nature … All energies and forms pre-existed in her and they were shaped and revealed through the arrival of night.' In the work he produced in the period 2006–08 he made a decision to move as far as possible from the information-strewn contemporary urban space and to seek instead a more primal world. His choice of the night-time world of the Mediterranean coast came partly because of the place in which he lives, and partly because it offered him the opportunity to explore a nocturnal world that for many people remains yet to be fully experienced.

Technically, the making of photographs at night is demanding, requiring longer exposures, the use of a tripod, and a good understanding of the effects of long exposures on colour rendition. It also requires an enhanced ability to 'see' in the darkness, and resolve what is there before taking the photograph. It requires a particular sensitivity and the willingness to be complicit with the whole process, as well as to accept that the unexpected may well come about. In addition it requires the ability to work slowly, and as such is the complete antithesis of those forms of reportage and documentary photography that

depend on the speedy reactions, so as to capture what Henri Cartier-Bresson called 'the decisive moment'. In an image made by Kissas that same moment comes after he has selected the position from which the image will be recorded, and judged (partly by guesswork and partly by experience) how much light the sensor in his camera will collect and how the colours he believes to be there will be registered. He may choose to use flash within his images, to highlight the foliage or objects close to the camera, or he may instead rely on the ambient natural light of the moon, or on artificial lights. Significantly, in the majority of the images it is only through such artificial lights, or the traces of habitation – buildings, distant city skylines, boats out on the water – that the human presence can be discerned. Human forms appear in very few of the images, and then only as silhouettes, or figures blurred by their movement during the long exposures that are necessary.

The resulting images carry poetic resonances: it is not difficult to align them with personal experiences of hot nights beside the Mediterranean, the sounds of crickets, the whisper of warm winds through the branches, the lapping of water on the shoreline, distant voices, the sound of bells on the sheep and goats on the hills. This evocation of memory is one aspect of photography that is not as readily available, if at all, in other printmaking mediums. A photograph is seen in a different way to, for example, a lithograph, since the making of photographic images, as well as the process of looking at them, has become part of our common experience of the visual world, of which Konstantinos Kissas offers us a unique vision.

http://interartive.org/index.php/2009/01/kissas/
(Environment, Memory)

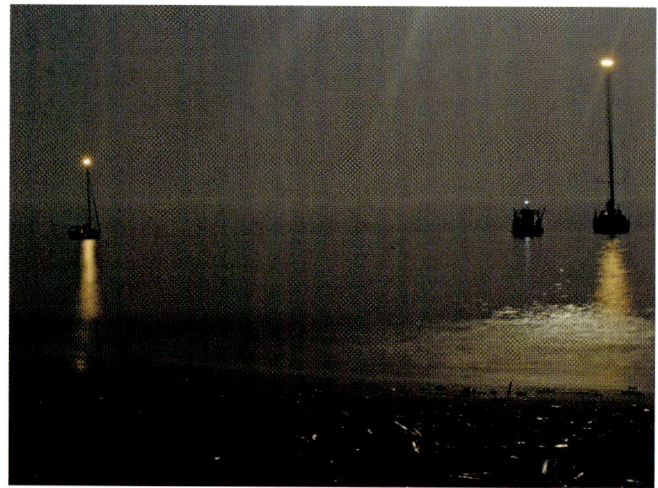

Konstantinos Kissas, *Untitled, (from Night-time series), 2006–08.*
Digital print on matt archival paper, 87 x 110cm. 34 x 43in.

KSAWERY KALISKI

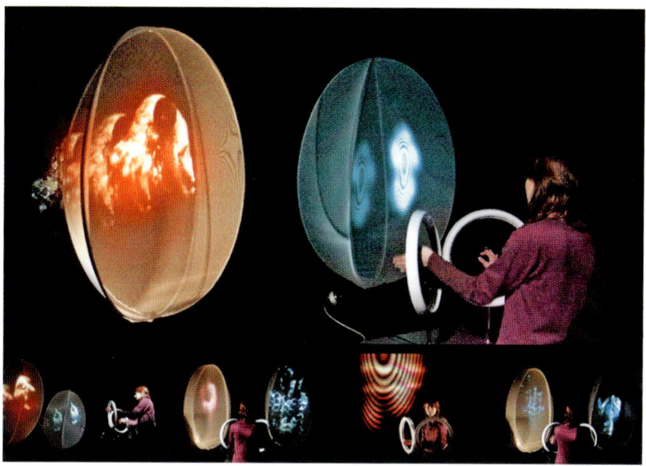

Ksawery Kaliski, *Against Nothingness (Montage), 2005/06.*
Installation with digital images and interactive rings, size variable.

Ksawery Kaliski studied graphics at the Academy of Fine Arts in Katowice, graduating with distinction in 2002, and since then has taught there in the new-media laboratory. Katowice, situated in Silesia in southern Poland, was formerly an important centre for heavy industry but in recent years has been the site of considerable regeneration, undergoing a gradual modernisation. In September 2009, the city council resolved at a meeting to dedicate the city to the advancement of culture. Kaliski's work has developed against this background, changing from the use of traditional flat techniques on paper to multimedia projects using advanced and experimental new technologies. His work has been seen in many countries around the world at film festivals, exhibitions of graphic arts and as site-specific presentations. He is also involved in the creation of a major interactive installation for the projected Copernicus Science Centre in Warsaw, and with the design for a mobile interactive Silesian pavilion, scheduled to tour a number of European cities in 2012.

It is a major leap from traditional printmaking to multimedia works, requiring an idiosyncratic imagination. Making such work may require less physical effort than the making of, for example, a conventional etching, but creating four-dimensional works demands a highly tuned imaginative and conceptual ability throughout what is a lengthy process, as well as a thorough technical understanding of what the software can achieve, the demands of the technology for presentation, and a sensitivity to the particular requirements of the spaces in which the presentations are to be made. Kaliski also works in close collaboration with the architects and designers of new buildings and spaces, and – because his projects are working with cutting-edge technology and new materials in the search for new solutions – with engineers and manufacturers. There

are still some traditionalists who insist that digital techniques – whether as images for print or as multimedia image sequences – cannot be considered as printmaking, in that the output is not on paper and there is no physical matrix through which an edition can be limited. Within a narrow definition, they have a point. But, as Walter Benjamin wrote (in 'The Work of Art in the Age of Mechanical Reproduction', first published in 1936), 'Mechanical reproduction of art changes the reaction of the masses towards art. The reactionary attitude toward a Picasso changes into a progressive reaction towards a Chaplin movie.' Experimental works in digital mediums can be considered in this context, and the digital file can be considered as the matrix from which come the images that are the equivalent of a print. Within these contexts it is also clear that Kaliski's work is indeed 'beyond the edge'.

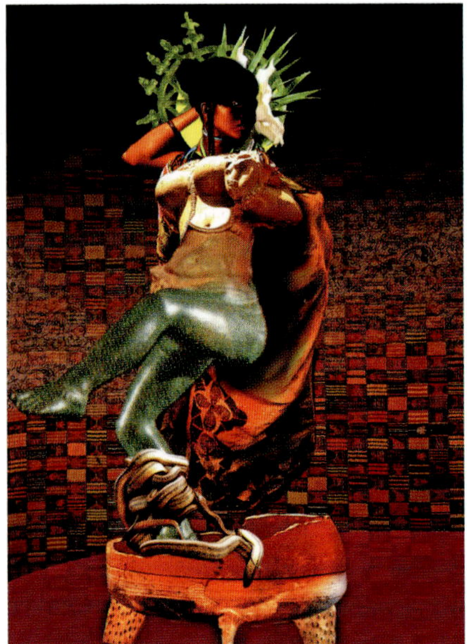

Ksawery Kaliski, *MARI3, Mary the Seducer, 2007/08.*
Interactive screen with digital imagery,
140 x 93.3cm. 55 x 37in.

'Against Nothingness – Entirety and Infinity' was shown in 2005/06, winning the first Honourable Mention for a multimedia work ever awarded by the Kraków International Print Triennial. In essence this work is based on the complexity of relationships between men and women, and the variable imagery is controlled interactively by the viewer via the use of specially designed rings. The imagery is derived from male and female dancers filmed underwater, whose movements can be controlled by the viewer. By learning the manipulation required the viewer can then bring them together to interact in a deeper relationship through the projection of moving images onto a cloud of steam.

'MARI3' is an interactive installation using three large touch screens and proximity detectors to cause changes that depend on the viewer's position and touch. It is based on three stages in the relationship of woman to man – as she takes on the successive roles of seducer, mother and teacher – and blends a wide range of cultural references from India, Africa and Japan as well as the classical symbols of Mary in Western beliefs. Together with other examples of Kaliski's work this was shown in 2008 as part of a major multimedia festival in Toruń, on a screen measuring 40 x 10m (131 x 32ft), hung on a wall of the town hall.

PR-OR-OK (Public Relations or OK-Prophet) was created in late 2008/early 2009 in response to the global financial crisis: based on the issue of investment, the main element is a male figure speaking the garbled language of finance, whose behaviour and appearance is determined by the proximity and movement of the viewer, becoming more complex if there are two viewers. Kaliski is also working on the design and making of a series of 'Stations of the Cross' for a 1960s church in southern Poland, to be constructed in plaster with coloured silicon skins. This work can be seen as a complement to the high-tech projects of an artist whose work is truly of the 21st century.

www.ksawerykaliski.com
(New technology, Large-scale printmaking and installation)

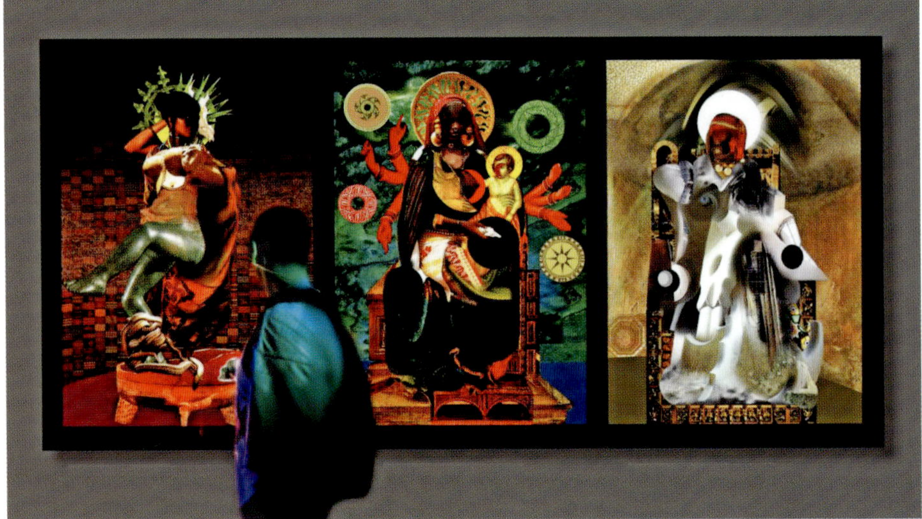

Ksawery Kaliski, *MARI3 (3 images), 2007/08.* Three interactive screens with digital imagery,
140 x 280cm. 55 x 110in. (overall).

LEONIE LANE

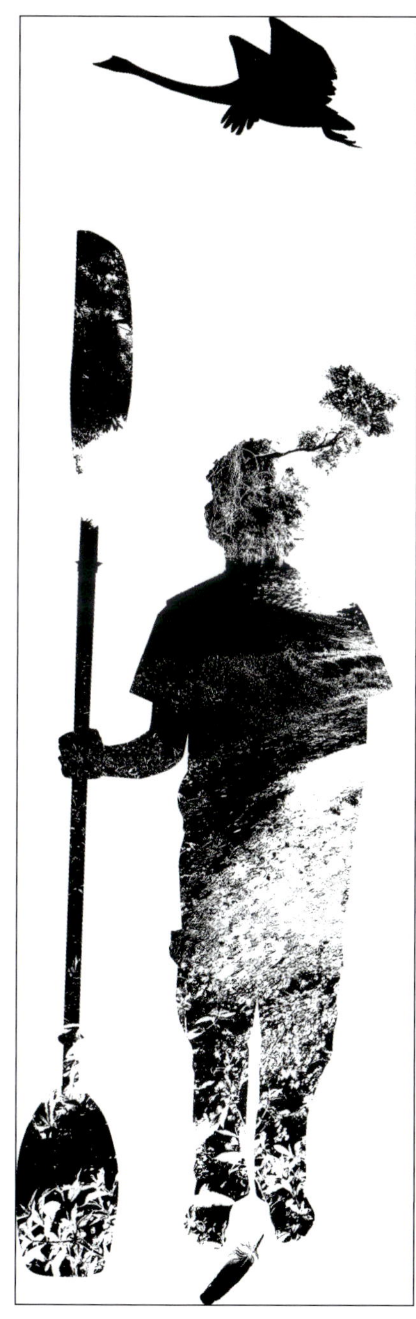

Leonie Lane, *Ghibli (from Down River project), 2007.*
Digital print on Hahnemühle paper. 141 x 61cm.
55.5 x 24in.

Leonie Lane was brought up in the Northern Rivers area of New South Wales, Australia, and completed her MA at Southern Cross University in Lismore, where she now teaches. Prior to this she worked with Redback Grafix, a socially engaged print workshop based in Sydney (which in 2008 was honoured with a major exhibition at the National Gallery of Australia), and worked as a freelance graphic designer. She has since returned to Lismore and lives in the same area as Jan Davis (q.v.), combining her personal work with graphic design. Her MA research project was based on '(un)folding landscape and identity' and 'notions of "place", personal narrative and social identity via digital imaging and installation'. A large part of her work in recent years has been involved with the process of coming to an understanding, by travelling through it, of the nature and meaning of landscape, with many of the journeys being made either on or beneath the surface of rivers.

The role of rivers in the way we relate to landscape, geologically and physically, has been a significant theme in both visual art and literature, as well as in music, for as long as these forms of expression have existed. Rivers have always been important to the Aboriginal peoples of Australia, as a source of food and water, and as a way through the landscape in both the literal sense and also as a vital constituent in their beliefs about the Dreamtime. With the expansion of urban settlement along the coastal fringe of Australia, the growth of irrigation farming, and the changes in global climate, in recent years rivers have become a central preoccupation for all Australians. Drought, combined with water extraction, is threatening ecological damage on a vast scale in the Murray and Darling River basins. As in many other parts of the world, where rivers with historic, cultural and environmental importance are threatened by climate change and human intervention, the role of artists in drawing attention to those threats has assumed a growing importance.

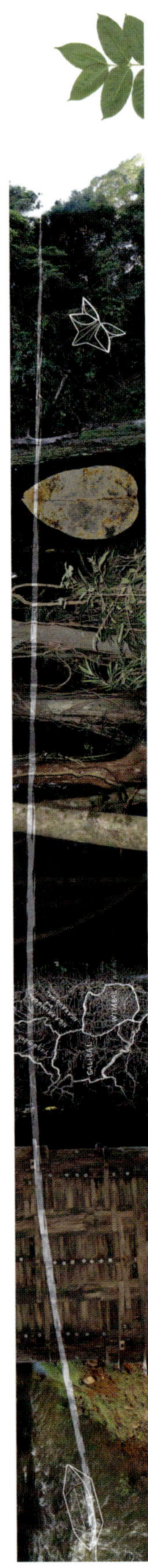
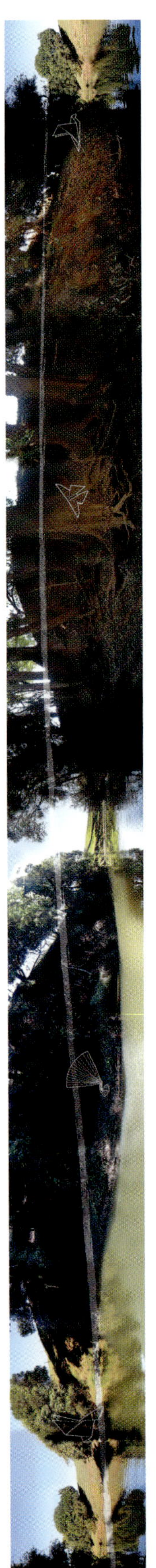
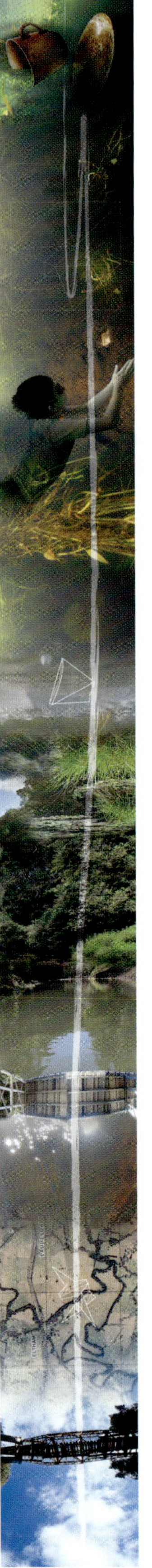

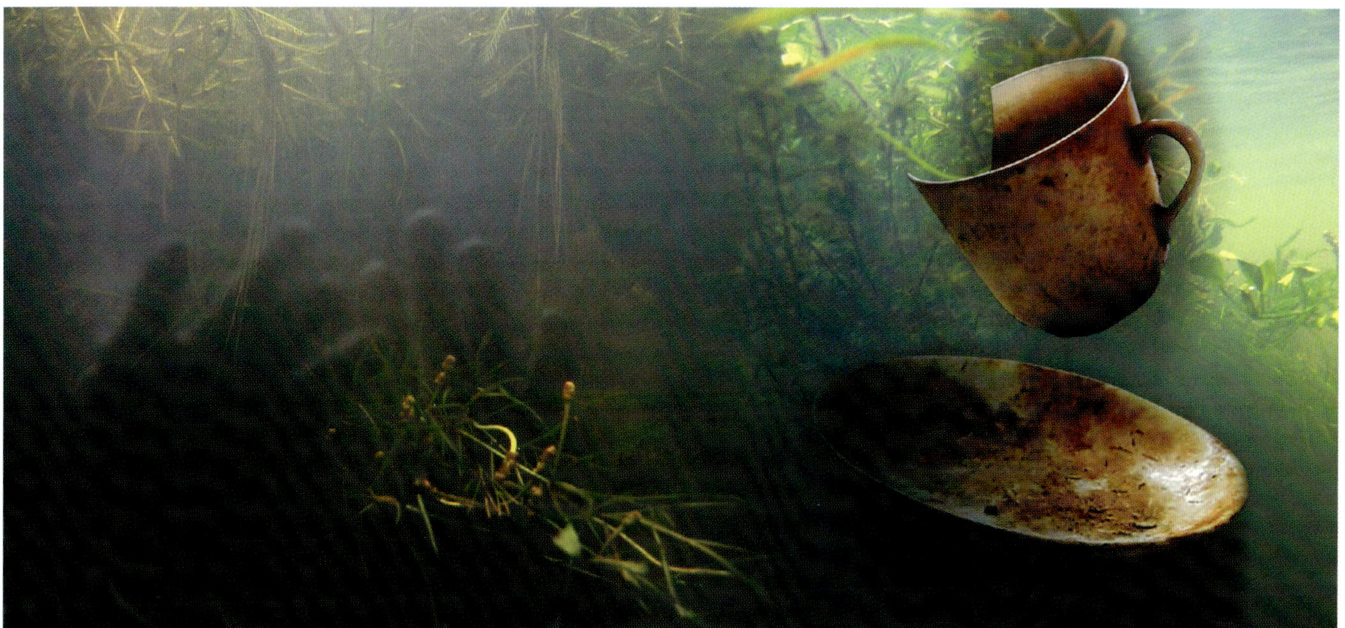

The role of rivers in Leonie Lane's work therefore gains an added resonance. Her major one-person exhibition at the Grafton Regional Gallery was titled *…down river…*, and explored a section of the Wilsons River between her home in Booyong and Eltham. This section of river is familiar to the artist from her childhood and her present life – 'a familiar and remembered terrain', as she puts it. The journey was made in a canoe used as both mode of transport and viewing platform, with still photography – 'the frozen moment' – rather than digital video being used as the main means of recording, thereby enhancing the qualities of stillness, reverie and peace that are central to Lane's understanding of the spirit of place. As well as making digital images she also collected fragments and ephemera connected with the locations through which she travelled, and made origami representations of animals and found objects, synthesising these collections with the images themselves to produce an autobiographical portrait of the river and the land through which it flows. The final composite images were used to produce a series of long works of variable size that were mounted on wave-rolled aluminium for subsequent mounting on the gallery walls, in a sequence that allowed viewers to follow the passage of the river from the beginning of the journey to the end.

The digital images were complemented by a series of large digital prints on paper that combined silhouetted figures with imagery from the journey, the collected ephemera and references to the Dreamtime stories of the region. *Landscape in a Figure – Ghibli*, refers to the moment in which Lane was paddling downstream and looked up to see a black swan flying overhead along the course of the river. This bird, known in the language of the Widjabal people, custodians of the land, as 'Bundjalung' (which is also the name of the nation of that people), is central to their creation story in which Ghibli becomes part of the constellation known as the Southern Cross. In the print the black feather that was collected recalls this moment and the feather is shown at the feet of the narrator. Other related prints recall incidents and observations along the course of the journey, and another aspect of the exhibition was the creation of a series of concertina-folded artist's books containing images of the journey. The installation was completed with a display of much of the ephemera collected, and the origami representations that were made. The intensive process of making and recording the journey, and then producing the range of prints to synthesise the experience, achieved the result of a thought-provoking and poetic meditation on the river.

www.booyongdesign.com
(Postcolonialism, Environment)

LINA RICA

At its most basic, the art of printmaking might be expressed as, 'Matrix + Intervention (by the artist) + Substrate (paper) = Print'. This process is well understood in terms of traditional techniques, and is widely accepted. But what happens if it is transmuted through the eyes of the new generation of artists in the postmodern (or even the post-postmodern) era? Lina Rica is one such artist, who, in search of the means of expression, has taken the equation in a new direction, applying very different definitions to the terms of that equation. She was born in Makarska in Croatia, and has studied both in London and at the Academy of Fine Arts in Zagreb in Croatia, which in 2008 awarded her its printmaking prize for the best postgraduate work. She has exhibited her work and made installations in many parts of Europe, and received the Special Acknowledgement of the jury at the 4th Triennial of Croatian Printmaking, an award that led to her work being included in the 5th International Triennial of Graphic Arts in Prague in 2007.

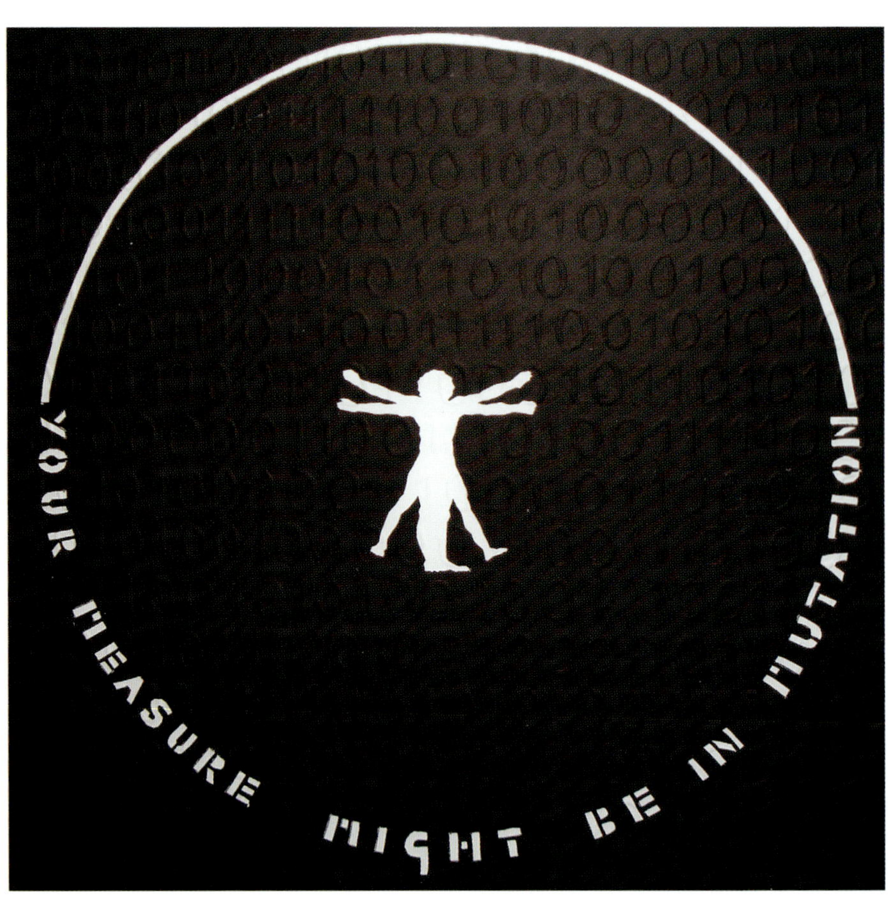

Lina Rica, *Metanoja (from Metanoja series), 2005.* Planography with blind embossing. 70 x 70cm. 27.5 x 27.5in.

The installation she made for the Prague exhibition was *The Line*, conceived as a means of creating the space for visitors to the exhibition to intervene in the work. It was her intention that through their additions to her work they should move from being passive observers to active participants. The work comprised a large area of black paper bearing the words 'This Triennale is …', with a box containing long rolls of self-adhesive coloured letters that visitors could peel off and then apply to the main area of paper, making words to complete the initial phrase. At the foot of the installation the words 'Trespass, Transmit, Transfer' appeared in large letters. The success of the proposition is measured by the large number of additions that were made during the course of the exhibition. While this contribution to the Prague Triennial was the most experimental, the artist also exhibited a series of works in blind embossing and planography that explored the relevance in

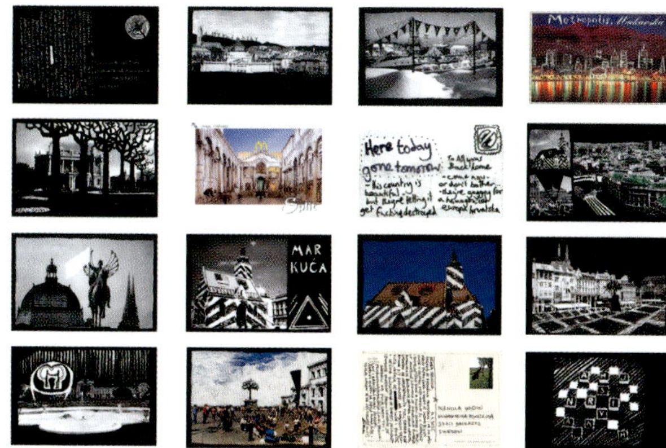

Lina Rica, *Greetings from the Future, 2008.*
Altered postcards, print, hand colouring, size variable.

the computer age of Leonardo da Vinci's Vitruvian Man. The work combined a sequence of images bearing binary code and variations on the iconic image of the human figure contained within the circle and the square – a juxtaposition of the ideal human form and the pervasive artifice of computer technology.

Since then her work has moved further away from what would, in conventional terms, be accepted as printmaking. But, as she writes in a statement about her recent work, '… the main concept of the work is alienation. That feeling I take as the matrix of the work, while streets, floors and other spaces I treat as "paper" on which I leave the traces. The formal backbones of presence are sentences that are used in different places and contexts, during which they stay unchanged – like the matrix in graphic discourse.' In summer 2008, as part of the Operacija Grad (Operation City) programme in Zagreb, which involved many independent cultural organisations, she devised *Greetings from Zagreb* as a project dealing with the issues of public space

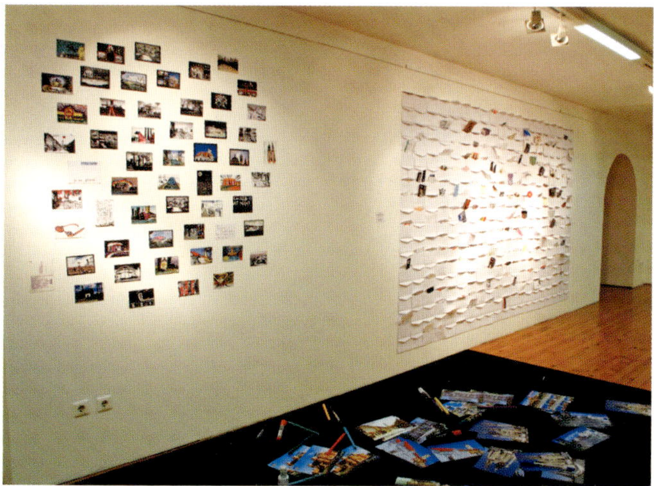

Lina Rica, *Greetings from the Future/Collective Mix, 2006–08.*
Altered postcards, texts, print, hand colouring, size variable.
Installation, Zagreb, Croatia.

and citizens' roles within it, the development of a post-socialist Zagreb in a future of neoliberal politics. Postcards of present-day Zagreb were displayed together with graphic materials with which visitors to the project could make interventions/alterations to the postcards to express their ideas for the future, which were then sent to addresses of the authors' choice, with a selection going to the offices of various authorities.

The *Campolis* project (2008), devised in conjunction with Tonka Maleković, proposed a utopian revitalisation of an abandoned military base on Cape Marin, which prior to 1990 was a forbidden zone for local inhabitants, and has not yet been opened up to tourist exploitation. Rica and Maleković made interventions on the base to suggest improvements for use as a 'wild camping' site, cleaning the site and mapping it for potential future development. After the site had been opened it was left to the local people and their informal guests to use and expand it. In 2009, another project devised by Rica, *Leksikon* (Dictionary), was based on the 'friends books' that are made by children. On each page there is a question and numbers for the answers with each contributor who wishes to give answers being given one of the numbers against which to write their answers. The form of the book remained the same but the artist devised new questions, 35 in total. Some of these were, 'Which Internet sites do you visit most?', 'What do you observe for a long time?' and 'What are you doing when nobody is watching?'. The completed pages were used to produce a suite of prints in silkscreen and drypoint.

www.komikaze.hr/wiki/pmwiki.php?n=Komikaze.
PozdravIzBuducnosti
(New technology, Large-scale printmaking and installation, The new generation)

LIZ INGRAM

'We live in an age obsessed with targets and goals, in which contemplation, deep philosophical thought and creative practice is often derided as a waste of time.' This sentence, from the lecture that Liz Ingram gave when she was presented with the Gordon J. Kaplan Award for Excellence in Research at the University of Alberta in 2008, goes to the core of her meditative work in printmaking and installation. She was born in Argentina and grew up in India and Canada, before studying art and printmaking, firstly in Toronto and then at the University of Alberta in Edmonton in Canada, where she gained her master's degree in 1975, and where she is now Professor in the Department of Art and Design. Her mentors at the University were Walter Jule and Lyndal Osborne, two celebrated printmakers whose enthusiasm and drive were central to the development of the Printmaking Department into the international centre of excellence that it is now. Liz Ingram has an extensive record of exhibitions in many parts of the world as well as awards from numerous institutions and competitions, and is a member of the Royal Canadian Academy of Art.

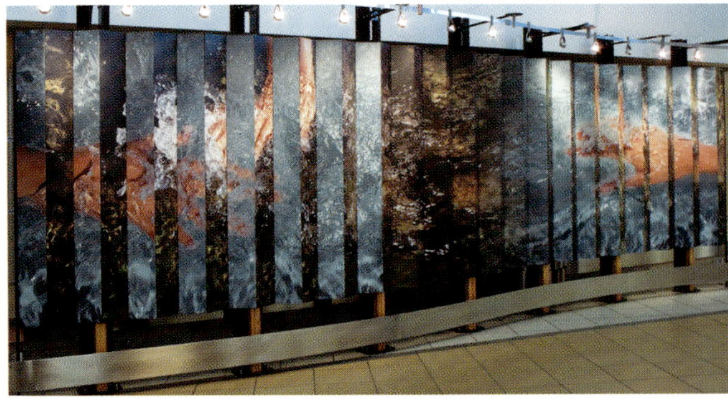

Liz Ingram, *Touching Water – Anticipation and Memory, 2004.*
Digital outputs on 42 aluminium panels, 200 x 700 x 71cm. 78 x 276 28in.
Installation at Edmonton International Airport, Edmonton, Canada.

For many years this artist's work has centred on her exploration of the transitional states between material presence and the 'spiritual'. She believes that her childhood in India gave her a strong impulse to explore ideas about human existence in both its physical and ephemeral aspects. She writes, 'Early exposure to extremes of physical deprivation, butted up against heightened sensuality, exotic rich colours, sounds, smells and ritual practices, have predisposed me to this continuing endeavour.' In exploring these dichotomies Ingram has in much of her work in recent years concentrated on imagery derived from water and the human body. She is deeply aware of the fragility of the global ecosystem, which obviously depends on water, and also the potential fragility of human life when set against a threatened environment. She understands also that many people no longer appreciate their place in the natural world, becoming ever more distanced from it by technology and urbanisation and the sense of deracination and alienation that these can bring. In addition she is concerned that the fragmentation of contemporary life deprives us of, 'first-hand experience, spiritual stimulus and connection with our natural biological pace'. Her work addresses the temporal nature of our

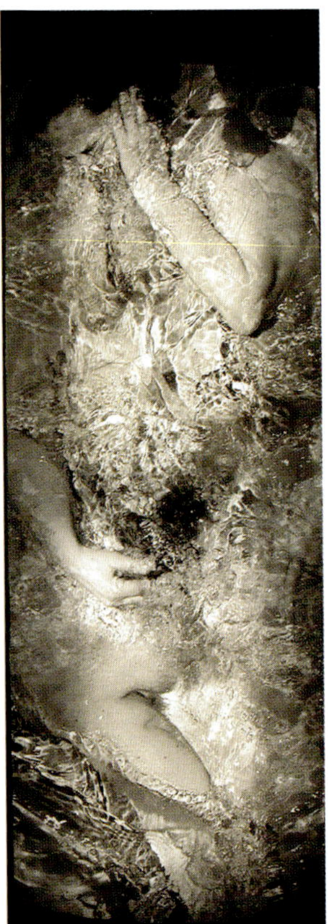

Liz Ingram, *Synectic Pulse, 2005.*
Layered digital prints on acetate, Plexiglas, wood, fluorescent light box, 211 x 97 x 11cm. 83 x 38 4.5in.

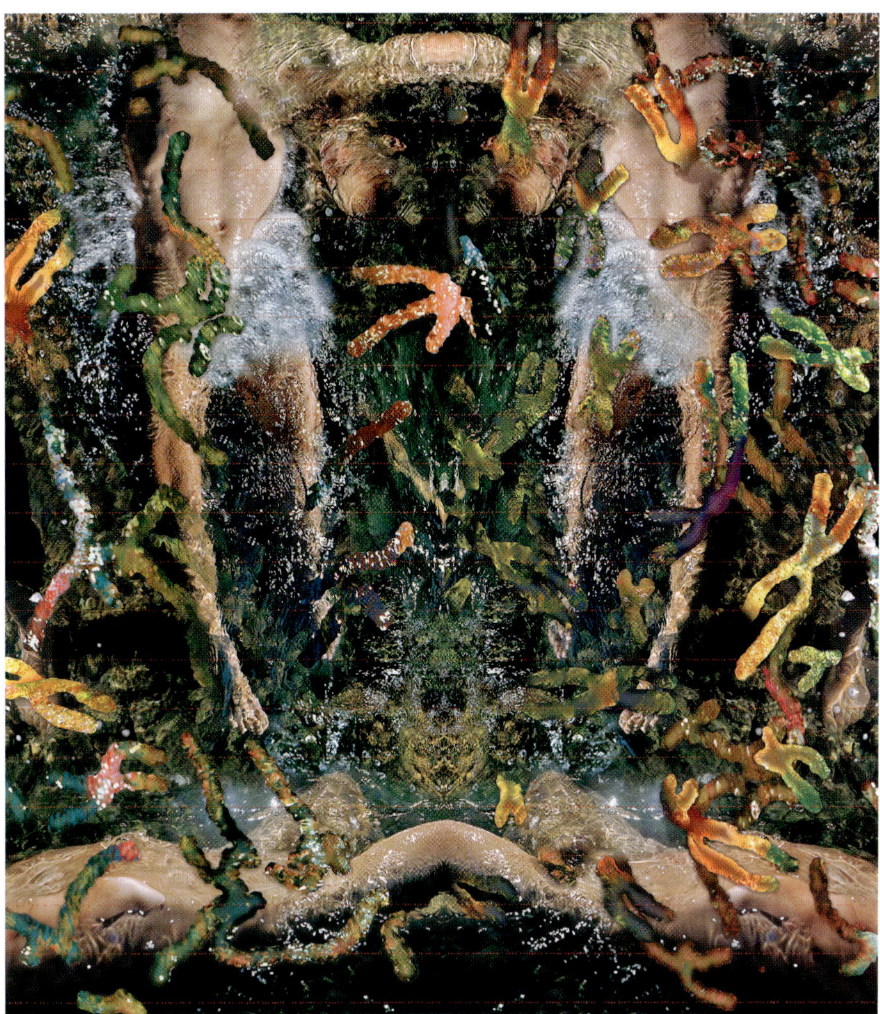

existence on this planet and the threats to the continuation of water resources and, in a different but connected way, to essential human intimacy.

Following a gradual evolution in her work from the mid-1970s to the late 1990s, a period during which she worked with lithography and screenprint, then with intaglio techniques and finally photo-intaglio, Ingram began to incorporate digital techniques with increasing frequency. At the same time the size of her works increased, from prints with dimensions less than 1m (39in.) up to installations that make use of new technologies enabling dimensions of many metres. In 2004, she was commissioned to create a major installation for Edmonton International Airport, comprising 42 panels of digital prints. *Touching Water: Anticipation and Memory* is suited to its location in an airport concourse, but it demonstrates well her concerns and preoccupations, showing hands in moving water, and with a concertina form allowing different images to be seen depending on the direction of observation.

In her Kaplan lecture the artist describes how years of working with lith-film images and light boxes led her towards exploring the making of images to be mounted in backlit boxes. She said that, 'The intangible flickering nature of these backlit images, which dematerialize into dots … speak directly to my fundamental interests in the intangible, fragility, memory and transience.'

Synectic Pulse (2005) is one in a series of images in which the artist had photographs made of herself in the bathtub, and subsequently reworked the images as layered digital prints on acetate and Plexiglas, to be mounted in wood and fabric, with fluorescent lights. In a darkened space prints such as these allow the establishment of a different relationship between the image and the viewer, a deeper intensity of identification with the vulnerability that is shown. As part of the interdisciplinary project Imagining Science, involving bio-ethicists, scientists and artists, organised by Sean and Tim Caulfield for the Alberta Art Gallery in 2008, Liz Ingram collaborated with her husband, Bernd Hildebrandt, in the creation of *Perplexed Realities I & II*, based on photographs taken at Obed Lake and Creek, and using the images of natural vegetation and Hildebrandt's body in the water to produce complex compositions that go to the core of her, 'belief that we are seamless and totally interconnected, that nothing has an end, and that truth lies in the never-ending mutability and mystery of life.' We become complicit with this belief through her work.

http://lizingram.com (Large-scale printmaking and installation, Environment, Memory)

MAŁGORZATA 'MALWINA' NIESPODZIEWANA

Małgorzata 'Malwina' Niespodziewana studied printmaking at the Academy of Fine Arts in Kraków in Poland, graduating in 1998, and subsequently being awarded her doctorate in 2007 for *Body: the Artistic Idea of a Universal Body.* The human body has for many years been at the core of her work, which has been shown in many exhibitions across the world. She has travelled widely, notably to India and Japan, where she took up a residency at the Mino Art Village Project. Her studies in Kraków, with its academic traditions and rich history of printmaking, provided her with a fertile context in which to develop her work. While the academy tradition in Kraków served her well in the development of her idiosyncratic work, giving her a sound background in figure drawing in the academic style, she has since evolved a style of her own in which the depictions of the human form are metaphors for the human condition, transcending strict anatomical references and sometimes gender. Her travels to India and Japan introduced her to different interpretations of human anatomy and medicine, and these have joined with her European-based studies to give her figures a wider frame of reference and presentation. She refers in her writing to the universal language of feelings, emotions and reactions, shared by cultures throughout the world. Through her exploration of this language she has produced a body of work that offers a profound insight and relevance.

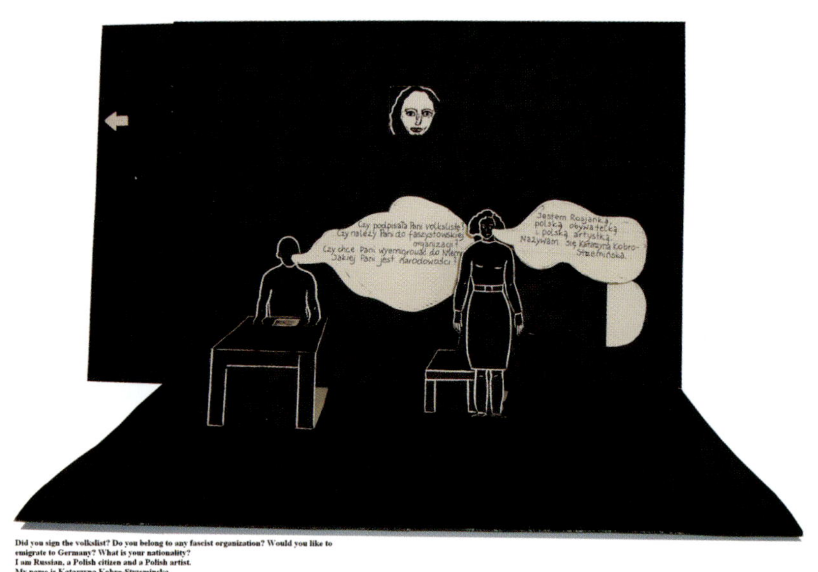

Małgorzata Niespodziewana, *Kobro – Cross-examination (from cycle Kate and Nika, 1936–1951), 2008.* Linocut, thread, pop-up book 25 x 25 x 35cm. 10 x 10 x 14in. (book).

In addition to her works based on printmaking techniques, Malwina has also worked with installation, three-dimensional objects, performance and photography, seeking the most appropriate means for extending her ideas and finding forms that give it the most powerful resonance. This may be, as in her 2003 exhibitions in Denmark, Poland and Japan, in the form of delicate full-size three-dimensional figures constructed from translucent washi, with threads and beads, in a meditation on the theme of life and mortality, symbolised by the addition of blood vessels and a foetus. *In The Boys cry…* (2005) she used linocut on dyed paper with the addition of tears made with thread, to produce a life-size print of a group of boys whose features put them beyond ethnicity or time. In these and other works the stylised depictions give a sense of universal relevance, vulnerability and strength.

Władysław Strzemiński was a celebrated painter in Poland in the early part of the 20th century, and a prime mover in the early avant-garde in Poland. He was married to Katarzyna Kobro, a sculptor who was Russian by descent and Polish by nationality, and who gained a certain prominence herself before sinking into obscurity. Her role in the avant-garde was reassessed in the 1980s, and she is now regarded as being one of the most important artists of her generation. Malwina has been inspired by Kobro's work, and her tragic life, for many years, and also by her innovative approach to sculpture; having studied both her works and accounts of her life and works, the artist sought ways to express the story and its relevance to the present day. During the research for the project Malwina considered the possibility of extending the traditional form of the flat print, and extending it into space so that it could interact with those looking at it. The final project to date (and more may come about) comprises a series of small linocut portraits, a life-size linocut portrait of Kobro on rice paper, a pop-up book, *Kate and Nika* 1936–51, and *The Black Box* K-S, which comprises a set of ten boxes.

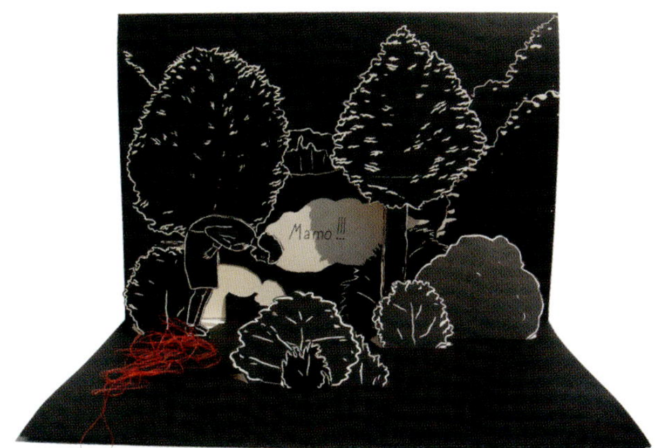

Małgorzata Niespodziewana, *Kobro – Forest (from cycle Kate and Nika, 1936–1951), 2008.* Linocut, thread, pop-up book, 25 x 25 x 35cm. 10 x 10 x 14in. (book).

The pop-up book was conceived to invite the interaction of viewers, offering them the chance to turn the pages and pull the tabs that animate the images – a chance rarely allowed in art galleries. Malwina describes Kobro's life as, 'a fairy tale gone wrong', being 'rich in such tragic events as the war, hunger, ethnic problems, poverty, cancer and finally death.' The time period of the book begins with the birth of Kobro's daughter Nika, and ends with Kobro's early death. The events are told in stark black and white, with the exception of red to symbolise blood and, in the scene depicting Kobro's funeral, the red skirt worn by Nika, which outraged others at the ceremony. The strength of the bond between mother and daughter, recounted in Nika Strzemińska's book, Art, *Love and Hate*, dedicated to the lives of her parents, is shown to powerful effect. *The Black Box* K-S presents the events of the break-up of the marriage of Kobro and Strzemiński in a stack of black cardboard boxes, each of which is open at the front, in which scenes of those events are shown. In this as in all her work, Małgorzata Niespodziewana seeks to bring out the universal relevance of the human situations she depicts.

www.niespodziewana.xwp.pl
(The third dimension, Memory)

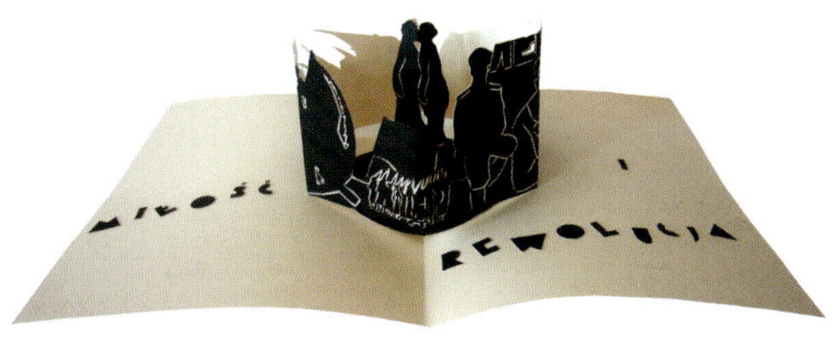

Małgorzata Niespodziewana, *Kobro – Love and Revolution (from the cycle Kobro), 2009.* Linocut, pop-up book, 20 x 20 x 27cm. 8 x 8 x 11in. (book).

MARCUS REES ROBERTS

Marcus Rees Roberts followed his BA in English from Cambridge University with studies in film theory and printmaking at the Slade School of Fine Art in London. He then taught at the Slade, and subsequently in Edinburgh and at the University of Central Florida, before returning to live and work in London. His work has been shown in many exhibitions in Britain and internationally, and is included in a number of important British collections. The scope of his work is wide, including paintings and drawings as well as prints and monotypes, and artist's books. His prints have been mostly in traditional mediums, such as woodcut and intaglio, but he has also incorporated digital chine collé.

His woodcuts are strongly expressionist in style, with images of faces and bodies drawn powerfully, employing a sombre palette. Rees Roberts has travelled in Spain for many years, and has developed a deep regard for its landscape, language and culture. Two series of prints in particular have provided a rich source of subject matter for his books and films: *Hostal de Francia* and *Catalunya*, both from 2007, contain stark faces and images of bodies, echoing the dark history of the Spanish Civil War in Catalonia. A set of three etchings with aquatint titled *Between Dog and Wolf* (2008) explores the passions of relationships, and the prints combine two or more images on the same sheet, setting up contrasts. The artist had also explored this technique to good effect in *A Silence* (2002).

By working with multiple images on a sheet, and through developing his themes in series, Rees Roberts has striven for the means by which to establish a narrative within his work. It is logical that he should have taken this a step further through the making of artist's books, in a range of mediums and formats that allow the narrative thread potential for development. The artist is deeply concerned in much of this strand of his work with the problems faced by human beings in extreme situations, and the tensions that result. There are strong links to Ezra Pound – in *White Wings of Time Passing* (2004) and *Ash to Dark Water* (2005) – and to Lorca – in *The Fountain of Tears* (2003) and *It is the Day Returning* (2007). These books are, as with most artist's books, produced in relatively small editions – no more than 130 and as few as 25.

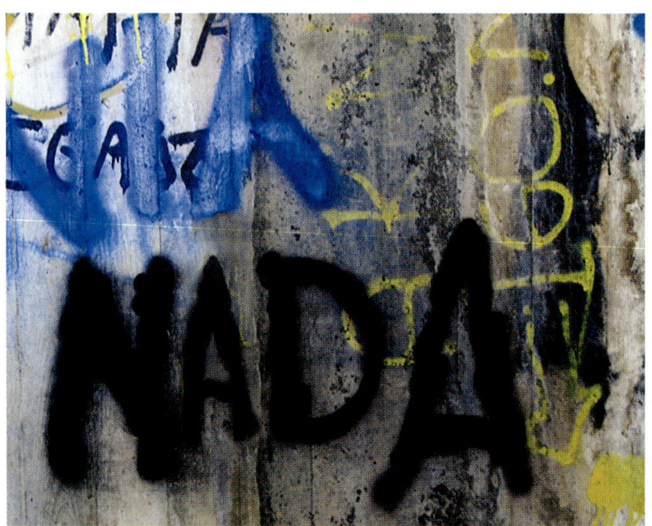

Marcus Rees Roberts, *Man at the Border (detail – Nada), 2008.*
Digital prints – from DVD Film, published by Pratt Contemporary.
Size variable.

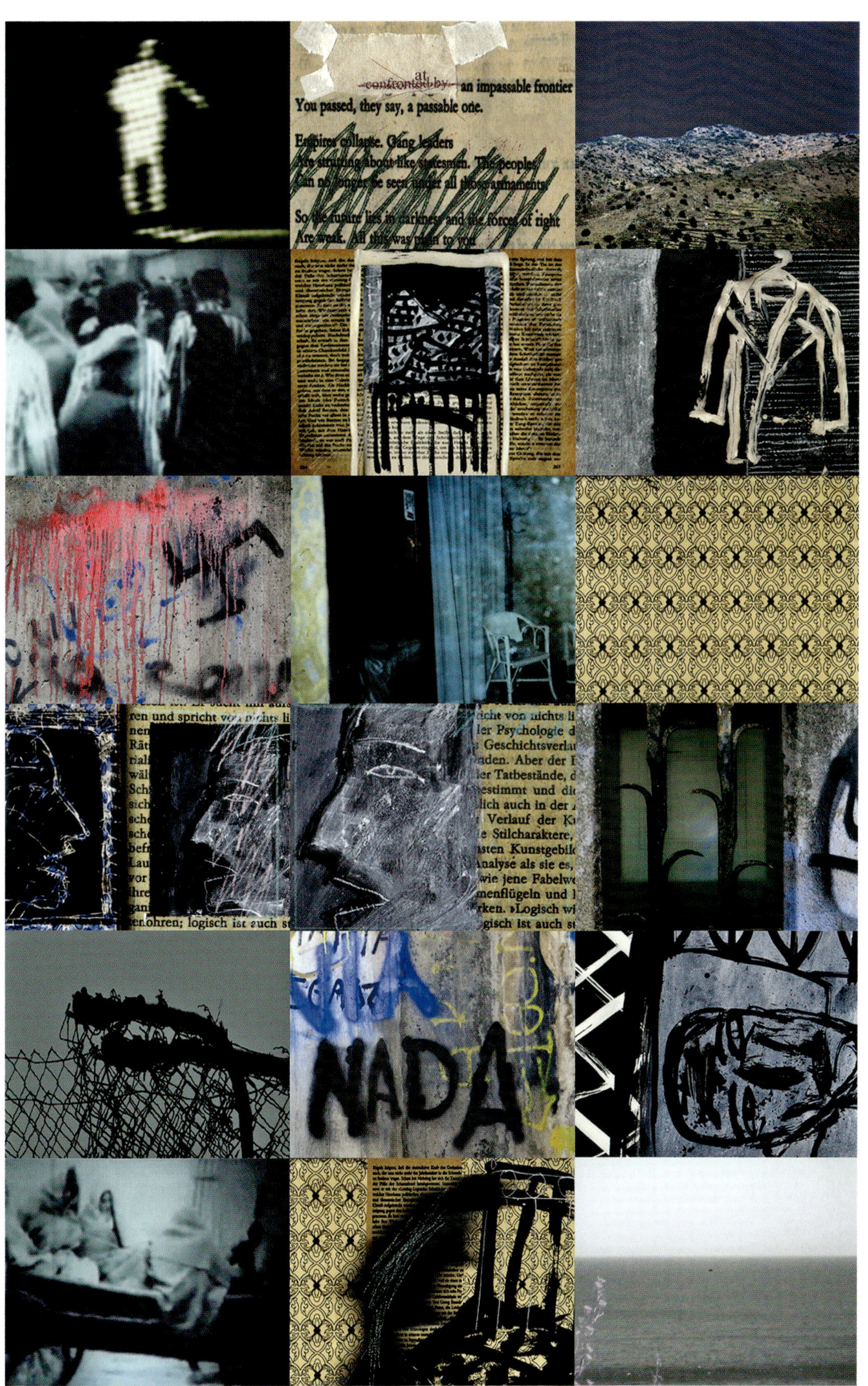

Marcus Rees Roberts, *Man at the Border (montage), 2008.* Digital prints – from DVD Film, published by Pratt Contemporary. Size variable.

Marcus Rees Roberts, *Man at the Border (detail – Head), 2008.* Digital prints – from DVD Film, published by Pratt Contemporary. Size variable.

The elegiac mood of the books is carried through to Rees Roberts's work in film, in the form of DVDs, a medium that offers him a greater sense of liberty and control over the way in which his chosen images and contexts are presented, as well as containing the possibility of being available for many to view. Films enable the camera to move across or into images, with effects such as cross-fades adding to this dynamic; sound can also be incorporated, as music or the spoken word; images can be held still or changed rapidly – the use of combinations of such techniques can add a richness that is not available in conventional prints or in books. Films are, however, just a part of this artist's work, in which all the mediums of expression that he chooses develop from the same sources of inspiration and the same techniques.

A series of 11 films, *The Winter Journey*, contains (as Part 4) *Man at the Border*, a haunting evocation of the last day in the life of Walter Benjamin as he strove to escape the risk of capture and death in the genocide of World War II by crossing from France into Spain through the border at Port Bou. There he was betrayed by an hotelier and, fearing being handed over to the Gestapo, he committed suicide. Rees Roberts conveys the desperation and claustrophobia of that final day through shifting images, and a final coda in which film of a boat out on a misty sea is accompanied by music and the text, 'at an impassable frontier you passed, they say, a passable one.' This is a memorable elegy to a writer whose work continues to be central to the art of printmaking. In *La Colonia: The Fountain of Tears* the artist takes as his theme the final days of Lorca, seized by the Guardia Civil, shot and buried in an unmarked grave in an olive grove. Sequences of images and music, including a photograph of a man being seized which is scratched over with the image of another man, itself to be scratched over, elide into a poem, 'It is the Day Returning', before coming back to a final sequence of music and images. This film provides a fitting elegy to the poet, but also offers a meditation on our own mortality.

www.prattcontemporaryart.co.uk/Marcus%20Rees%20Roberts/Marcus%20Home.html
(New technology, Memory)

MARIAN MAGUIRE

Sometime in the 13th century Polynesian voyagers made the hazardous journeys across the South Seas and discovered the islands that in time became known to those first Māori settlers as Aotearoa – the Land of the Long White Cloud. In 1642 the Dutchman, Abel Tasman, made a perilous journey to become the first European in the islands; Captain Cook made three voyages of exploration through the South Seas, including a landing in New Zealand, in the mid-18th century; and in 1840 the Treaty of Waitangi brought the islands into the British Empire. Those islands on the farthest side of the world from Europe have been subject to colonisation for centuries.

To create links between the Ancient Greeks, the Māori and the European explorers and settlers in New Zealand might seem strange. But that has been the central theme in the work of Marian Maguire for the past decade or more, resulting in three major suites of prints. Maguire was born in New Zealand and studied there at the University of Canterbury before going on to complete the Professional Printer Training Programme at the Tamarind Institute in New Mexico. She returned

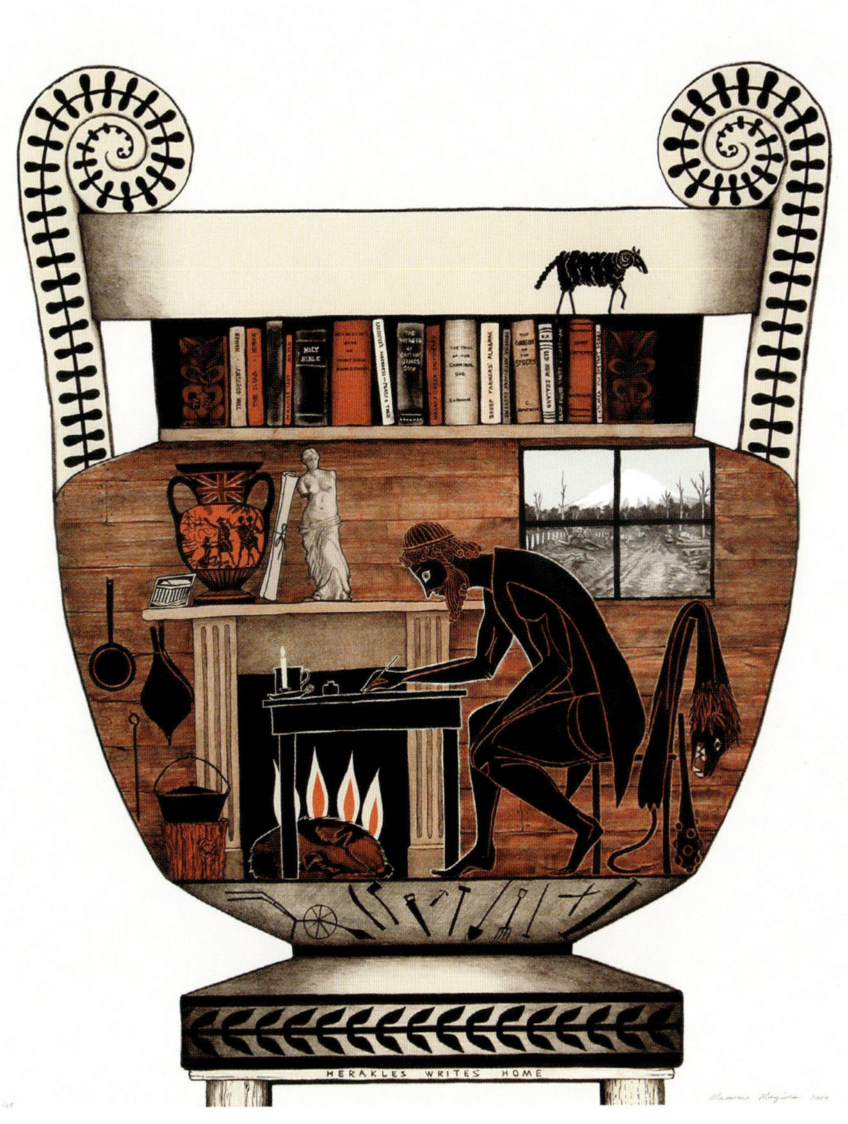

Marian Maguire, *Herakles Writes Home, 2007–08.* Lithograph, 72.7 x 57cm. 29 x 22.5in.

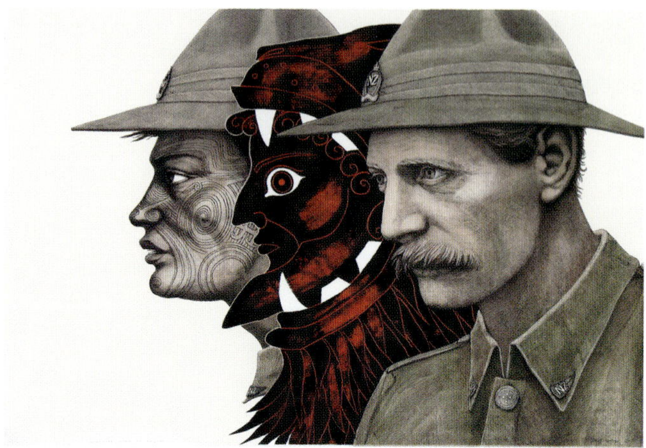

Marian Maguire, *Herakles goes to Gallipoli, 2007–08.*
Lithograph, 52.5 x 76.5cm. 21 x 30in.

to New Zealand in 1987, and since then has been deeply involved in printmaking there, running her own fine-print studios, teaching and selecting exhibitions, as well as pursuing her own work, which has been widely exhibited in her own country and is held in numerous public collections. She writes of how part of her degree in art was accompanied by religious studies, which included intensive scrutiny of the artefacts of the native peoples of the Pacific region as well as studies of the Italian Renaissance and Ancient Greece. In turn this led to an abiding interest in the history of how her own country was colonised, and the artistic records of that period, and then to a consideration of how the world of the Ancient Greeks and the world of the European explorers, each with their own myths and stories, might be combined. She writes, 'I decided that it was perfectly OK to have more than one set of myths for one country that overlaid each other, and they didn't have to be logical together.'

The first of the three suites of prints was *Southern Myths* (2001), which transferred the myths of Achilles and Ajax to New Zealand, and combined elements of the landscape and fauna of that country with imagery that owed much to the silhouetted figures on Greek vases, resulting in a masterly and yet unsettling sequence of images. This was followed by *The Odyssey of Captain Cook* (2003–05), a series of highly detailed lithographs that took the principle of combination further, with Maguire appropriating images from historical New Zealand art as well as inventing her own versions of classical Greek figures. Thus a lithograph of a volute crater shows in fine narrative detail the arrival of Captain Cook in the South Seas and incidents from his life and death. Another shows the face-to-face meeting of a classical Greek helmeted figure

with the profile portrait of the tattooed chief Natai, from an original 1833 lithograph, while her version of the landing of Captain Cook shows him being met by warriors, not Greek but Māori. The apparent discontinuity between the sources of the imagery the artist uses is overcome by virtue of her skills in appropriation and composition, as well as her fine lithographic technique and subtle use of colour, to create a memorable and haunting series of images.

The third suite, which features lithographs and etchings, is *The Labours of Herakles* (2006–08), in which Herakles, the hero who carried out the instructions of the gods, is transported to colonial times in New Zealand. The fusion of seemingly disparate imagery is still there, but is taken to a new level through the skill with which Maguire appropriates carefully selected imagery for combinations that perhaps should not work, but most emphatically do. So we see Herakles uprooted from the mythic locations in which his story is told and placed in situations that would have been just as alien to him as they were to the early settlers. He is seen signing the treaty between the Māori and the British, witnessed by Queen Victoria and a Chief in ceremonial dress; he is shown writing home, while sitting in a settler's house beneath a shelf of books including the Bible, Mrs Beeton and The Origin of Species; and at Gallipoli, not far from the legendary site of Troy, his classical profile is shown between the Chief Natai and Robert James Scott, a celebrated New Zealand wrestler – both of them wearing WWI Army uniform – in a poignant image that connects this mythic and historic conjunction of heroes. Marian Maguire's work repays detailed examination and reveals the historic roots of a shared heritage.

www.papergraphica.co.nz
(New uses for old technology, Postcolonialism)

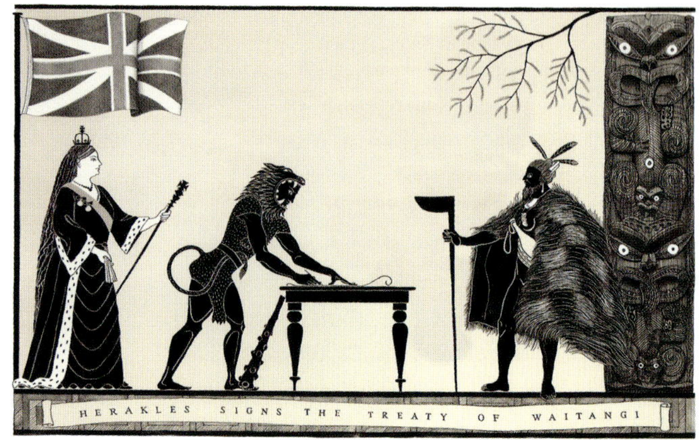

Marian Maguire, *Herakles Signs the Treaty of Waitangi, 2006/07.*
Lithograph, 39.4 x 61.4cm. 15 x 24in. (plate) on 57 x 76.5cm.
22 x 30in. (paper).

MARINA NÚÑEZ

To a child born half a century or more ago the notion of the 21st century was the stuff of science fiction, an inconceivably distant place, a comic-book world as strange and unreachable as the world of the Middle Ages, and as odd as the world of the Victorians. Science-fiction books proposed robots and space ships, and dystopian worlds that satirised a future that seemed in peril during the time of the Cold War. We now live in a 21st-century world that is less resolved than ever, in which some of the predictions of science fiction have come to pass, to be joined by technologies and events that were not foreseen. Science and technology are driving the world towards a future that seems to be as far away as ever but which, paradoxically, is approaching at increasing speed. While we take for granted many of the advances in technology that would have astonished our grandparents, and communicate across the planet with the flick of a finger, we are also in danger of losing touch with our humanity.

This is the context in which Marina Núñez works. She was born and studied in Spain, lives in Madrid, and since 1989 has exhibited her work in Spain and internationally. Her early exhibitions featured objects with surrealist references, hyperrealist paintings on cloth, and drawings that prefigured her more recent work with digital mediums. In 1993 she produced a series of versions of faces from art-historical sources, painted on linen napkins. By the turn of the century her work had evolved into paintings combining oil and digital, paintings of neurons, light boxes with digital images and fluorescent paintings requiring ultraviolet light. Throughout this period, and continuing up to the present, Núñez was deeply interested in the fundamental scientific, technological and philosophical concerns surrounding the relationship between humans and machines. It is therefore not surprising that her work relates directly to these issues, developing in conjunction with the emerging field of 'technoscience', which denies the historical

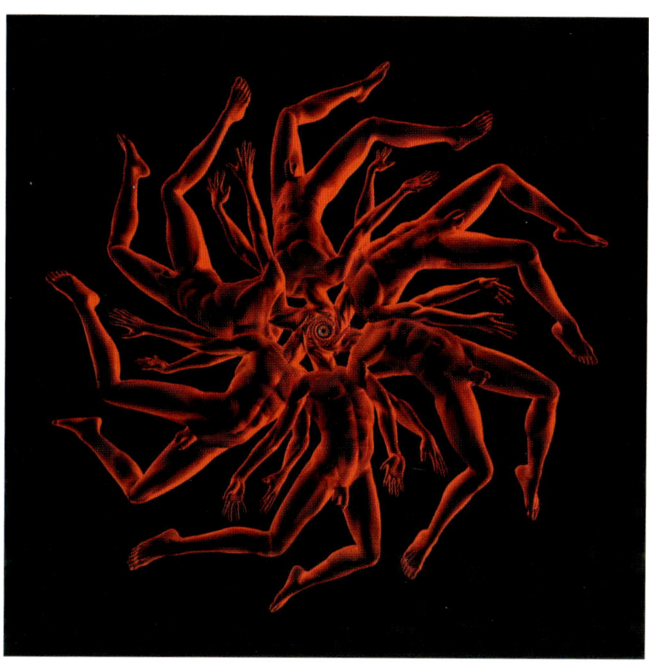

Marina Nuñez, *Explosión 2, 2008.* Infography on light box, 100 x 100cm. 39 x 39in.

separation between science (as theory) and technology (as practice), and by extension the distinctions between nature and society, natural and artificial, organic and inorganic. While much of the thinking in this field has in itself been theoretical, developments in technoscience are leading to extraordinary developments in prosthetics, human/machine interfaces, and sensory aids, as well as the application of robotics in general.

While Núñez's work has sprung from and is positioned within the art world, it clearly also has its place in the emerging worlds of biotechnology, post-silicon computing and global communication technology. Interestingly, in this context printmaking has always harnessed cutting-edge technology in the service of artistic expression; it is just that the technology has moved on further and faster than could have been envisaged in the middle of the last century. Virtual reality has moved out of the realm of fantasy films and into the real world; computer simulations have moved from the Star Trek 'holodeck' into

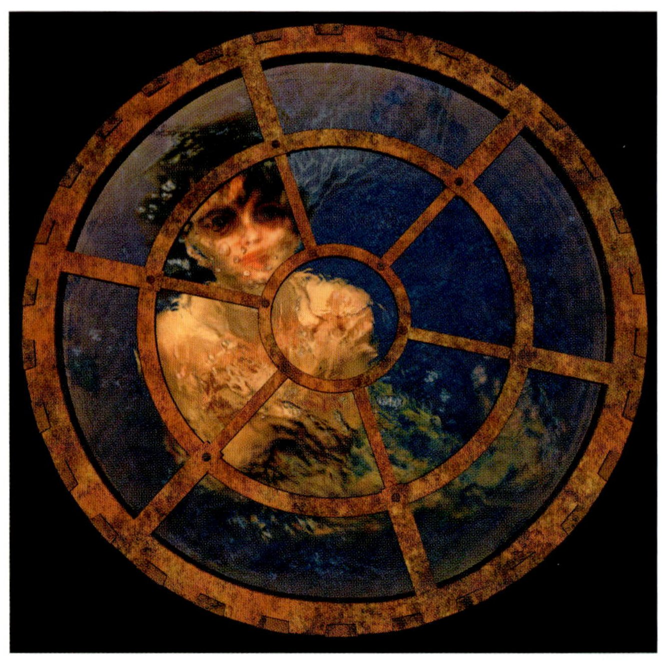

science and industry, and sooner or later will become part of domestic life as well. As an artist who is closer than many to the world of technoscience, Núñez is aware of her role in counteracting the conservatism of thinkers such as Francis Fukuyama, who call for new forms of state regulation of the emerging technologies that he foresees as offering a threat to democracy itself. Artists, like writers (Shelley's 'unacknowledged legislators of mankind'), can work to counteract that incipient conservatism and offer a credible choice somewhere between the dystopian and utopian visions of the future, in which democratic and beneficial developments may be possible.

Marina Núñez uses the term 'infography' to describe her digital works, either on paper, in light boxes, or as projections. It is a term appropriate to the techniques she uses to express her ideas, which are almost entirely dependent on computer technology and software for their realisation. She is prolific in her output and meticulous in the means she uses for exhibiting her work. We are presented with images from a world that is hard to imagine, but which once seen appears to contain its own logic, not so far from the daily worlds in which we move. There are post-apocalyptic cities, skeletal masks with multiple eyes, visions of silent hells, fallen angels, Vitruvian spiders, and mermaids trapped beneath city drainage covers. Her vocabulary of images and techniques is extensive, and the worlds that she presents are disturbing yet fascinating, offering visions of strange purgatories and implied warnings of the destinations that might await us should a balance not be found between the emerging technosciences and the renewal of the humanity upon which our survival depends.

www.marinanunez.net
(New technology, Large-scale printmaking and installation, Science)

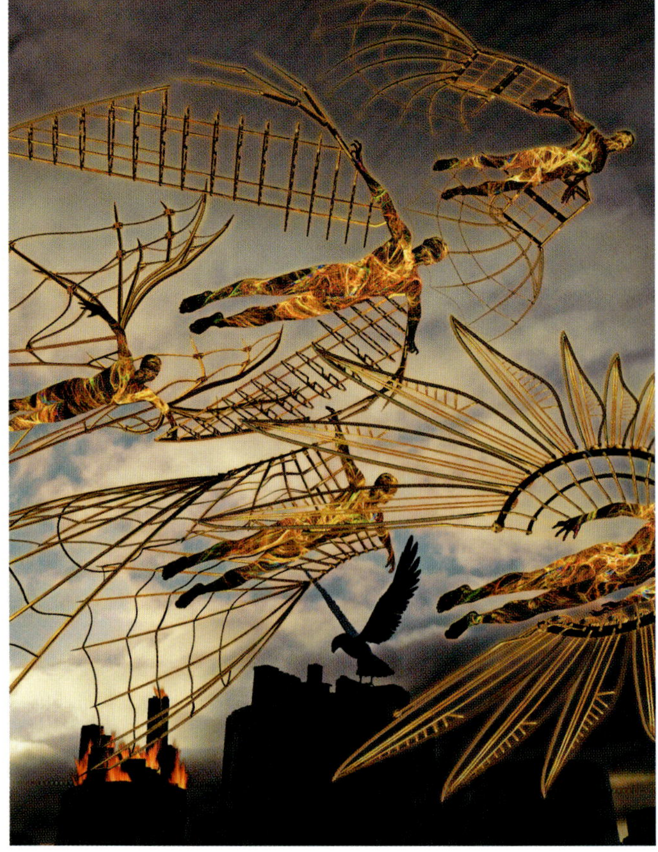

MICHAEL BARNES

The American Midwest, being far from both coasts – with their distinctive printmaking scenes – has for many years offered something different. The nature of the environment – cities interspersed with wide areas of open farmland – has been the seedbed in which idiosyncratic art and music traditions have developed. Michael Barnes studied in Iowa and in Michigan, and is now Associate Professor of Art at Northern Illinois University in DeKalb, some distance from Chicago. Since the late 1990s he has gained a considerable international reputation, exhibiting widely and winning a number of awards, with work included in many international collections.

The first reaction when encountering this artist's work is its 'otherness'. His preferred medium is lithography and he is a perfectionist in this technique, combining excellent drawing skills with a subtle control of tone and a sombre palette of colours, all of which contribute to the essential nature of his prints. He offers us a strange vision that is not quite the world we are used to, where mutations are commonplace, and there is an overwhelming sense of melancholy and resignation to the cruelties of a world that that has eventually succumbed to human greed and thoughtless neglect. We are drawn into the images that he creates, fascinated by the detail they offer, and repelled by what we find there. And yet, at the same time, we are drawn back into the world he describes, to meditate on what might have happened there and to reflect on what we might have done to bring it about. There are no solutions to the situations Barnes offers us; there is no hope of resolution, and the images remain as they are, caught in a cold stillness beyond the hope of redemption.

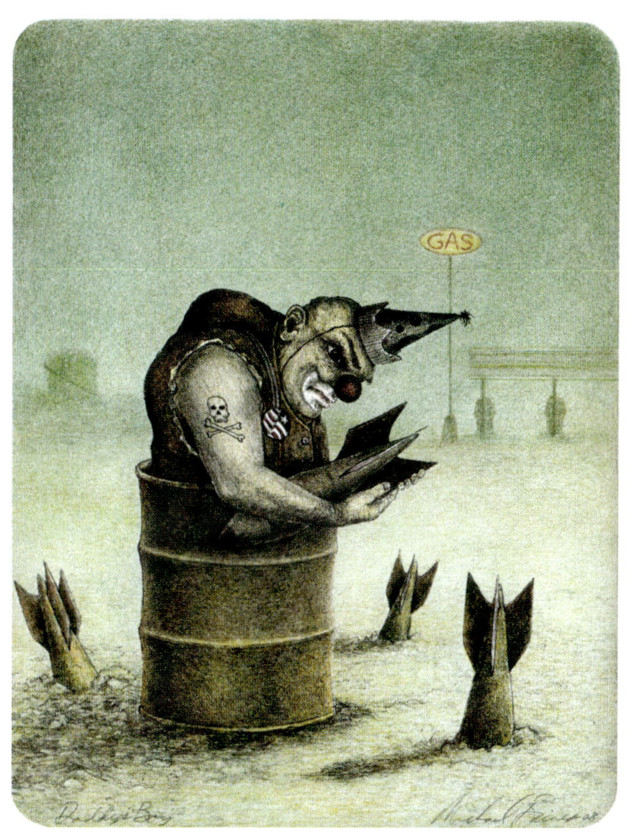

Michael Barnes, *Daddy's Boy, 2008.* Lithograph, 29 x 21.5 cm. 11.5 x 8in.

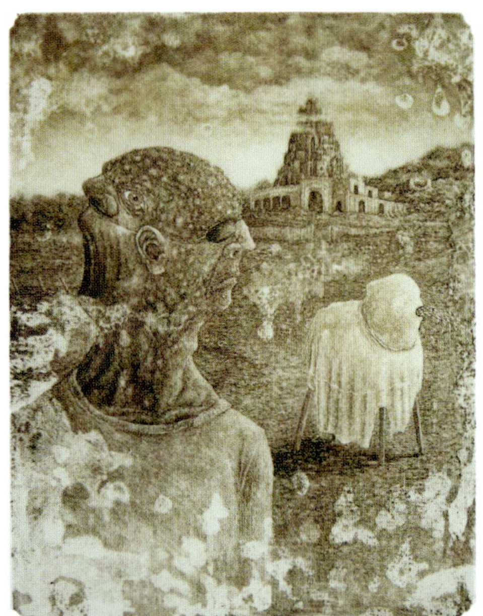

Michael Barnes, *The Blessing..., 2009.*
Lithograph, 27 x 20cm. 10.5 x 8in.

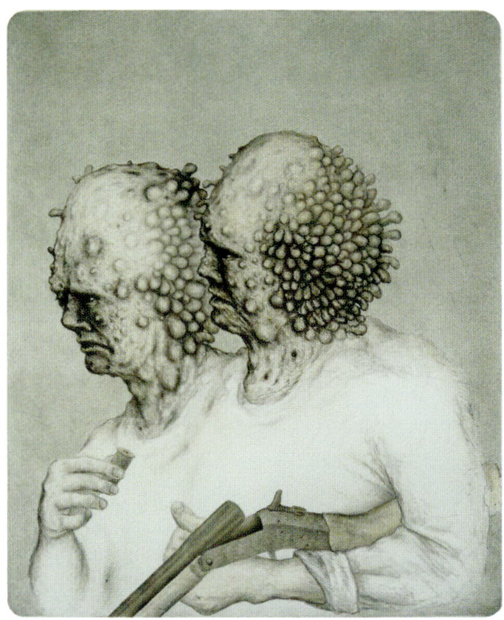

Michael Barnes, *The Accomplice, 2009.*
Lithograph, 56 x 46cm. 22 x 18in.

Barnes says of his work, 'My daily entertainment includes science fiction literature and cinema, record collecting – punk rock and heavy metal – growing cacti. I enjoy drawing, making prints and using my imagination to create stories. In general, I am inspired by all around me – the movies I watch, the books I read, the video games I play, the politics of my job and the greater world, my family and my friends. My art is the centre of my life where it all melts together.' What emerges from the rich fertility of this melting pot is a narrative from beyond the dark edges of the subconscious, replete with more questions than answers, posing psychological dilemmas and mysteries to which there can be no single solution, and perhaps no solution at all. The certainty of Barnes's technique and skill leads to an uncertainty in our interpretation of his work.

Something has clearly gone wrong in the world he offers for our contemplation. In his *Malignant Arsenal* series (2007 onwards) he addresses the issues of violence and corruption in the developed world, entities that he considers to be inseparable from each other. The weapons in this series, depicted in profile against blank backgrounds, are rendered impotent by cancerous growths from within, turned into grotesque versions of what they once were, their potential for violence mutated into malevolent infections through which their threat continues: we cannot, it seems, escape. Mutations, or genetic alterations, are shown in another series, *Invasive Species* (also 2007 onwards), in which plants have changed into barely recognisable simulacrums of those with which we are familiar. The question of who is responsible for these mutations remains unanswered.

In, *Preparing for the Worst* (2008) Barnes offers us a figure that might perhaps once have been a priest, armless and changed into a mutant larval form, balanced precariously in front of a bundle of sticks of explosive connected to a detonator, its plunger raised. There is a misty tower in the background, and on the detonator the initials 'MB': the circle of destruction is suggested, but we cannot be certain of its completion. The narrative form in such work is bleak, remorseless and pregnant with slow inevitability, reminiscent of the writing of the American novelist Cormac McCarthy. This is shown in other works, such as *Daddy's Boy* (2009), in which a hunchbacked clown, tattooed and wearing a patriotic badge, is stuck inside an empty oil barrel, cradling a bomb, while other bombs are embedded in the ground around him. In the background is a deserted and silent gas station. This is one of the least ambiguous of the artist's prints: it is a clear and unequivocal condemnation of the incestuous relationship between war, oil and capitalism in recent military adventures, an angry condemnation of the politics of greed.

Michael Barnes does not present us with a comforting world. For him redemption of our dystopian future is some distance away. The calm assurance of his technique and the power of his imagination suggest a place for him among such artists as Bosch, Daumier and Goya.

www.michaelbarnes.us
(New uses for old technology, politics)

MICHAEL REED

Michael Reed is a printmaker, a textile, medallion and mixed-media artist, and an exhibition and portfolio curator who was born and educated in Christchurch on the South Island of New Zealand, where in 1999 he gained his master's degree from the School of Fine Arts in Canterbury. He has travelled widely, exhibiting in galleries across the world, with work now held in a number of major international collections. Central to his work is an exploration of the visual arts in terms of his personal journey as a Pākehā (a New Zealander of European origin) in the context of New Zealand and Pacific art. His work follows two main strands: an exploration of the cultural history of the South Pacific, and a social and strongly political commentary. In earlier work completed towards the end of the 1990s he made screenprinted images that alluded to the French nuclear tests in the Pacific and their impact on Polynesian communities. He also produced a major body of work that condemned the international arms trade fuelled by the major global arms producers and sellers, who are based in countries that, ironically, are members of the UN Security Council. This work, shown in his exhibition *Business as Usual*, staged in Christchurch in 2000, included artist's books, medallions and screenprinted panels, all expressing Reed's anger and concern at the implications of brutal global conflicts. His central powerful work on this theme, *Binding Statements* (2000), consisting of screenprinted texts on cotton bandages, attracted favourable endorsement from the then New Zealand Prime Minister and Minister of the Arts, Helen Clark, and was subsequently purchased for the Christchurch Gallery. It is somewhat unusual for work of such an overtly critical nature to achieve recognition at this level, but the episode is a good indication of the political climate in New Zealand at the time.

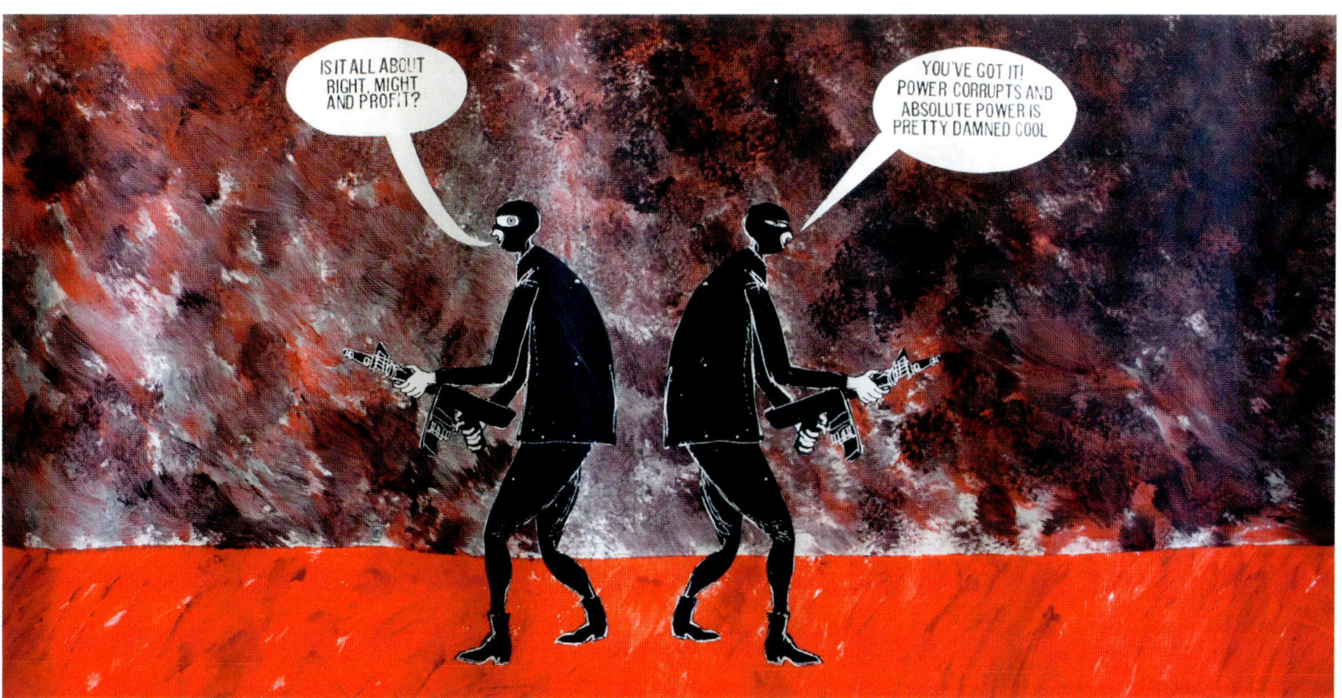

Michael Reed, *Think on the Job (detail) (from Drapes for Real Men series), 2009.*
Screenprint, stencil, painting and stamps on textile 1600 x 400cm. 630 x 177in. (full piece).

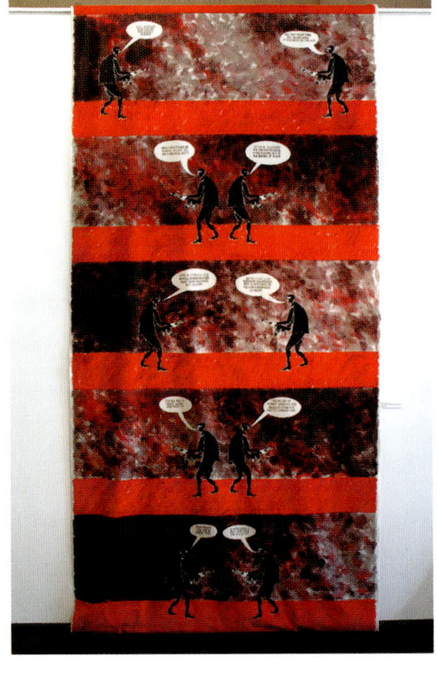

Michael Reed, *Think on the Job (from Drapes for Real Men series), 2009.* Screenprint, stencil, painting and stamps on textile. 1600 x 400cm. 630 x 157in.

The political strength that lies at the core of Reed's output since that exhibition gives his work a potency that is missing in much work produced within the traditional canons of printmaking. But, as the New Zealand critic Dorothee Pauli pointed out in the catalogue for Reed's major 2006 exhibition at the Rangiora Library Gallery, 'As early as the 15th century the woodcut, the first widely used medium in the European context, served to disseminate pictorial statements of religious dissent or moral instruction to a largely illiterate audience.' She also wrote of how art in the service of political propaganda had not featured strongly in historic New Zealand art. Printmaking there in the 19th century, mostly as engraving, served to chart the progress of colonisation in the islands, capturing 'the sights of a strange and distant land for a disbelieving European audience'. While there were changes in the early 20th century, with some artists adding printmaking techniques to their other chosen mediums, it was not until 1967 that the country had a print council, which lasted until 1976. Michael Reed's activity within that context was mainly in the medium of screenprinting. As with artists who were part of the Pop Art movement in the USA and Britain, the medium was attractive for its relatively low set-up costs and versatility, and for Reed it became the main means for the development of his sharply focused work, whose social and political comment were unparalleled in printmaking in New Zealand.

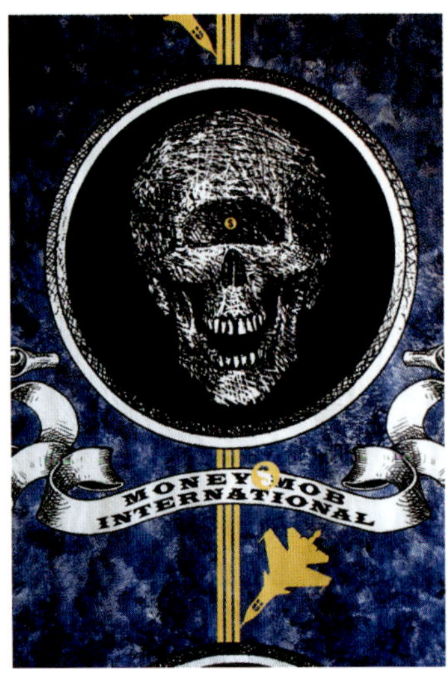

Michael Reed, *Money Mob International (detail) (from Drapes for Real Men series),* 2009. Screenprint, stencil, painting on textile, 1600 x 450cm. 630 x 177in. (full piece).

While this artist has chosen to locate much of his work in the political arena, he has also made work of a more personal nature, as in *3 Laments* (1999), which marks his parents' passage into frail old age in a poignant and touching manner, demonstrating his equal skill in the use of images and words. Another work of a less bleak nature comes in the *Raro/Sweet Raro* suite of 2005, which records his impressions from visits as a tourist to Rarotonga in a light-hearted and sometimes humorous manner. He has returned to strongly political comment in his recent output, two sets of which from 2009 demonstrate the artist's skill in creating large-scale works with unusual printmaking techniques. In *Runners for Corridors of Power* his designs were reproduced through digital dye injection on tufted nylon carpet, to be exhibited on the gallery floor. *Carpet Bombing* is a self-explanatory depiction of bombs falling to earth; while *Power, Right, Might, Profit* shows targets at either end, with, in between, the repeated text of the title reading from one end, and a text celebrating the political power of guns reading from the other. *Drapes for Real Men*, with lengths of screenprinted and painted textile is a condemnation of the connections between money, terrorism and violence, while in *Thinking on the Job* two terrorists consider what this means to them. In all these works there is a warning that it would seem foolish to ignore.

www.cityart.co.nz/reed.html
(Large-scale printmaking and installation, politics, Postcolonialism)

MICHAEL WALKER

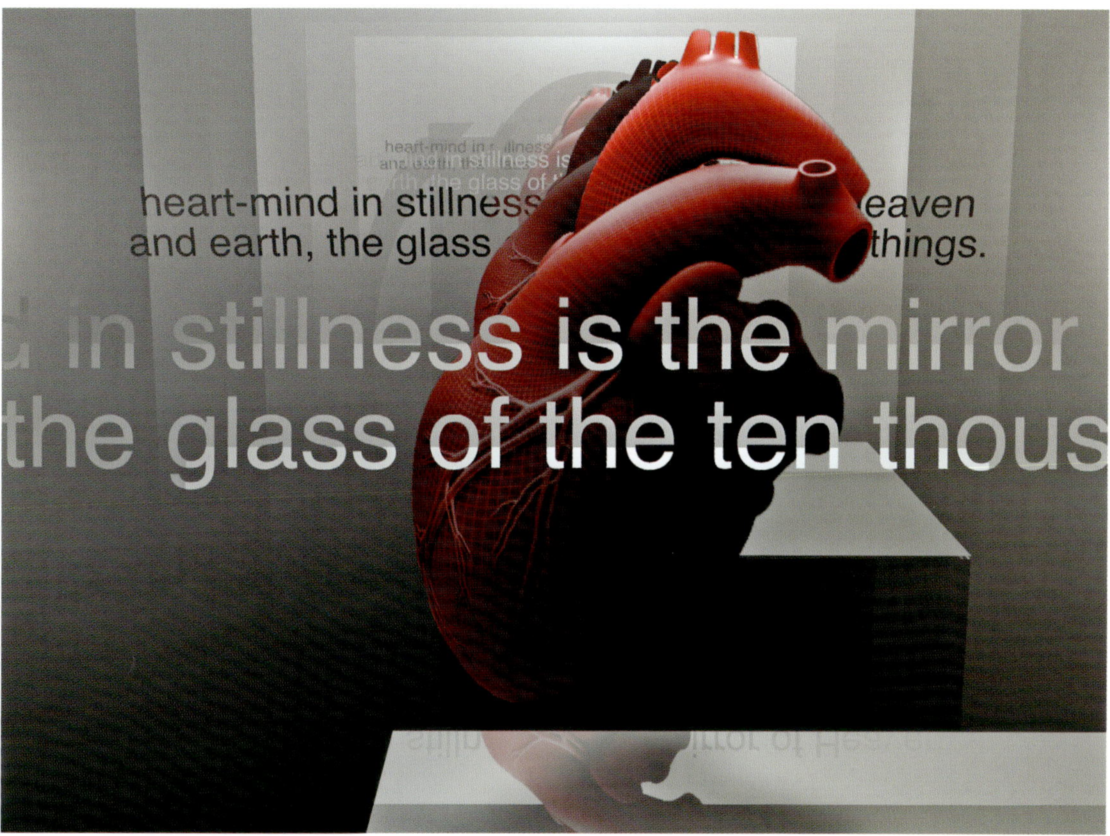

Michael Walker, *from Book 4 (detail), 2009.*
Digital still from interactive online digital artist's book, size variable.

The artist's book is an aspect of printmaking and the graphic arts that in recent years has grown to become one of the major genres of expression. The inherent physical qualities of a book – the choice of papers for text and covers, the methods of binding or presentation, the format and the choice of images – offer the visual artist a rich vein of inspiration as well as methods of production for the dissemination of ideas and concepts. The collectors' market for such books is considerable, and growing, while international competitions and exhibitions present opportunities for the makers and the public to increase their understanding and appreciation of such books. However, there is a major problem in achieving this end, in that it is seldom possible to handle the books when they are on exhibition. The viewing public are left to admire them – they are often shown within glass museum display cases – from the outside without being able to experience them by touch, and without the possibility of examining them in detail and so comprehending the richness of the artist's intentions or the chosen materials. This can, of course, be achieved by purchasing one of them; but that inevitably restricts the intimate knowledge of such books to an elitist clientele able to afford the high prices that many will fetch, rendering them largely inaccessible to a wider public.

However, just as the dissemination of printed books is being aided by technological developments, and e-books are becoming more widespread with the increasing availability of pocket-sized readers using digital ink technology, so too can technology be utilised to bring digital artist's books to a much wider international audience via the internet. With the rapid evolution of laptop computers and handheld devices such as smartphones giving access to the internet and its ever-increasing content, access to digital artist's books are now a reality. Michael Walker is one of the pioneers in the creation of this new form. He was born in Brazil, where he now lives and works, and studied in Switzerland and Mexico before achieving his doctorate after studies in Spain. He has exhibited internationally, and is Professor of Printmaking at the Federal University of Bahia. His earlier work in printmaking was through the medium of lithography, but in the early 1990s he began to experiment with innovative and alternative methods of making prints, taking his work into the expanded field of printmaking as an integral part of the widening field of contemporary visual art. He has continued to explore the potential in printmaking through a range of work in both printed-paper and digital forms, and writes of his approach, 'I work with different materials, concepts and at the same time concentrate on the idea of the print, whether physical, spiritual, marks left or memories.'

In his works on paper he has developed a way of incorporating positive latex forms made in plaster moulds, which he believes adds a depth that enhances the observer's relationship with his work. In *Shadows 1* (2009) he combines 84 digital images with 16 latex-relief prints, based on the same shadow profile, some of which are reversed, and which combine to replicate in pixelated form a larger version of the profile. Each shadow has beneath the inscription 'ID Number: 0', reflecting the idea that while they are all the same none offers any hope of identity or otherness, despite the changes that come about in the latex over a period in time. This is the first in a continuing series of prints on the theme.

Walker's use of latex goes back to a series of prints from 2007, *Contours of the Earth*, which explored the nature of our understanding of the surface of the planet on which we live. Some of the images in this series appear in the first of his

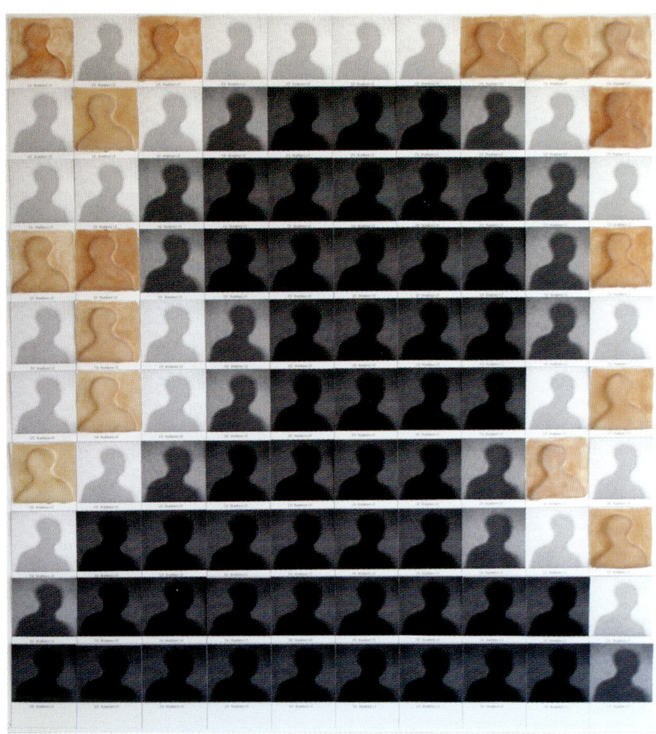

Michael Walker, *Shadows Fading and Materialising II, 2009.*
Digital print and latex on Hahnemühle paper, 80 x 71cm. 31.5 x 28in.

interactive digital books, which he describes as, 'micronarratives – non-linear – memories or projections, composed of images or animations, made using 3D modelling, video and photographs, using Flash software'.

In *Book 1* Walker presents a book with simple page-turning animation, flipping through images of geological forms until one page resolves into a looped animation, before leading to the final page in which passport stamps mark man's authorised passage across the earth. *Book 2* offers a greater degree of movement and transition, encouraging interactive exploration, while *Book 3* offers a cyclic reiteration of day/night and summer/winter, with passing shadows. In *Book 4* we are taken into a more complex realm, the 'glass of the ten thousand things', in which change is the constant. These books, readily accessed through Walker's website, offer a sense of ownership to those who interact with them, and a developing perception of their meaning. The coming developments in digital technology will undoubtedly present artists with increasing possibilities for the communication of their ideas in this form.

www.michaelwalker-art.com
(New technology, Memory)

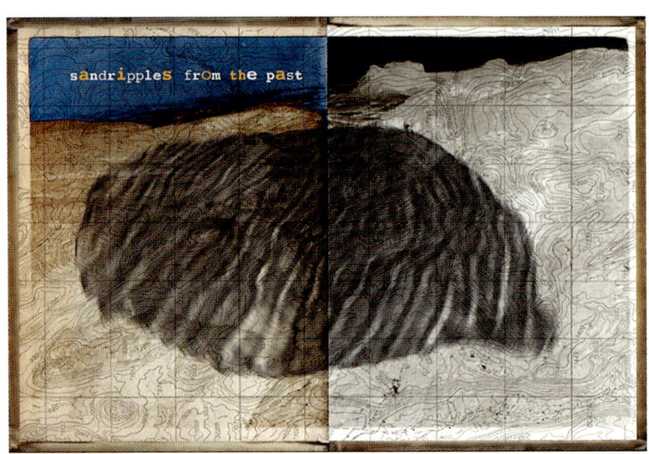

Michael Walker, *from Book 1 (detail), 2009.* Digital still from interactive online digital artist's book, size variable.

MICHAEL WEGERER

In art all is not what it seems to be: appearances can be, and often are, deceptive. All art is a form of representation – and re-presentation – giving the viewer, observer or participant the opportunity to think again about the nature of what seemed to be so certain. In Magritte's celebrated painting of the pipe the words 'Ceci n'est pas un pipe' are correct – it is not a pipe but a painted representation of one. Visual tricks and sleight of hand have long been part of the armoury by which artists defend their position. The arts of printmaking were harnessed to the service of disseminating a painted image through the making of engravings: thus a painting of a real (or imaginary) scene or person could be converted through the skill of a craftsman engraver into a form that could then be reproduced in large quantities, changing the medium, the scale and the aura of the painting (which was in any case a simulacrum) into something entirely different. Illusion and simulation have long been an integral part of printmaking, albeit one that has not always been acknowledged.

Michael Wegerer was born in Austria and studied there, first in electronic engineering and subsequently in art and design, graduating in 2008. He has exhibited widely in Austria and internationally, and has been awarded a number

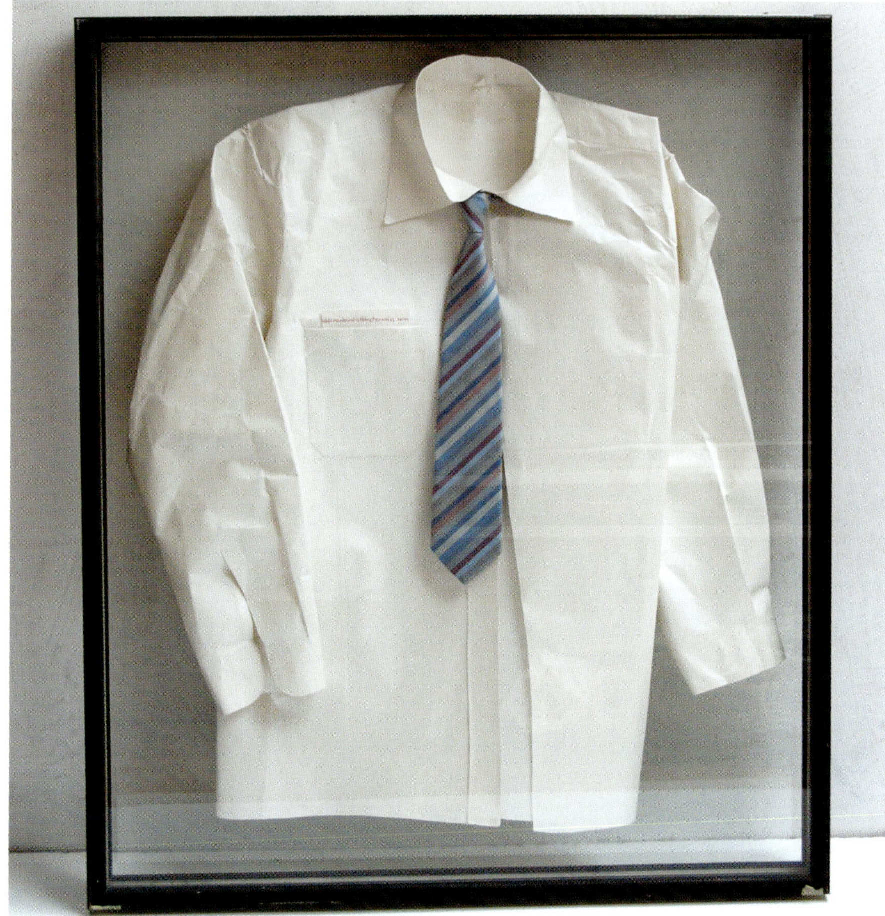

Michael Wegerer, *Displayced (detail, Shirt), 2007.* Brocade print with Mica powder on Zerkall Büttenpapier 150gsm, glass case, size variable.

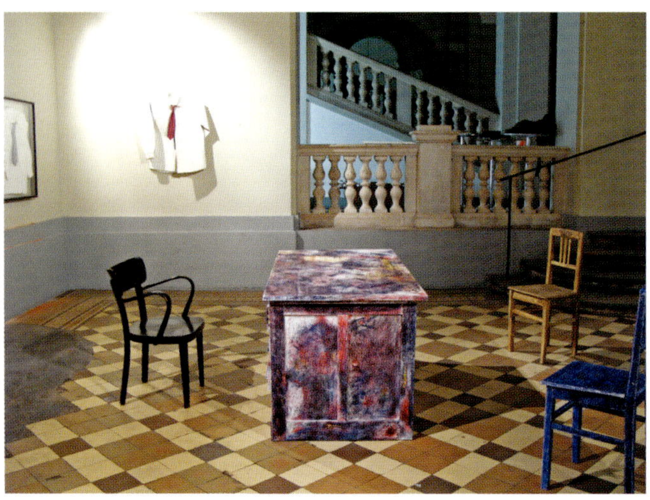

Michael Wegerer, *Displayced, 2007/08.*
Installation: hybrid paper sculpture with scribble print, Hahnemühle
Büttenpapier 300gsm and Canson Aquarelle 250gsm, size variable.

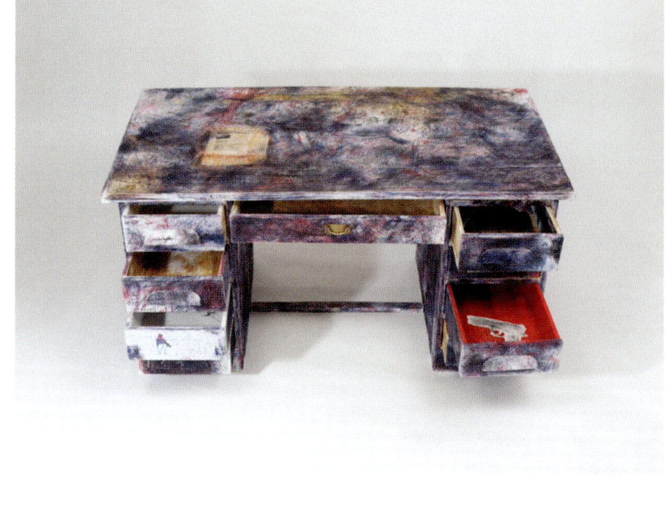

Michael Wegerer, *Displayced (detail, Desk), 2007/08.*
Hybrid paper sculpture with scribble print, Hahnemühle Büttenpapier
300gsm and Canson Aquarelle 250gsm, size variable.

of prizes. In the summer of 2009 he was Artist in Residence at RMIT University in Melbourne, Australia, and he is currently undertaking a postgraduate course in printmaking at the Royal College of Art in London. Central to his work for a number of years has been the nature of illusion and reality, and his work – which succeeds in the simultaneous blending of levity and seriousness – plays with the question of how real reality really is, drawing visitors to his exhibitions into complicity with what he presents, and in some of his pieces into active participation.

At the International Print Triennial exhibition at the Künstlerhaus in Vienna in 2007, the artist showed *Obviously*, which comprised a full-sized stepladder made from paper printed by woodcut with highly detailed wood grain, and with simulated metal hinges likewise made with paper. This sculpture encapsulated with precision the way in which Wegerer approaches the questions about reality. His 2009 exhibition at the Kunstraumarcade in Mödling in Austria also included a stepladder, again made from paper and simulating aluminium, but in this form without treads – not only an illusory reproduction but one stripped of any pretence of being useful. The same exhibition included another work involving simulation but taking it further. Wegerer made a woodcut from a real door, and then asked participants in an international symposium, *Baghdad in Love*, to add their comments and thoughts or leave drawings: the results included an Iraqi love poem. The artist then used these results as the matrix for a further print in which the writings, whether in Latin or Arabic scripts, were reversed. The door made from this latter print then became a symbol for our present cultural confusion, and alludes also to the fact that the biblical Tower of Babel is presumed to have been close to present-day Baghdad.

For his final degree show Michael Wegerer produced a paper sculpture installation with the title, 'displayced::space::power', which 'investigated and represented power structures in relation to space and order.' He was aware that in making this piece in the form of an installation he was taking his work into the realm of theatre, by setting up resonances between the objects he chose to re-present – a desk, chairs and business shirts, together with a 'real' chair behind the desk from which the installation could be viewed. One of the shirts, made from paper printed in the 'brocade process' that gives it a pearly sheen, was displayed in a glass case to preserve its unimpeachable spotlessness. Two others were hung, one on the wall and the other on a coat-stand. The desk was completed with a detailed underframe and opening drawers whose inside surfaces were printed with symbols of the business world; this and two chairs were constructed from paper printed in his signature style, and the desk was then covered with what the artist refers to as 'scribble print', a technique he devised by means of a mixture of monoprint and frottage using watercolour, and printmaking papers printed directly using bundles of ballpoint pens. The high level of detail included in this complex work drew attention to the multi-levelled thinking process required in business and industry in order to reach informed decisions, and also the need for an equally multilayered individual responsibility. This installation, in which printmaking is a constituent element, symbolised the game of power, and also the power of games: levity and seriousness are finely balanced.

www.mikewegerer.com
(New uses for old technology, Large-scale printmaking and installation, The new generation)

MIRTA KUPFERMINC

Mirta Kupferminc was born in Buenos Aires in Argentina, was educated and still lives and works in that city. She has a long record of international exhibitions, and has been the recipient of many awards. Her work is held in major collections in her own country and others. Her parents both survived the horrors of Auschwitz, and following the end of the war they moved around Europe before settling in Argentina in 1948. Among the artist's earliest memories are the numbers tattooed on her parents' forearms, and her curiosity about their meaning. She remembers her mother telling her, 'I have this not to forget'; she also remembers growing up with a longing for grandparents and family photographs. The tragic depth of this family history, and the power of survival, have been the inspiration for much of Kupferminc's work, which relates not only to those events but also to the events she herself witnessed in the disappearance of thousands of dissidents in the late 1970s and early 1980s. While much of her work, with its roots in the Holocaust, her Jewish history and the injustices of her own country's past, deals with her response to these specific dark events, it has evolved further to address the wider problems of the world, and the need for tolerance, justice and human freedom. The range of her work covers painting, printmaking in both traditional and digital mediums, installation and sculpture, and the production of major book works in collaboration with writers. There is a profound, meditative quality in her work, which is often obscure at first encounter but is not without touches of dry humour and conspiratorial glances that offer hope of redemption from the darkness it evokes. The work seeks close engagement from those who come into contact with it, whom it duly rewards for such attention.

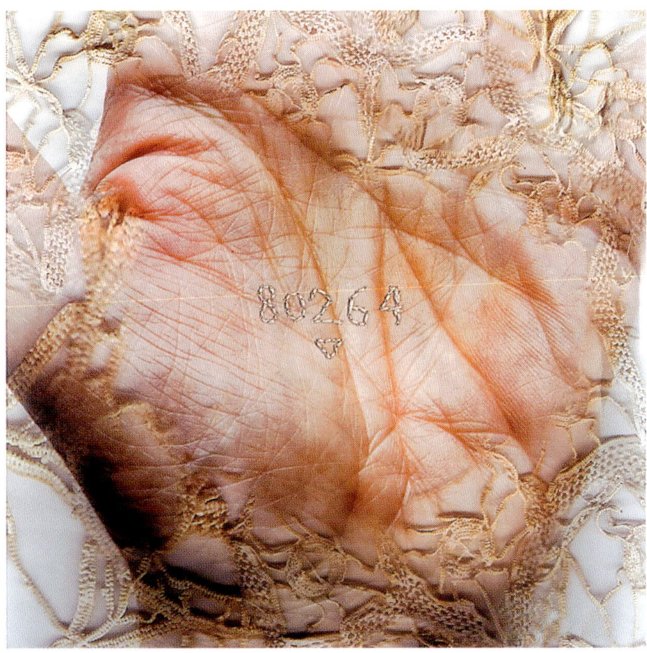

Mirta Kupferminc, *Embroidered onto my skin, 2009.*
Digital print embroidered with silk, 40 x 40cm. 16 x 16in.

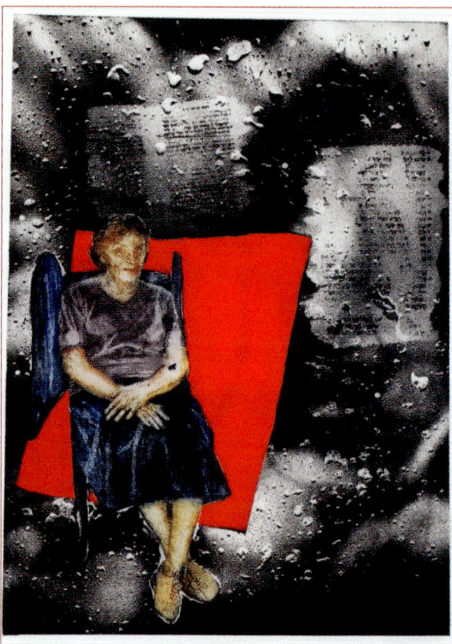

A number of her etchings with aquatint dating from 1999 onwards incorporate processions of figures, reminiscent of the medieval images of the Dance of Death. Some of the figures are familiar from documentary photographs of the Second World War, such as those in *Ghosts of the Łódź Ghetto* (in memory of Daniel Kupferminc) (2000), which is dedicated to her half-brother, who was killed at Auschwitz. Another, *En Camino* (On the Way) (2001) shows six people carrying trees, and another crouched figure, perhaps an orthodox rabbi, carrying buildings on his back. The significance of these characters is shrouded in mystery, so that they might be compared with those encountered in the magical realism novels of such writers as Gabriel García Márquez and Jorge Luis Borges. The title of this print was also used for a mixed-media work published on disc in 2005, in which Kupferminc collaborated with the animation artist Mariana Sosnowski and the musician Luciano Dyzenchaus. Images from the artist's work are presented in a continuous cycle, moving and shifting in form across a changing landscape of fragments from other works. An old woman struggles on her way through this strange space–time, carrying her belongings in a case and a sack, encountering other mysterious characters in an evocation of the eternal return.

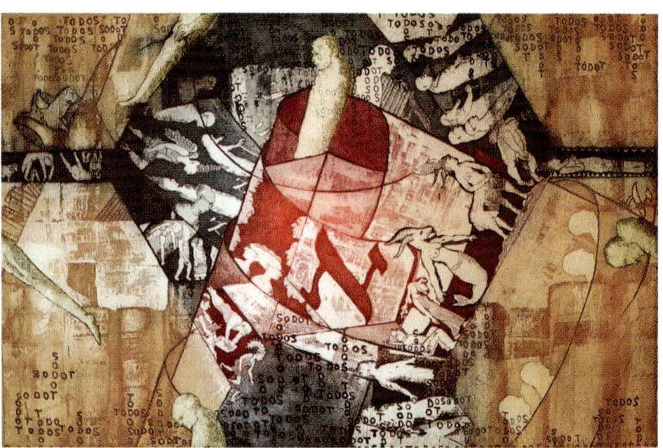

Mirta Kupferminc, *The Library of Babel, 2004.*
Etching, 57 x 76cm. 22 x 30in.

The link to Borges continues in Kupferminc's collaboration with Saúl Sosnowski, the poet and scholar, in a major artist's book, *Borges and the Kabbalah: Paths to The Word*, published in 2006 in an edition of 25. Containing text by Sosnowski, incorporating texts by Borges and excerpts from the Torah and rabbinical teachings, together with a suite of 29 etchings by Kupferminc, this handmade bibliophile's edition with an embossed cover is presented in a folder and accompanied by a CD and a number of Ex Libris prints. It is a richly layered and complex work that explores the mystical nature of the Kabbalah. The book gave rise to an exhibition at the University of Maryland in 2008: *Borges and the Kabbalah: Seeking Access* continued the dialogue between Kupferminc and Sosnowski, delving back into the source texts and incorporating new and existing works in two and three dimensions to create what Sosnowski described as 'a conceptual journey of our book's spirit. Through prints, texts, installations, lights and a video, visitors are invited to enter a world of appearances, of truths, and of veiled secrets.' Just as the Kabbalah requires deep and expanding study to reveal the truths it seeks, and the writings by Borges on this text and others require thoughtful reading, so too does the work of Kupferminc require a willingness in those who see it to become complicit in its many levels of meaning. There is immediate visual fascination in a new world of colourful and complex images, followed by a curiosity about the meanings of those images and their connections within a print, and to each other. Printmaking, as practised by Mirta Kupferminc, achieves a rare engagement with the human spirit.

www.mirtakupferminc.net
(New technology, Large-scale printmaking and installation, Memory)

MOISES YAGÜES

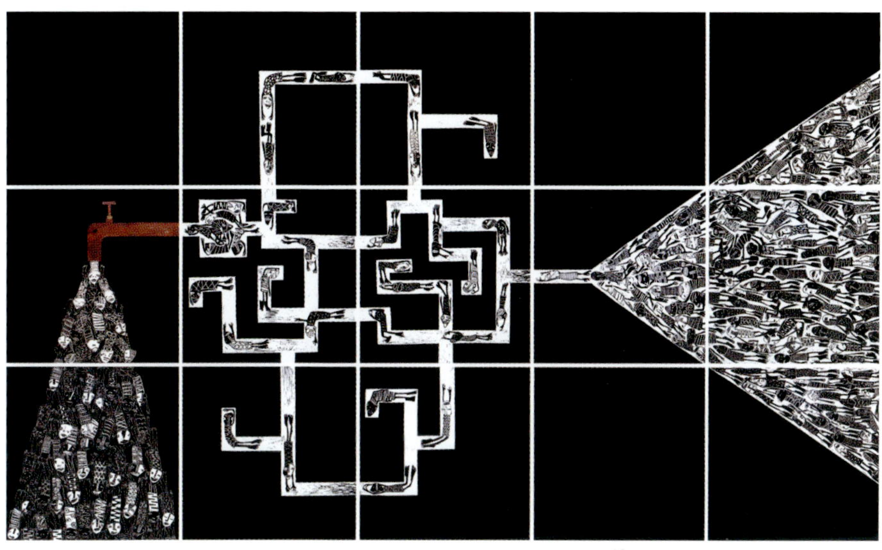

Moises Yagües, *Traffic Men, 2008.* Fifteen woodcuts, collage, 180 x 300cm. 70 x 118in.

The borders between the traditional and the new techniques have in the past caused heated discussion in printmaking circles. Thankfully, those artificial borders have largely dissolved, leaving a more open and creative atmosphere. National borders, including those based on geographical features, are the result of social and political divisions established over centuries, and are responsible for much of the human misery that has blighted our history. There is something of a paradox in the human condition at the beginning of the 21st century: on the one hand there is increasing globalisation and the dissolving of borders by means of electronic technologies, but on the other there is a hardening of attitudes in the defence of those arbitrary national boundaries against economic migrants or those fleeing oppression.

Moises Yagües, a self-taught artist, was born and lives in Murcia in southern Spain. He is a Master Printer, resident at La Persiana Naranja art-studio space in that city, and has exhibited widely in Spain and elsewhere. He has been the recipient of prestigious awards, including in 2009 a scholarship to the Casa Falconieri Workshop in Sardinia, and an invitation to be Guest Artist at the Guanlan Print Art Centre in China. In February 2008 in Murcia, Spain, he showed a large series of mixed-technique works, many based on woodcut, under the title *Inhabited Head*, which showed variations on diagrammatic profiles of the human head, each containing elements alluding to aspects of human experience and emotions. These works, mostly in the 56 x 56cm (22 x 22in.) format, demonstrated

well the approach that Yagües take to his work, combining seriousness with a leavening of sardonic humour: in *Houses in the Head*, for instance, the area usually occupied by the brain is full of small black silhouettes of symbolic houses, while in *From My Window* the eye is replaced by a cartoon depiction of an open window in which a cartoon face appears.

In 2006 the artist began a series of prints that have established him as one of the most outspoken artists in Spain and in Europe. Under the general title, *Traffic Men (*A Moving World), he has created a body of work that addresses the plight of those who attempt to cross borders where they are not wanted, seeking a better life or an escape from persecution. Yagües writes, in a description of this work, 'Here, you can see people who intend to cross borders, who want to cross to the other side of the line … Human history is also the history of human mass movement and immigrations cannot be controlled either by walls or weapons'; and, 'In these woodcuts I am taking up again the nature of documentary printing, which decreased in the second half of the 20th century, by expressing the social reality, the migratory flows, and the difficulties that people find, all of these related to art, human movements and borders.' It is not surprising that this powerful body of work was shown during 2008 in the Spanish colony of Ceuta in North Africa, and in Albuquerque in New Mexico in the USA, both being locations in which the issue of human migration is complex and controversial, and clandestine crossings are commonplace events. Significantly, the Albuquerque exhibition was supported by Amnesty International.

The artist cites among his influences comics, ethnic art and Goya, a combination that serves to explain why his works contain a degree of humour and irony. So it is that on seeing these works we can simultaneously think deeply about the explicit and implicit horrors he depicts, the controversial political responses to illegal immigration, and the raw humanity of those involved, experiencing the full range of emotions evoked by these daily and far from rare occurrences. A characteristic of the series of the addition of collaged elements to the black and white woodcuts. So in '¡Volando Voy, Volando Vengo!' a plane with many people crowded onto its fuselage and wings flies across a black sky on which are collaged clouds made from cotton wool; while in *La Isla* (The Island) a multitude of people with their hands raised are crowded together on collaged strips of thin rusted iron sheet, neither understanding nor escaping from their predicament. In *Traffic Men*, clustered figures force themselves through a triangular space and into a narrow opening that leads to a labyrinth of tunnels, leading in turn to a metal tap (again, collaged sheet iron) from which other clustered figures pour in a triangular stream. The process is as endless as it is heartless, so that the work can't help but draw attention to our responsibilities as human beings.

www.arthaus66.com/online-art-gallery/moises-yagues
(New uses for old technology, Large-scale printmaking and installation, Politics)

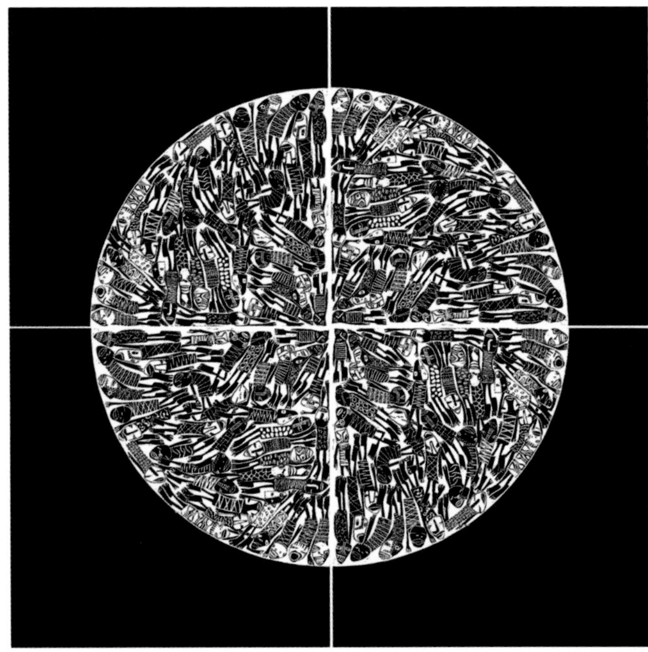

Moises Yagües, *Go Out If You Can, 2009*. Woodcut, 120 x 120cm. 47 x 47in.

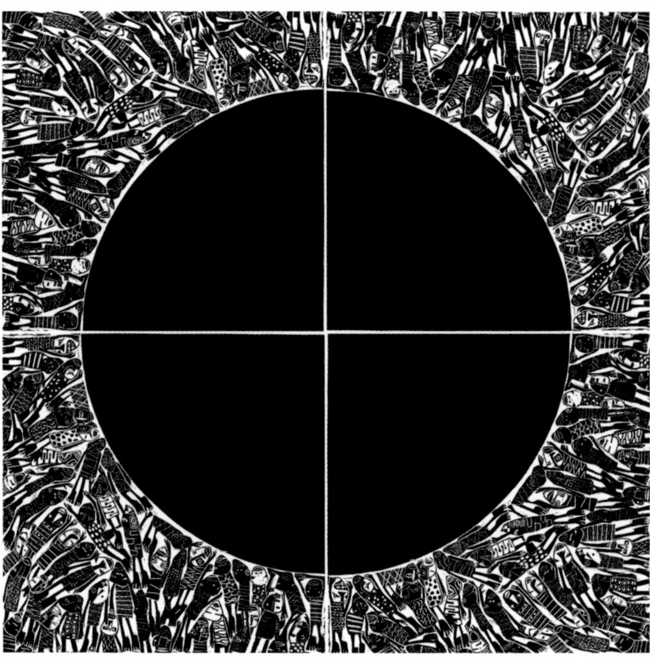

Moises Yagües, *Enter If you Can, 2009*. Woodcut, 120 x 120cm. 47 x 47in.

MYEONG-GOOG JUNG

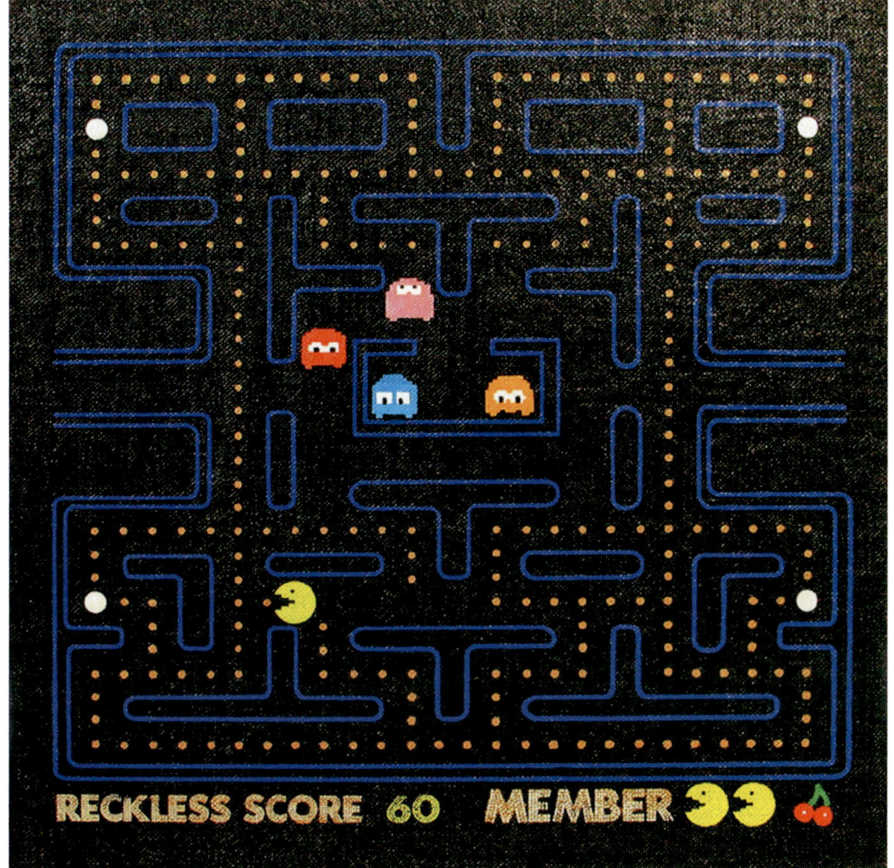

Myeong-goog Jung, *Game, 2008.*
Silkscreen on canvas 40 x 46cm. 16 x 18in.

Frottage is one of the first methods by which children make prints. By placing a coin underneath a sheet of paper and rubbing a pencil over the paper a detailed image of the coin can be produced, the right way round. Max Ernst took this a stage further when, fascinated by the images he perceived in the old scrubbed floorboards in his studio, he used the same method to produce images to incorporate into his drawings and later his lithographs. Myeong-goog Jung uses frottage to create full-size images of vehicles. The process is the same – paper is secured on the surfaces of vehicles, and the impression of what lies beneath is transferred on to the paper through the use of graphite, with text added to some of the images. Graphite, especially when used on a large scale in this manner, produces an image with a high sheen that reflects light in an echo of the reflection from the painted metal panels of the buses, trucks and cars from which the artist works. His intention is not to reproduce the vehicles: he presents them as ghosts of themselves, taken out of their usual context and exhibited in the alien space of a gallery, drawing attention to the paradox they bring to urban life. While cars are often symbols of status or achievement, and buses and trucks carry signage to advertise the products or services of the operator, they are also the means by which city streets are becoming ever more congested and polluted. These works sum up the love–hate relationship the contemporary world has with vehicles.

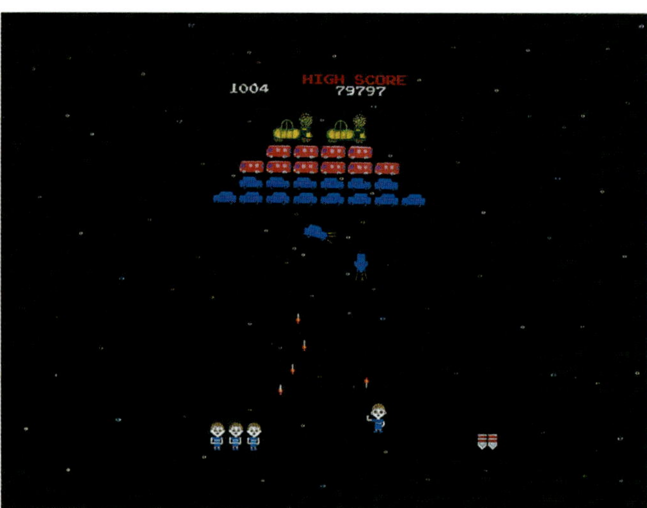

Myeong-goog Jung was born in the Republic of Korea and has had numerous exhibitions in that country. He lives and works in Seoul, a vibrant and modern city with a long history and a unique culture, but also a place where the problems of traffic congestion are a daily fact of life: hence his fascination with creating full-size reproductions of vehicles. This major Asian capital city is also a centre of the electronics industry, with a high concentration of manufacturers; the shops, which sell an astonishing range of these electronic devices are clustered together in multi-storey buildings, providing an equivalent to the souks of the Middle East. The prevalence of digital electronics, particularly in games, is the root of the parallel aspect of Jung's work – images that explore the nature of electronic games and our fascination with them.

He comments that we live in a digital era in which computer games are a major form of entertainment. While electronic devices, with operations based on binary mathematical code and pixels on a screen, can make life simpler, drawing us into working and playing with them, they can also have the effect of detaching us from social interaction. He is concerned that people living in cities are becoming like robots moving in accordance with the rules of the city, which is itself becoming less and less human and more like a vast computer program. His view of city life, with its reliance of vehicle transport, is critical, and he asks in his work what it is about that life that is so brilliant and splendid and what lies concealed behind the shiny surface.

At first glance, Jung's images of the screens of games machines are instantly familiar: we are presented with versions of Pac-Man, Asteroids and Space Invaders that are deeply embedded in the subconscious of anyone who has passed hours playing such games in arcades or on the early domestic games consoles, or for that matter on sophisticated computers for which such games have been rewritten while still retaining the necessary retro look to give them cult status. The images on his screenprinted or stencil-printed prints have the same pixellated contours as the original games, the scores and game data are there in the same basic typefaces, and the overall appearance has the same primitive look which made the games so attractive when they were the height of sophistication and make them so attractive now on account of the nostalgia they evoke.

But the images repay further consideration: in place of alien spaceships that descend at increasing speed and in growing numbers, we are presented with the silhouetted shapes of cars and trucks that are out to attack the player. In *Galagcar 7* (2007) the defender is a line of small children, and in others a set of robots. The only winners in the original games, apart from the user's potential temporary status as highest scorer, were the programmers and manufacturers of the games; the only winners, it can be argued, in our traffic-choked cities are the manufacturers and sellers of the vehicles, and the city authorities who collect the taxes on their use. These works amuse, and have a powerful message.

www.cyworld.com/goog22
(New uses for old Technology, New technology)

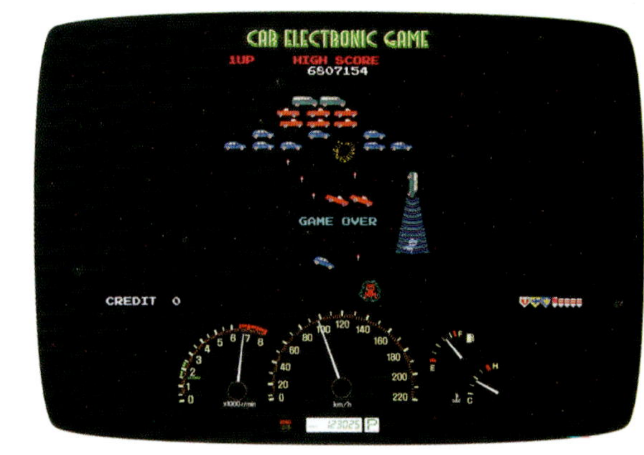

Myeong-goog Jung, *Game-Car, 2009.* Silkscreen on paper. 70 x 100cm. 70 x 100in.

NATHANIEL STERN

Printmaking today involves a wide variety of mediums and methods, and has long since moved out of the confines of the printmaker's workshop and the artist's studio. The dark arts of traditional printmaking are still practised, but the world of digital printmaking has broken the exclusivity of the past to the extent that anyone with a laptop and a domestic inkjet printer in the corner of a room can legitimately claim to be making prints. It would, however, come as something of a surprise to hear someone who was wading through a lily pond in your local park with a strange contraption around his neck, tell you that he was working on making prints. But this is one of the things that Nathaniel Stern does in his extensive search for the best means of capturing innovative images of the world around him.

Nathaniel Stern was born in the USA and studied at an engineering high school before, 'having got bored with what computers could do at that point', going on to study fashion design and music at Cornell University, and later gaining a master's degree in interactive communications at New York University. In 2009 he completed successfully his studies for a Ph.D. at Trinity College, Dublin. The range of courses he has studied, together with the variety of fields in the arts with which he has been involved, mark him as something of a 'renaissance man', bridging with ease the gaps between art and science, performance and conventional flat prints, installation and interactive video arts. He has exhibited, performed and taught widely in the USA, South Africa and other countries. His early work was based on the creation of interactive video installations that relied on the participation of the viewers as part of the performance, in which their unconscious movements affected what was projected on the gallery screens or wall, leading to viewers learning how to control their movements and thus create new iterations of the basic imagery. It was a relatively short step from this work to becoming the man in the pond.

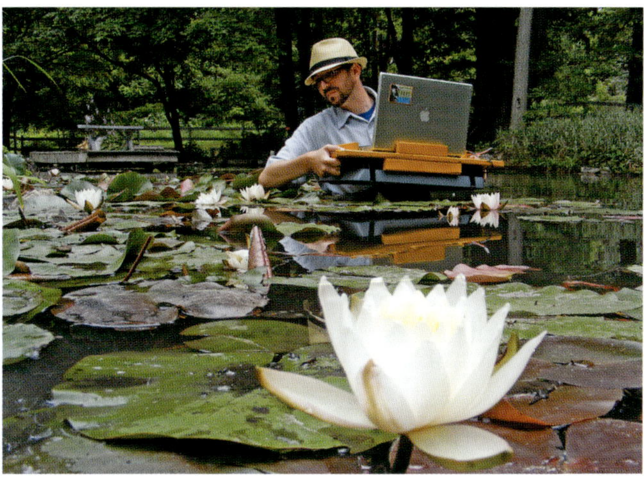

Nathaniel Stern, *Nathaniel Stern, scanning waterlilies in Indiana, 2009.* Photograph, size variable. Photo: by Jesse Egan.

What Stern was doing there was capturing images of the water lilies and water surface by means of a converted scanner linked to a laptop computer and battery pack. Scans were made as he moved – either himself or the scanner – through and across the water, recording images that contained some measure of the effects of that movement as well as photographic records of form and colour. The images thus captured were compressed from the reality in which they were made, leading him to call the process 'Compressionism'. In variations of the technique he has scanned bodies, landscapes and objects and has developed a range of movements through which these can be captured by what he calls, 'performing them into existence'. Once the scans are made they can be stretched, cropped and coloured using computer software, resulting in a digital matrix from which prints can be produced. In addition to these digital prints he has used the matrix as the starting point for

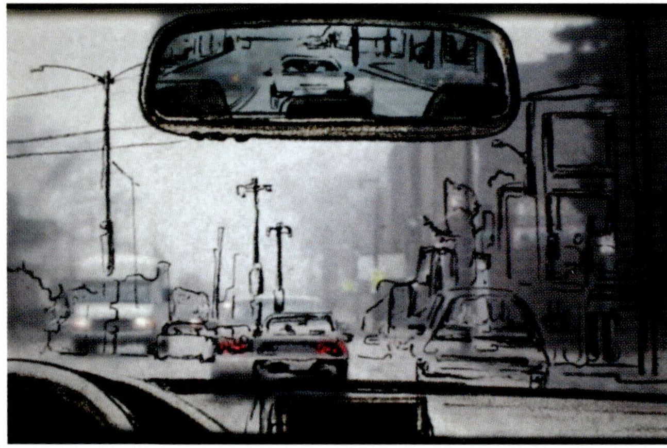

printmaking in a variety of traditional techniques, including engravings, lithography and screenprint. Stern concedes that this is still an experimental process, and one that is capable of further development, although the results he has achieved to date demonstrate to an impressive degree the way in which the unconventional use of machinery can mediate between the artist's vision and the observer's experience to offer a new range of impressions of the familiar world.

In 2009 Stern took up a post as Assistant Professor in the Digital Art Studio at the University of Wisconsin in Milwaukee, and began a collaborative project with his colleague Jessica Meuninck-Ganger, Head of Printmaking and Narrative Forms at UWM, that takes this work in another direction. Their joint project, *Distill Life*, combines old and new mediums to achieve moving images on paper. Translucent prints, made using one or more of a range of traditional techniques, including woodblock, screenprinting, lithography, photogravure and drawing, are mounted directly onto the surface of digital photo frames, into which are downloaded looped video recordings captured from the real world, 'or from the virtual world of Second Life'. The digital screens are taken from their frames to be placed within or behind the translucent prints. The fusing of disparate imaging methods, and the combinations of material and content – print/video, paper/electronic, real/virtual – allow for the creation of works that are in turn humorous, seriously playful and through-provoking. This strand of work is in its early stages, and will no doubt be developed further, as it allows for the addition of other technologies and mediums. Stern approaches printmaking from an unusual direction through new techniques that are a long way from the conventional ones, and yet he has proved that the innovative approach he takes can achieve intriguing results that combine poetically with traditional forms.

http://nathanielstern.com
(New technology, Environment)

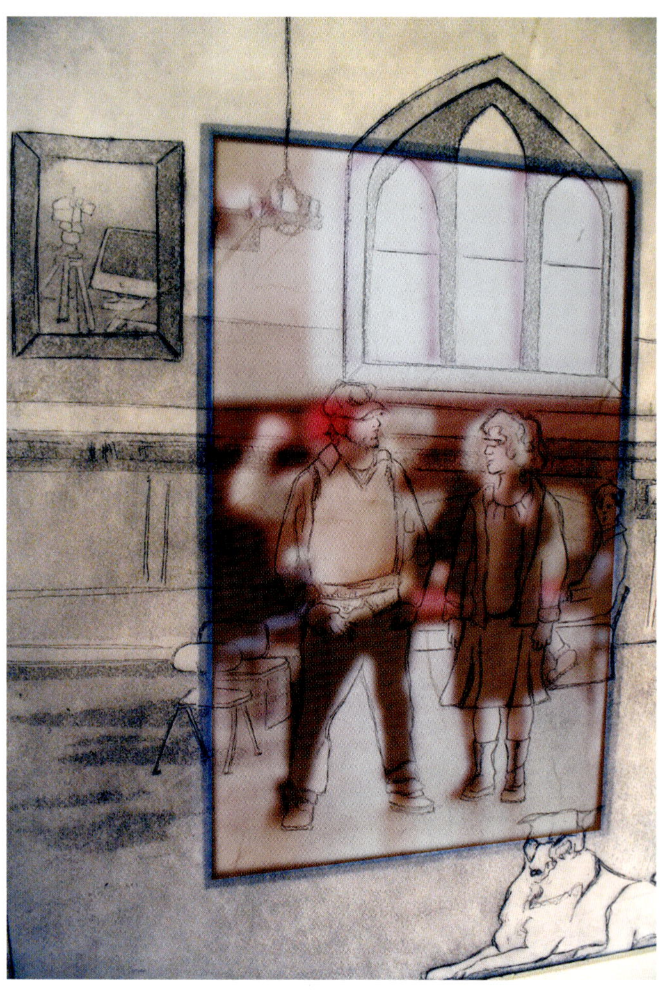

PATRICIA OLYNYK

Patricia Olynyk lives and works in Saint Louis, Missouri, where she is Director of the Graduate School of Art, and the Florence and Frank Bush Professor of Art, at Washington University. Her professional experience has covered not only work in art and design but also interdisciplinary work in the life-sciences and humanities departments. She studied at the Alberta College of Art and Design in Canada, and gained her master's degree in fine arts at California College of the Arts in Oakland, before spending four years in Osaka in Japan, and subsequently for a period as Research Scholar at the Kyoto Seika University, where she studied the traditional making of paper and books by hand. She has exhibited and lectured internationally, and her work is included in many public and private collections.

Olynyk's art investigates our human culture in relationship to science and the environment. She states, 'My work calls upon viewers to expand their awareness of the worlds they inhabit, whether those worlds are their bodies or the spaces they occupy.' Her work is essentially based on layers of experience, influenced to no small degree by the time she spent in Japan, and also by her active involvement in cross-disciplinary work with scientific institutions. The artificial separation between the arts and the sciences that led to a mutual mistrust at times in the 20th century has been replaced by a growing awareness of the commonalities between the two disciplines, led by a deepening understanding of human physiology and perception, and a greater awareness of the aesthetic beauty of the natural world. Scientific advances have combined with new technologies for recording and transmitting images, covering everything from the deep-space images gained by the Hubble telescope to extreme magnifications of atomic and cellular structures. The visual power of such images has influenced many areas of the arts, from movies to the work of artists such as Olynyk.

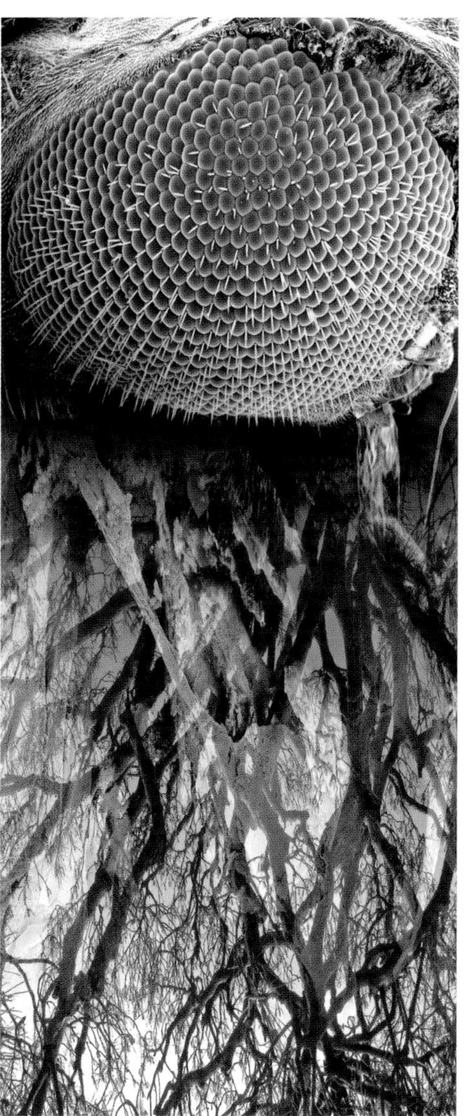

Patricia Olynyk, *Cenesthesia No.1, Sight, 2006.*
Digital print on Chinese silk, 366 x 112cm. 144 x 44in.

In an exhibition of her work at the Institute for the Humanities of the University of Michigan in 2000, the artist exhibited a series of mixed-media collage works on handmade paper. The process of making these works began with drawings of skulls, seedpods and archaic scripts that were then made into lithographic and digital prints to provide an archive of material. This was then collaged onto paper produced by hand using traditional Japanese methods, and finally combined with further layers of print, with persimmon tannin and oil to enhance the diaphanous quality of each layer. The resulting works transmuted and metamorphosed the imagery into a new and coherent form. In 2006 she exhibited a major new body of work, under the title *Sensing Terrains*, at the National Academy of Sciences in Washington, DC. This multimedia exhibition combined Olynyk's prints with an evocative soundscape based primarily on sounds recorded in Japanese gardens. The imagery in the large-scale prints on Chinese silk was derived from two sources: images of cellular structures made with a scanning electron microscope combined with macroscopic photographs of spaces in Japanese gardens. The microscopic images were taken from the sensory organs of a range of animal species –

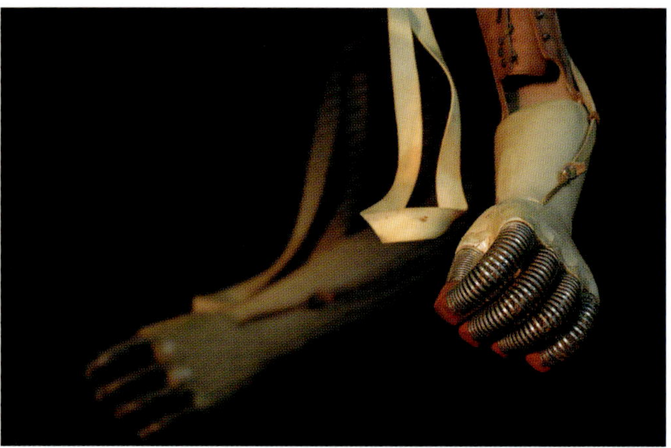

Patricia Olynyk, *Extension III, 2008.* Digital print, 61 x 114cm. 24 x 45in.

human corneas (for sight), wild-mouse taste buds and olfactory epithelia (for taste and smell), guinea-pig cochlea (for sound) and drosophila (fruit fly) feet (for touch) – to demonstrate that sensory experience is not limited to human beings. The combination of this imagery with that obtained from Japanese gardens, which are in turn the product of sensitive design, sought to offer an interpretation of nature as highly abstracted and structured, presenting an indeterminate space in which scale, dimension and time became skewed. The soundscape added a further 'tickle to the senses', another aspect in the exhibition's intention to explore 'cenesthesia', defined in the Merriam-Webster Medical Dictionary as 'the general feeling of inhabiting one's body that arises from multiple stimuli from various bodily organs.'

For her recent series of large digital pigment prints, *Probe*, the artist accumulated a large collection of historical prosthetic devices and medical instruments used to supplement or probe into the human body. Her intention in using such objects as the starting point for her images is to comment on the human desire to fetishise and even to anthropomorphise such objects, in the service of manipulating or controlling the human body. There is, as noted elsewhere in this book, a widespread interest in the possibilities of cyborgs; Patricia Olynyk's recent work, while superficially similar, addresses alternative concepts with a different psychological dimension that explores another level of function and fantasy. On a more general level there are similarities: the historical desire of human beings to know more about ourselves, to know more about the world in which we live, to understand why we are as we are, and also to strive to become more than we are.

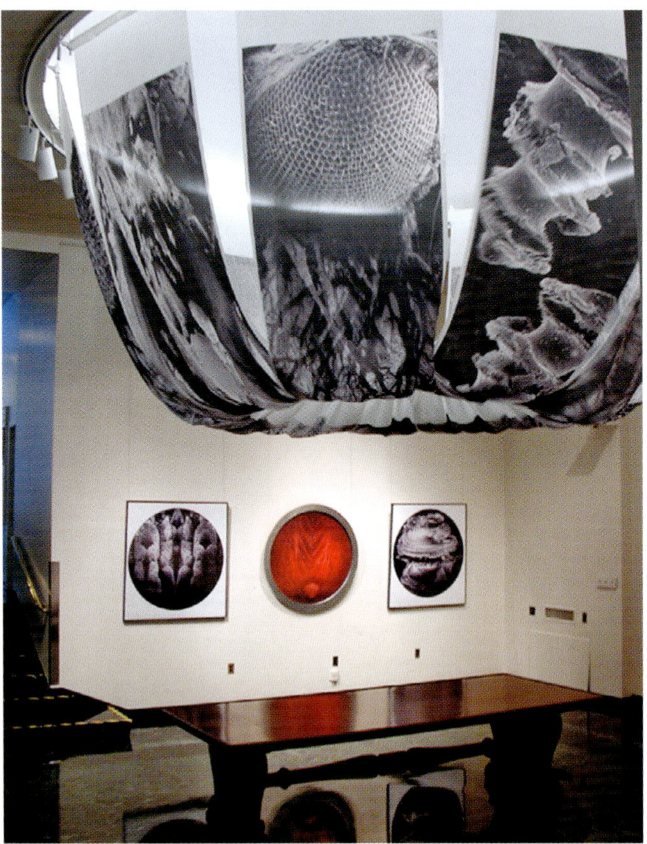

Patricia Olynyk, *Sensing Terrains, 2006.*
Digital prints, fittings, size variable. Installation in Rotunda,
National Academy of Sciences, Washington, DC, USA.

www.brunodavidgallery.com/artistDetail.cfm?id_artist=46
(New technology, Science)

PAUL CROFT

During the 2007 opening of the exhibition Stone•Plate•Grease•Water at MOMA Wales in Machynlleth on the west coast of Wales, it was instructive to listen to comments made by the large crowd attending the event. Looking at the diverse works on show, some people commented that this one must be a watercolour, or that one a drawing, yet another a photograph, before, upon looking at the information cards, realising that they were all, in fact, lithographs. It is probably the case that, for many people viewing this exhibition, this was the first time they had seen so many lithographs – by 64 artists from nine countries – in one exhibition, as major printmaking exhibitions are, sadly, infrequent in that part of the world. Such reactions are therefore understandable given the versatility of the lithograph print, but they are also a credit to Paul Croft, who curated the exhibition, for selecting artists from around the world whose use of the medium is marked by a wide range of innovative approaches.

Croft graduated in drawing and painting at Edinburgh College of Art in Scotland, before continuing with postgraduate studies that included printmaking at the same institution, as well as subsequently in Belfast in Northern Ireland. In 1996 he became a Master Printer at the Tamarind Institute in Albuquerque at the University of New Mexico, and in 2008 was elected as a Fellow of the Royal Society of Painter Printmakers. He is now Lecturer in Fine Art Printmaking at the School of Art, Aberystwyth University, in Wales. In addition to showing his work in a large number of international exhibitions he has a considerable record of publication on printmaking, notably two standard works on stone lithography and plate lithography respectively. Croft is, in short, a passionate advocate of lithography in all its forms.

His personal work is largely concerned with symbols and language, and with the communication that these enable. The two years he spent in New Mexico gave him time to explore the petroglyphs in the American Southwest, in particular at the Three Rivers site, made by the aboriginal cultures that inhabited that land in the past. As well as depicting animals and humans these extensive traces of ancient communication

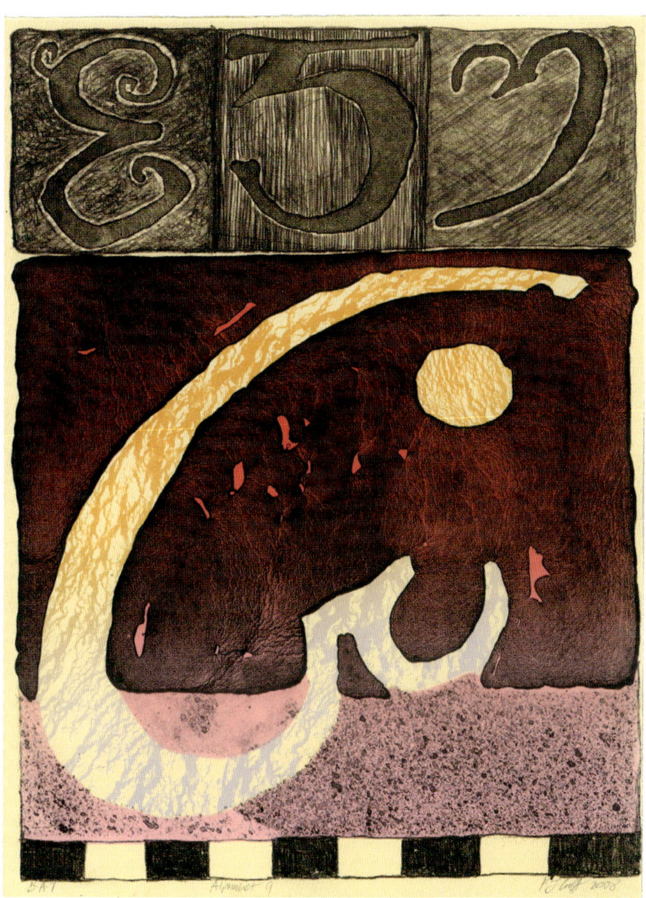

Paul Croft, *Alphabet G, 2008.* Lithograph, 40 x 29cm. 16 x 11.5in.

contain many symbols, the meaning of which can in many cases only be guessed at. This experience, supplemented by his studies of calligraphy during a visit to Japan, gave him a profound interest in the signs and symbols by which human beings communicate with each other.

A series of prints made around 2005 is based on fishing boats seen in Welsh harbours; these are not images of whole boats, or boats against harbour walls and buildings, but instead concentrate on sections of the boats, their painted identification marks, and the flags and buoys that indicate position. Others take elements from the boats and fishing gear and reduce them to semi-abstract compositions in which geometry and colour are the main constituents.

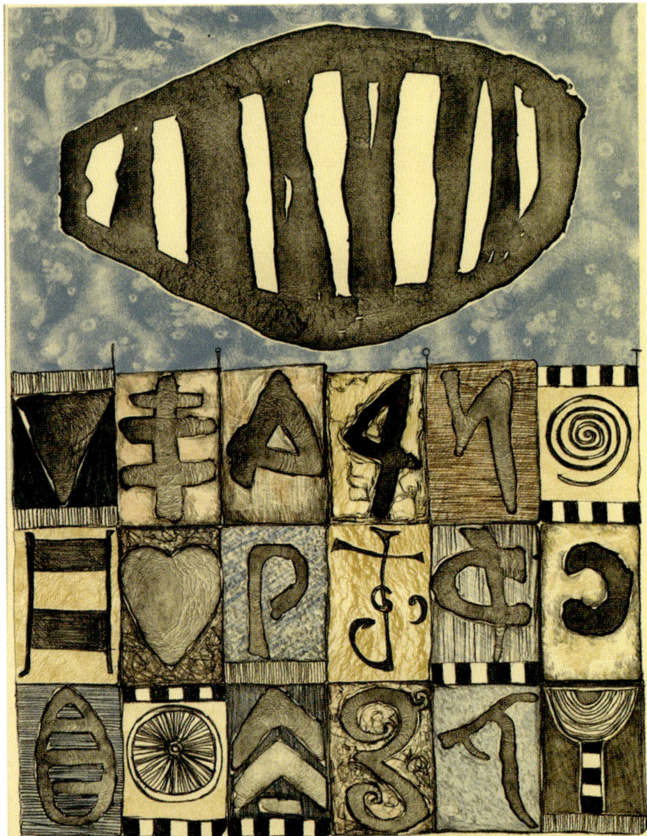

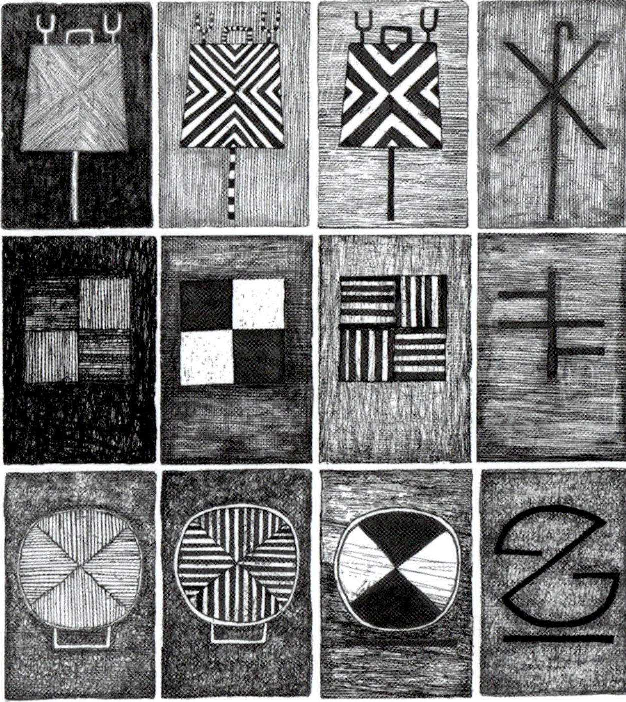

A subsequent series of work, which is still ongoing, deals more directly with his passion for studying the visual language through which early communication was made possible. In the *Alphabet* series he explores the development of symbols and letterforms, from Assyrian, Phoenician and other sources, and from those included on amulets, pottery and other artefacts seen in the British Museum. The sources, which could have been treated in a scholarly way, are in fact transmuted in Croft's hands into abstract forms in which colour and texture – in the form of highly controlled tusche washes – are melded into evocative and mysterious images in which historic and imaginary symbol forms are united. A recent development in Croft's work has been his *Greganyce* project, which takes a step further his exploration of the development of letter and symbol forms. Through a process of logical ordering and iteration he intends to create one or more computer fonts through which an abstract language can be expressed, for incorporation into the matrices for lithographic prints.

During his time at Tamarind, the artist researched a paper with the title 'Developing Customised Wash Palettes and Brush Tools', a study that he has recently revived through a consideration of how computer software might be used to create tusche washes with almost infinite variations, using digital technology as a tool to be included in the more conventional toolbox for mark and texture making. The fusion of new technology with traditional methods of making lithographs has in recent years been one of the most interesting developments in printmaking, allying the development of non-toxic and waterless methods with developments in photoplate, and more recently the Solarplate™ technique developed by Dan Welden, processes that allow virtually any graphic form to be incorporated into a print. It is research like this that will ensure lithography continues to develop and to inspire new generations of artists seeking ways to express their ideas in a reproducible form.

www.paulcroft.org
(New uses for old technology, New technology)

RŪTA SPELSKYTĖ

Rūta Spelskytė was born in Vilnius in Lithuania and studied printmaking at the art academy in that city. She is in the early stages of her career but has already had five solo exhibitions of her work in Lithuania, as well as participating in numerous group exhibitions in her own country and in many other parts of Europe. In addition she completed two residencies at the Cité Internationale des Arts in Paris in 2008/09, with a major installation in 2009. She was awarded First Prize at the Printmaking 2008 exhibition at Vilnius Graphic Art Centre in 2009, and her video Mechanism 2 won First Prize in the ENTER 6 Multimedia Art Festival in Šiauliai in Lithuania in the same year. In addition to her work in printmaking she works in sculpture, video and photography – with many of her photographs being made during her travels in Europe – in which she captures the effects of fleeting light and movement, as well as the emotions of human relationships.

The title of the project for her graduation as a Bachelor of Fine Art in 2008 was *Nesusikalbejimai*, translated as Misunderstandings or Failure of the Conversation. Her work for this project comprised a series of prints, together with two pieces of sculpture entitled Mechanisms, which have also been the subject of her video pieces. The sculptures relate to the prints both thematically and as the subject of two of the series, while at the same time retaining their autonomy. The artist comments, 'I tried to give them some warmth by using paper instead of plastic. But paper is not suitable for long-term use. The mechanisms spin for only a few hours and then I have to replace the damaged parts with new ones. But on the other hand I love the ephemeral side of the constructions. They are more like those investigated situations, short moments that come and go. For me this is a personal situation with my own questions that need to be answered. But the same situations can easily be lifted to a much wider social level.' These mechanisms,

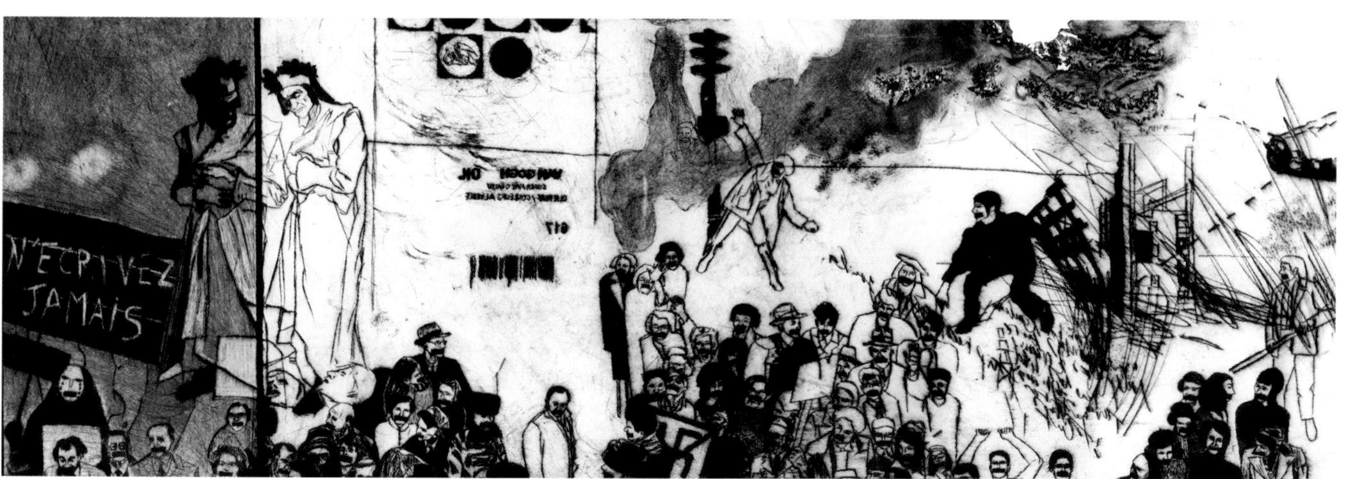

Rūta Spelskytė,
Unsuccessful Dialogue of the Crowd
(from the Misunderstandings series), 2008.
Drypoint, 22 x 58cm. 9 x 22in.

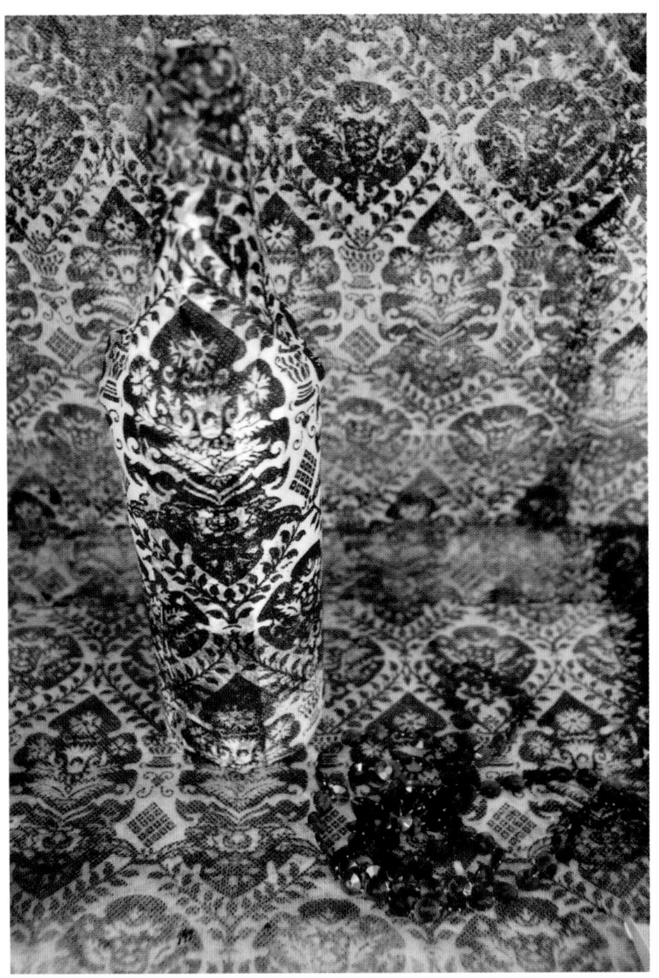

By contrast, the relationships shown in *Unsuccessful Dialogue of the Crowd* are more complex: there are references to one of the 'street events' of Guy Debord and the Situationists, with the wall graffiti, 'N' Écrivez jamais' (Write no more) summing up the anger directed by the Situationists at the establishment, and ultimately their lack of success in changing the system. Spelskytė contrasts this failure of communication by including the image of Dante, his proximity to the graffiti rendering it even more absurd. Other prints in the series chart the breakdown in relationships, or the failure to establish them in the first place through the choice of silence. The compression of the images, and the simple graphic drawing, renders these prints as a permanent record of events in relationships, of the transient success of meetings and subsequent partings.

As part of her 2009 residency in Paris the artist made an installation in the studio in which she worked. Prior to going to Paris she screenprinted 126m² (151yd²) of paper with a design based on a 16th-century Italian silk fabric, and used this to cover the surfaces of every part of the studio, its furniture and the objects in the room, resulting in a complex visual spatial illusion in which surfaces and objects changed in their visibility as the viewer moved around the space. This installation was the subject of a subsequent solo exhibition in Vilnius. Rūta Spelskytė is charting an original path through printmaking, with results that mark her as an artist with an idiosyncratic view of its potential.

http://spelskyte.googlepages.com/graphics
(The third dimension, Memory, The new generation)

which call to mind the work of Jean Tinguely, are carefully designed to function, and equally to fail, and in this they have characteristics that take them beyond the usual coldness of machines, relating of one part of the machine to another in a quasi-human way, and their whole character to those who encounter them.

The paradox of strength and fragility within the Mechanisms is also an important constituent of the human relationships that are the subject of her prints. *Working Example of Mechanism No.1* shows the encounter in diagrammatic form of two people becoming a couple and then splitting, framing an embracing couple in the centre, with a torn playing card to the right. Spelskytė makes reference in this work to a long history in the details and the contrast between the roles of the pantomime roles of King and Clown. In *Unsuccessful Dialogue of the Two*, a man and a woman are shown in three frames, as in a comic strip, in three stages of a dialogue. The situation of this couple can be read from left to right or right to left; either way, the lack of success in communication with each other is the same.

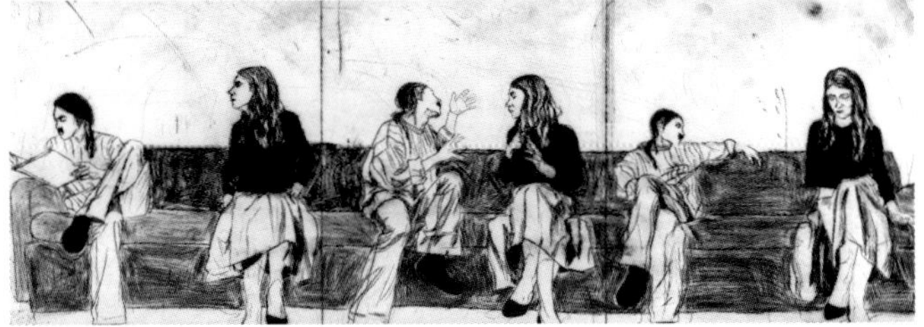

Rūta Spelskytė, *Unsuccessful Dialogue of the Two (from the Misunderstandings series), 2008.*
Drypoint, 23 x 57cm. 9 x 22in.

SANDY SYKES

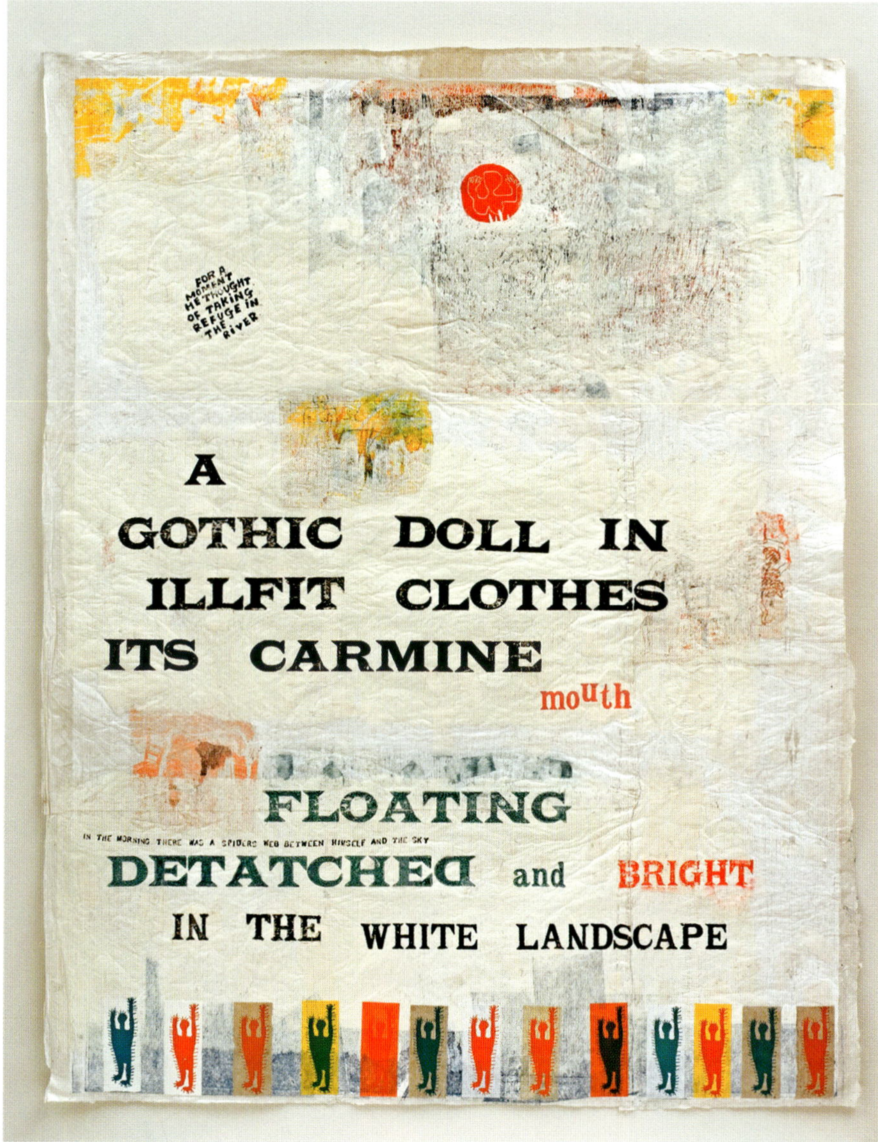

Sandy Sykes, *A Gothic Doll... (from the Manuscripts series), 2007/08.*
Hand-rubbed woodcut and mixed media, 150 x 100cm. 60 x 39in.

The bleak marshes of Essex on the windswept east coast of England, at almost the same level as the North Sea, are steeped in history that has been laid down in layers by successive invasions and settlements. This is where Sandy Sykes now lives and has a studio in an old barn. It is some distance from Yorkshire, the county of her birth, where she graduated from Leeds College of Art, before going on to take an MA in Printmaking at Wimbledon College of Art in London. The landscape of Yorkshire is very different to that of Essex, falling from the rocky heights of the Pennines eastwards to the cliffs that face across that same North Sea, but with a history that is laid down in layers that are equally rich in meaning. The artist writes: 'I love the areas of margin, where the sea meets the land, and earth and sea meet the sky; as we humans push or are pushed to the margins of passion, anger, despair and longing where the edges bleed or blend as does colour in water on paper.'

Sykes's work over the years has encompassed painting, printmaking and the making of artist's books, all firmly based on the disciplines of drawing: she has maintained sketchbooks throughout her career, recording in them visual and verbal observations of the world around her and its events. She reads widely; the books she encounters are a continuing influence on her work, which is in major

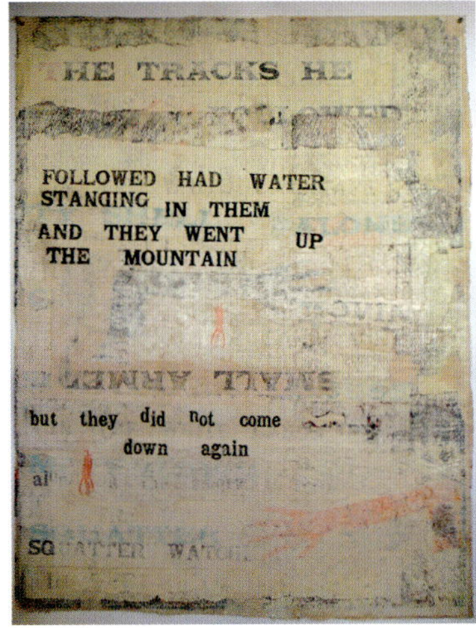

Sandy Sykes,
The Tracks he Followed...
(from the Manuscripts
series), 2007–08.
Hand-rubbed woodcut
and mixed media,
150 x 100cm. 60 x 39in.

museum collections in Britain and America. She exhibits widely, being the recipient of numerous international awards, and her travels have taken her to many countries. It is, however, to the flat lands of Essex that she returns, and from which she derives both the inspiration for her work and the space in which to bring it into being.

In *Cover Me*, a series of large drawings begun in 2008, there are clues to her approach. Large sheets of translucent Indian khadi paper, joined together as required, are covered with many small drawings that at first glance are deceptively simple. Cowboys brandish guns on horses, some of which have five legs; they are clustered together with other cowboys astride tanks, women waving flags, and children and teddy bears – the innocent victims of endless senseless wars, melded together inexplicably and irretrievably, in an endless litany of violence and its inevitable results. The composition of *Cover Me – Rifle* is made more complex with the addition of fighter planes and other deadly weapons, and the individual drawings overlap; there are also words printed onto the paper from individual wooden letters from old printing blocks.

The words appear in another series of works, begun in 2007. The *Manuscript* series takes the artist's work, and the use of printmaking, in new directions, and can be seen as the present culmination of much of her work in recent years. In essence these prints are hand-rubbed woodcuts on large sheets of paper constructed from handmade Indian papers; but the technique she uses is far more complex than this might suggest. Other mediums are involved, laid down and partly scraped off; other prints – linocut, etching, chine collé – are collaged onto the surface, hand-burnished with a wooden spoon or baren, or rubbed down with a cloth; thick and thin inks are used, fragments of other papers are added, or sanded away, or patched from the back; colour is added, words are composed from individually printed wooden letters, tears are repaired, or left as they are; images are drawn into or erased. The result is a complex multilayered image, a rich palimpsest of fragmented narratives that can be read differently each time the prints are seen; the history they contain lies both in the choice of materials used and the evidence of how they were made.

The short texts that the artist uses are taken from the novel *Child of God* by Cormac McCarthy, winner of the Pulitzer Prize for his most recent novel, *The Road*. These poetic novels are set on the margins of America in situations where life is tenuous and the raw wilderness is perilously close. For Sandy Sykes there is a close connection between the imagery in the work of McCarthy and the imagery and themes that she addresses in her own work: in both there is the threat of endings but in both there is also the hope held out by the thread of humanity, the centuries of history in which people have managed to cling to the promise of civilised life despite seemingly inhospitable conditions. Of the landscape she inhabits she writes, 'I am aware and in awe of earlier generations, each of which have devised solutions which are assimilated endlessly into the grand pattern of the next.' Her powerful work is the evidence of her absorption into this pattern.

www.sandysykes.co.uk
(Large-scale printmaking and installation, Memory)

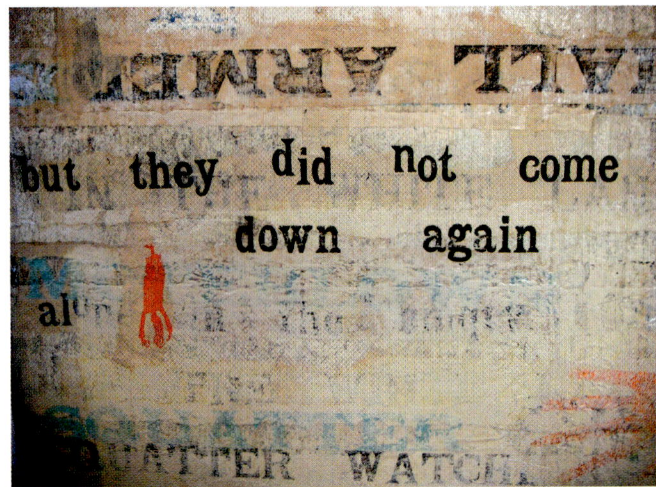

Sandy Sykes, *The Tracks he Followed... (detail) (from the Manuscripts series), 2007–08.* Hand-rubbed woodcut and mixed media. 150 x 100cm. 60 x 39in.

SHELAGH MORGAN

Landscapes of Exile – the past is a foreign country is the title of a digital video film by Shelagh Morgan. It shows bare walking feet and hands making sign language, overlaid with images of documents, in particular postage stamps, documenting the artist's family history, and tracing the long journey that family has made over the course of 176 years, from Wales, via Africa and the South Pacific, to New South Wales in Australia. The stamps, collected from the letters sent home over four generations of expatriation, construct the family history and the changing political face of the former British colonies in which the family lived. They also serve to chart part of the history of white people as they crossed distant lands and oceans, uprooted from the place that was once their home. For the artist, these stamps,

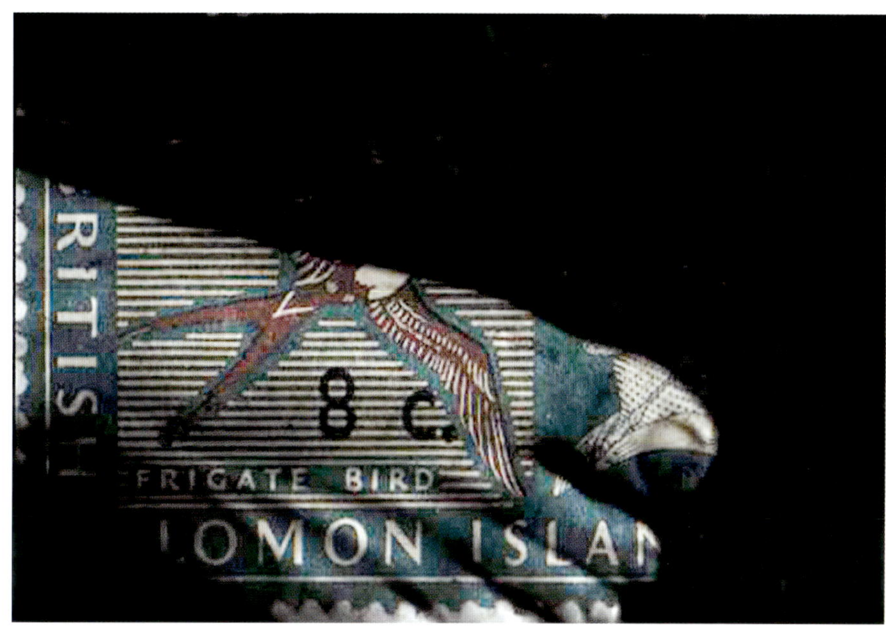

Shelagh Morgan, *British Solomon Islands (from the Landscapes of Exile series), 2007-08.* Digital print on Magnani paper, size variable.

'become like tattoos on my white foot, an indelible history that I carry forward as I now walk on Aboriginal ground'.

Shelagh Morgan was born in what is now Malawi, in Africa, and gained her doctorate at Southern Cross University in New South Wales, where she now teaches. Her work has been exhibited throughout Australia and is included in many public and private collections in that country. Like Jan Davis (q.v.) she lives close to where the artist Geoff Levitus lived, and in common with Davis her work is predicated on searching for the appropriate ways and medium to chart her changing relationship with the land that she now occupies. The journey that Morgan, and her family before her, made, always through countries in which she was not only a foreigner but also a colonist, has given her, 'a dispersed/displaced sense of belonging, as there is no right of return to any of the places I have called home'. Her awareness of both the history and the political and cultural contexts of the journey has led her to give her work the umbrella title *The Science of Whereabouts*, attempting to give shape to 'the intention and the unsayable nature of locating oneself in space/place'. This represents an understandable desire to make sense of the journey and through that to reach a fuller understanding of the place where she now lives. This desire contrasts greatly with the knowledge of the land held by the historical Aboriginal guardians, whose unwritten history reaches back tens of thousands of years. In her search for the most suitable means of expressing her ideas she will use

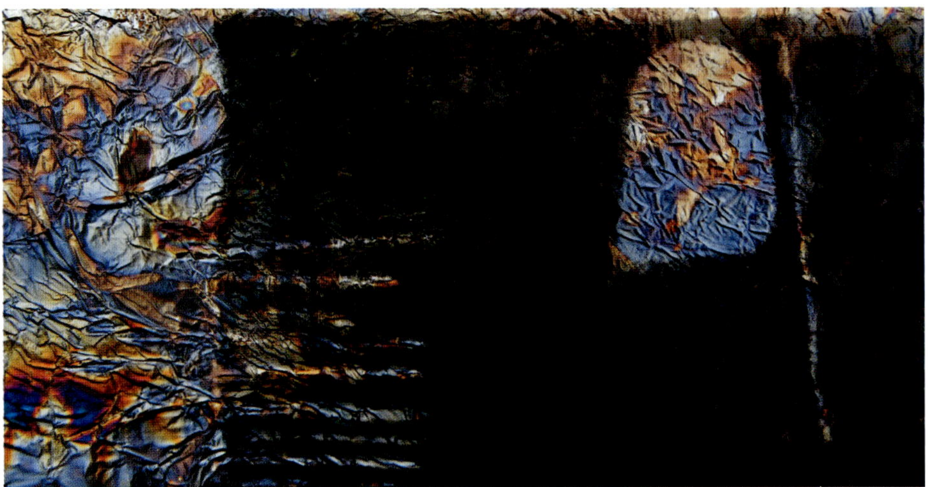

Shelagh Morgan, *Camphor Residue (from The Charcoal Burner's Diary series), 2009.* Digital print on Magnani paper, 28 x 21cm. 11 x 8in.

print techniques – both the traditional in which she trained, or the digital – or painting, drawing, photography or video, employing whichever of these is best suited to realising her ideas. She describes herself as neither painter nor printmaker, but rather a maker who uses whatever materials and processes are available to articulate an adequate visual language.

Her series from 2008/09, *The Science of Whereabouts II*, consists of 12 artist's books containing digital prints, 260 miniature oil paintings and a large number of kiosk-printed photographs. She set out in 2008 to take a photograph every morning at sunrise from the same spot outside her studio and always in the same direction. In the end she made 260 photographs, and recorded the azimuth, the time of sunrise and the length of day for each. By making small paintings she is not only changing the medium but also incorporating the process of passing time. The project stemmed from the desire she developed during her childhood travels to fix the position of her bed in relation to all the other places she had slept in, so that she could imagine those locations and come to understand her place on the surface of the world.

At the same time she has pursued another project, *Charcoal Burner's Diary*, in which she used wood from the trees in the valley around her home to make charcoal. Her sensitivity to the environmental history of the place was based on the notion that such a history was tied up in the molecular structure of the carbon of those trees. She describes the processes she used as being not so much image-making but rather a way of collecting place on paper. One tree in particular, the camphor laurel, makes excellent charcoal, but is an alien species that she describes as 'one of the most noxious weeds in Australia'. For the artist, understanding this came to symbolise the alien presence of settlers in the ancient land of Australia over the past 220 years, as well as offering a way to make work suggesting carbon credits and trading. Her work for this project has consisted of mixed-media works on paper, some incorporating digital print, and an artist's book of digital prints of drawings done in her homemade charcoal on paper. The work of this artist touches deep seams of understanding of the land that is at present the place called home.

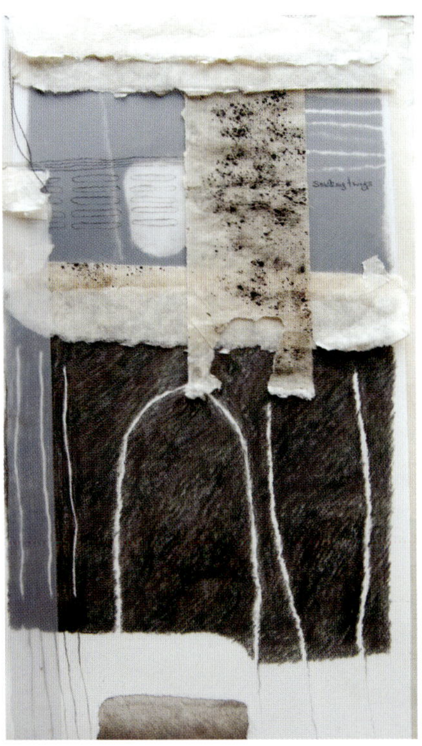

Shelagh Morgan, *Chimanea, 2009.* Mixed-media including camphor charcoal on handmade paper from sugarcane, size variable.

http://visualartsnetwork.net.au/artists/artists_gallery/index. php?show=artist&id=56
(New technology, Environment, Postcolonialism)

TOM HUCK

Potosi is a small town in rural Missouri, 70 miles southwest of St Louis, where printmaker Tom Huck grew up and attended high school – not perhaps the most likely starting place for someone who has since then gained the reputation of being one of the most remarkable artists in America. He taught printmaking at Washington University in St Louis, from which he gained his master's degree, where his unparalleled skill in woodcut and his outspoken opinions on the injustices that remain in America marked him out as an inspirational teacher. Like many of his generation he welcomed the ending of the Bush presidency with relief; he believes, however, that despite the positive changes there is still a negative aspect to America that is in need of healing and exorcism. The dark underbelly of his country has fascinated him for a long time and remains the source for his work. Asked to list the artists who inspired his interest in woodcut and his commitment to printmaking he lists Dürer as the artist whose work introduced him to the possibilities of this physically and mentally demanding technique, followed by Hogarth, Daumier, Ensor, Beckmann, Posada and Robert Crumb – all of them artists with strong social consciences and the ability to portray in uncompromising terms the social ills of their times and the violent injustices that lie not far beneath the surface of civilisation. Huck chooses, as these artists did, to represent the most grotesque aspects of society in ways that are politically provocative and possessed of a dark and grim humour. His website is proof of the reputation he has gained for the hardworking/hard-playing approach he takes to the serious business of making art and the equally serious business of enjoying life to the full.

His print shop, Evil Prints, is in a former industrial building near the centre of St Louis. It has large rooms, with ample space for his studio and for the large presses that he needs to pull his prints; there is also room for the classes he gives in a variety of print mediums. It is big enough to contain some of the social events for which Evil Prints is renowned, including the regular Dr Sketchy's Anti-Art School, which blends life drawing, burlesque and celebrated partying with considerable success. As with any studio it is the evidence around the place that offers clues to the artist's work: as well as his prints on the wall, and matrices leaning against the walls, there is a lot of ephemera, and there are bookshelves on which Jimi Hendrix, Matisse, Lovis Corinth, the Bible, Piranesi, Egon Schiele and Andrew Wyeth are found side by side. But his personal studio space is what is most indicative of the dedication he puts into everything he does: he works with the board vertical, sitting or standing to cut the matrix for each print on Maine birch plywood, first drawing in intricate details with consummate skill, and then spending weeks and months cutting away to reveal the image to be printed: the evidence is there of the hard-won image.

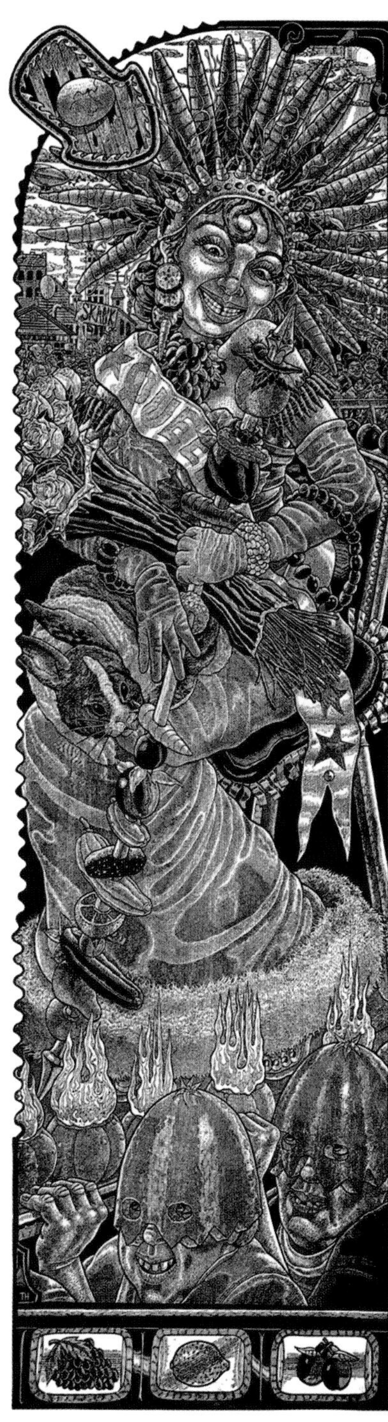

Tom Huck, *Brandy Baghead, Part I: Beta-Caro-Teen Queen, 2007–09.* Woodcut, 209 x 61cm. 82 x 24in.

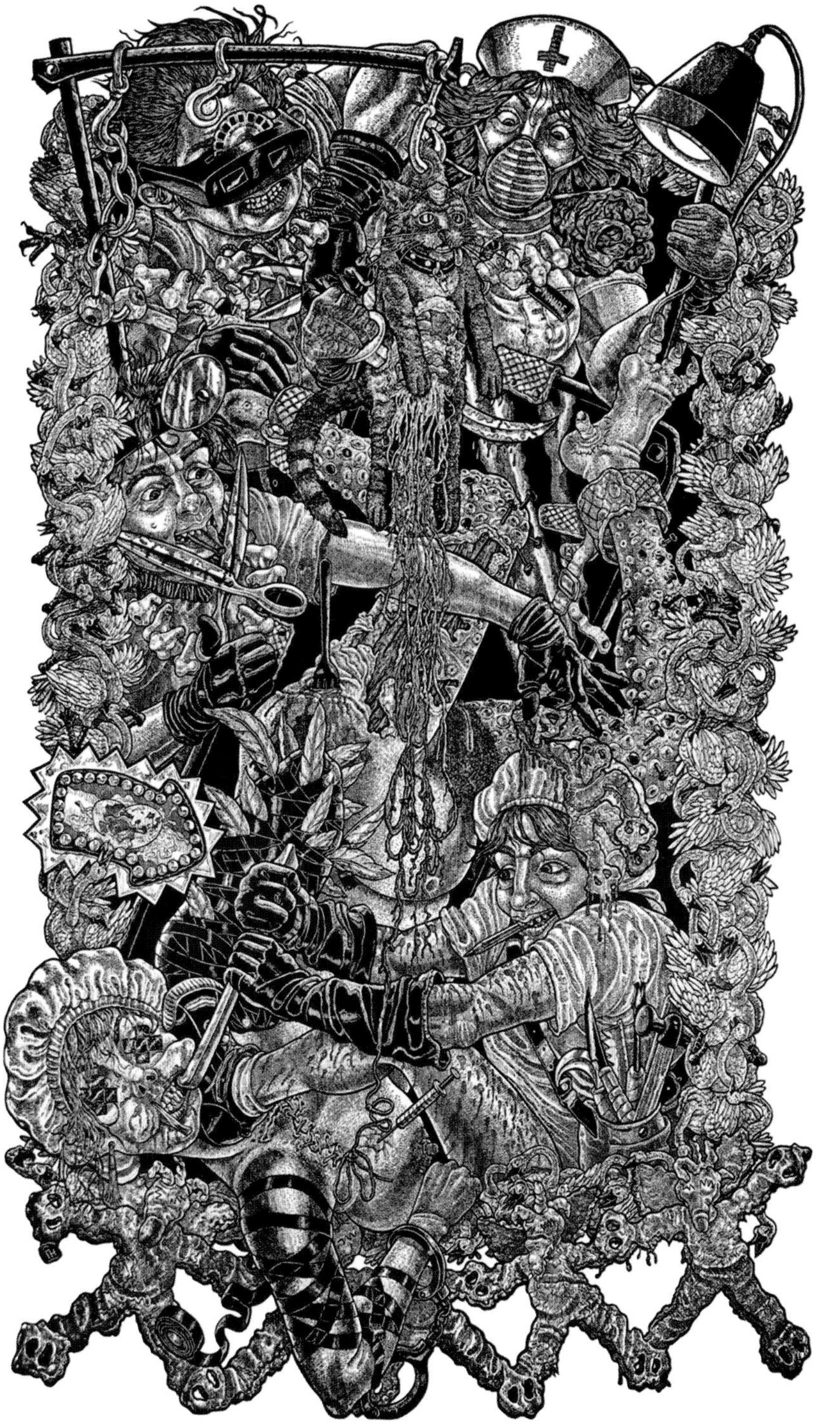

Tom Huck, *Brandy Baghead, Part II: America's Next Top Omelette, 2007–09.* Woodcut, 209 x 122cm. 82 x 48in.

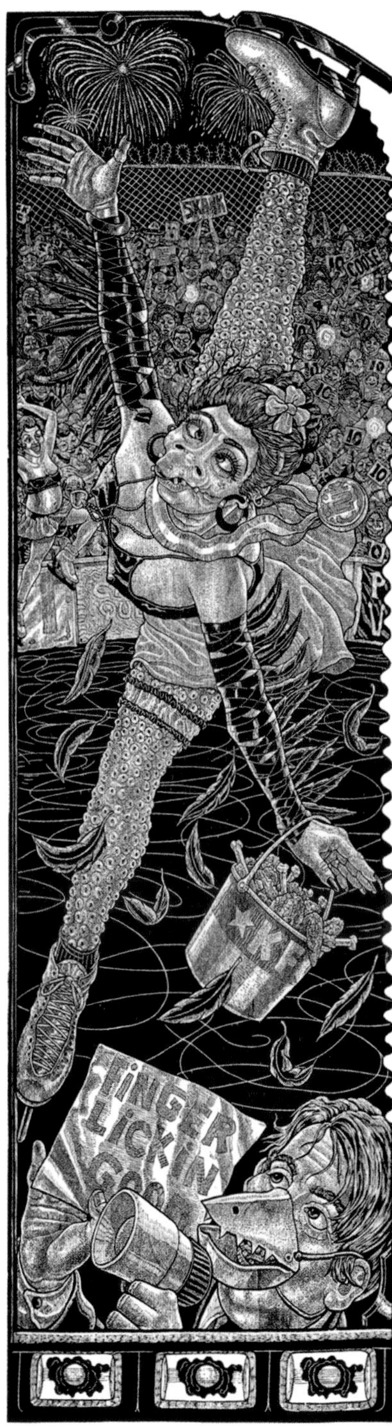

Two series of prints have won the artist considerable acclaim and are included in a number of major American public collections: *The Bloody Bucket* is a series of images of a bar that existed in the Potosi area for three short years from 1948 to 1951, which was the haunt of Second World War veterans, tales of whom were told to Huck by his grandfather. The images are of violence and drunkenness, graphically portrayed, while *Two Weeks in August: 14 Rural Absurdities* portrays tales, some taller than others, from the rural areas of Missouri. In both of these series the artist addresses the small-mindedness of the area in which he was brought up. He says, 'Small-mindedness is the one thing I cannot tolerate in this world. There's nothing more evil than that.' Both sets of prints reveal the depraved and ridiculous stories from Potosi's past through grim humour, exposing the hypocrisy that is also typical of rural communities in other parts of the world. In his most recent series the scale is even more ambitious: *The Transformation of Brandy Baghead* is the first in a planned series of triptychs, *Booger Stew*, which Huck thinks might take 15 years or more to complete. Brandy Baghead portrays episodes in the life of the eponymous anti-heroine, who is turned into a chicken so that she can enter an ice-dancing contest. It is a bitter indictment of the global phenomenon of mindless reality TV and the obsession with plastic surgery. It is dark, funny, thought-provoking and unsettling – and wonderfully well made. The gruesome world that Huck portrays is both beyond the edge and nearer to us than we may care to consider.

www.evilprints.com
(Large-scale printmaking and installation, Politics)

Tom Huck, *Brandy Baghead, Part III: Skating with the Scars, 2007-09.* Woodcut, 209 x 61cm. 82 x 24in.

XENOPHON SACHINIS

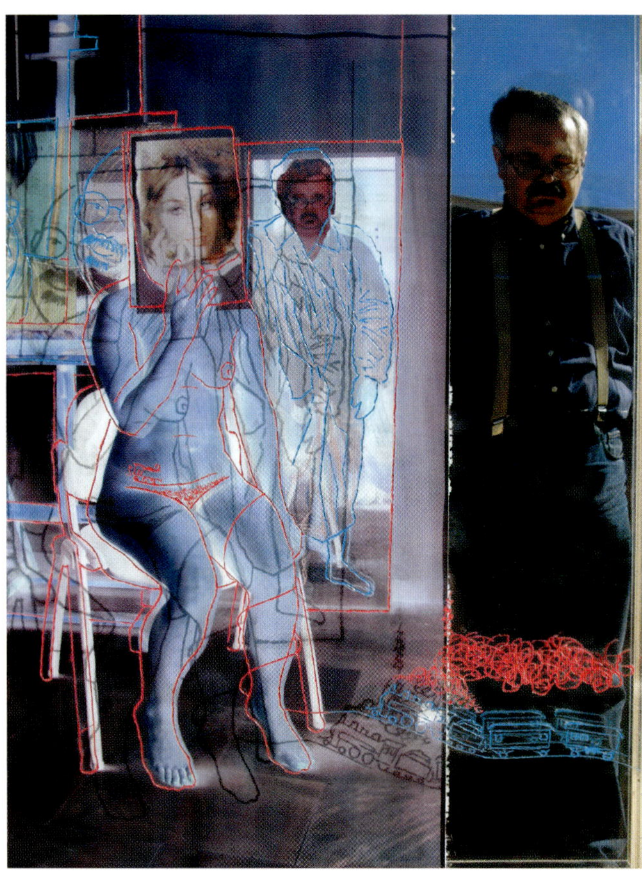

Xenophon Sachinis, *Self-Portrait and Model, 2008.*
Drypoint on Plexiglas, mirror, digital print, 105 x 80 x 5cm. 41 x 31.5 x 2in.

Xenophon Sachinis was born in Thessaloniki in Northern Greece, where he lives and works and is Assistant Professor at the School of Fine Arts at Aristotle University. He is also Co-Founder and Director of the Helios Printmaking Centre in the Neapolis district of the city, which in 2008 hosted its first international printmaking triennial. Sachinis studied at the School of Fine Arts in Athens and at the École Nationale Supérieur des Beaux-Arts in Paris. His work has been exhibited throughout Europe and the United States, and he participated in the IMPACT international conferences from 2003 to 2007. In addition he has a strong commitment to the importance of artist and student exchanges through the Erasmus programme of the EU. His activity in all these fields has helped to raise the profile of printmaking in Greece and to enhance that country's presence internationally.

His own work has followed a conventional trajectory, from traditional mediums to digital, and further into experimental forms. His quest for the best means of expressing his ideas is charted in his writings. In a statement about his work he writes, 'Is it possible to focus our artistic interest on the matrix, or is it forbidden to enjoy the work performed on the plate as if it were the forbidden fruit that no one must perceive as a work of art?' This goes to the heart of much of the discussion about the role of printmaking in the context of contemporary art. The work on the matrix – be it wood, stone, metal or lino – is naturally central to the printmaker's involvement with the creation of work, and is evidence of a high level of aesthetics combined with craft skill: but it is rarely seen by those who do not go into print workshops. When it is shown – as part of an exhibition, for example – the viewers' fascination with the object from which the print has been pulled leads to a greater sense of engagement with the process and a deeper appreciation of what the medium can achieve. This has happened increasingly in recent years, and is leading to a demystification of the 'dark arts' of printmaking. The role played by the emergence of digital techniques, with their greater and more democratic accessibility, has doubtless had something to do with this, as has the growth of the number of print workshops and the range of instruction courses they offer.

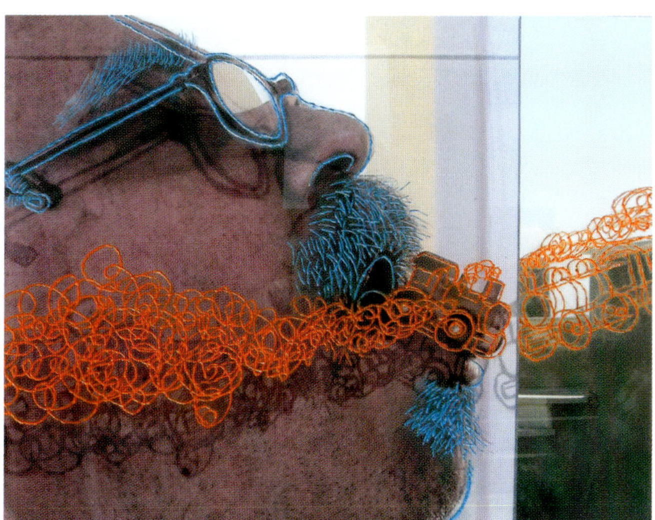
Xenophon Sachinis, *Figure 1, 2007.*
Mixed media, 148 x 60 x 5cm. 58 x 24 x 2in.

Sachinis has arrived at a thesis that underlies his work: 'Always be respectful to the idea of a matrix and its tangible memory – the print.' In the mid-1990s he started using Plexiglas as the matrix for his drypoint prints, finding in this transparent and yet resistant material a metaphor for the fight between oblivion and memory. Whatever he cut or marked into the surface became permanent – it could not be burnished out or obliterated without further material being removed. This factor gave him the flexibility to see printmaking as serving the idea of memory. While the initial works used Plexiglas as the matrix from which prints on paper could be pulled, he also explored the use of engraved sheets of the material assembled into cubes, in which the image from one side could be transmitted onto the other side by the action of light, and then sequences of these cubes could be made into installations. The addition of mirrors as part of the constructions was the next constituent, allowing the observer or the environment to be reflected within the work.

In his more recent work the artist has melded together digital prints, most of which are self-portraits, on one side of the Plexiglas, with engraved and inked drawings almost – but not quite – following the outlines of the digital image on the other. So in one work we see the artist with a train emerging from his mouth: a reference to a painting by Jannis Kounellis and to his own pursuit of railway modelling; another has the artist holding the image of a cat's head in front of his face: he is a cat-lover; and in yet another a ship emerges from his mouth: an allusion to the maritime history of his city. In a recent series, he uses a digital print of a seated model in front of an easel, with himself reflected in a mirror, to which he has added engravings as before, together with a train. The final part is the mirror that reflects the viewer, creating an image that reflects upon art history and the artist, and also those who encounter this work. Such works are set up as a form of psychodrama, with references to the dilemmas of art and reality, and those of contemporary society in which behaviour and identity are reflected and judged.

www.americasbiennial.org/Selections/2008/pages/Self-Portrait_II.htm
(New uses for old technology, New technology, Memory)

Xenophon Sachinis, *Self-Portrait, 2007.*
Mixed media, 60 x 75 x 5cm. 24 x 29.5 x 2in.

FURTHER STILL

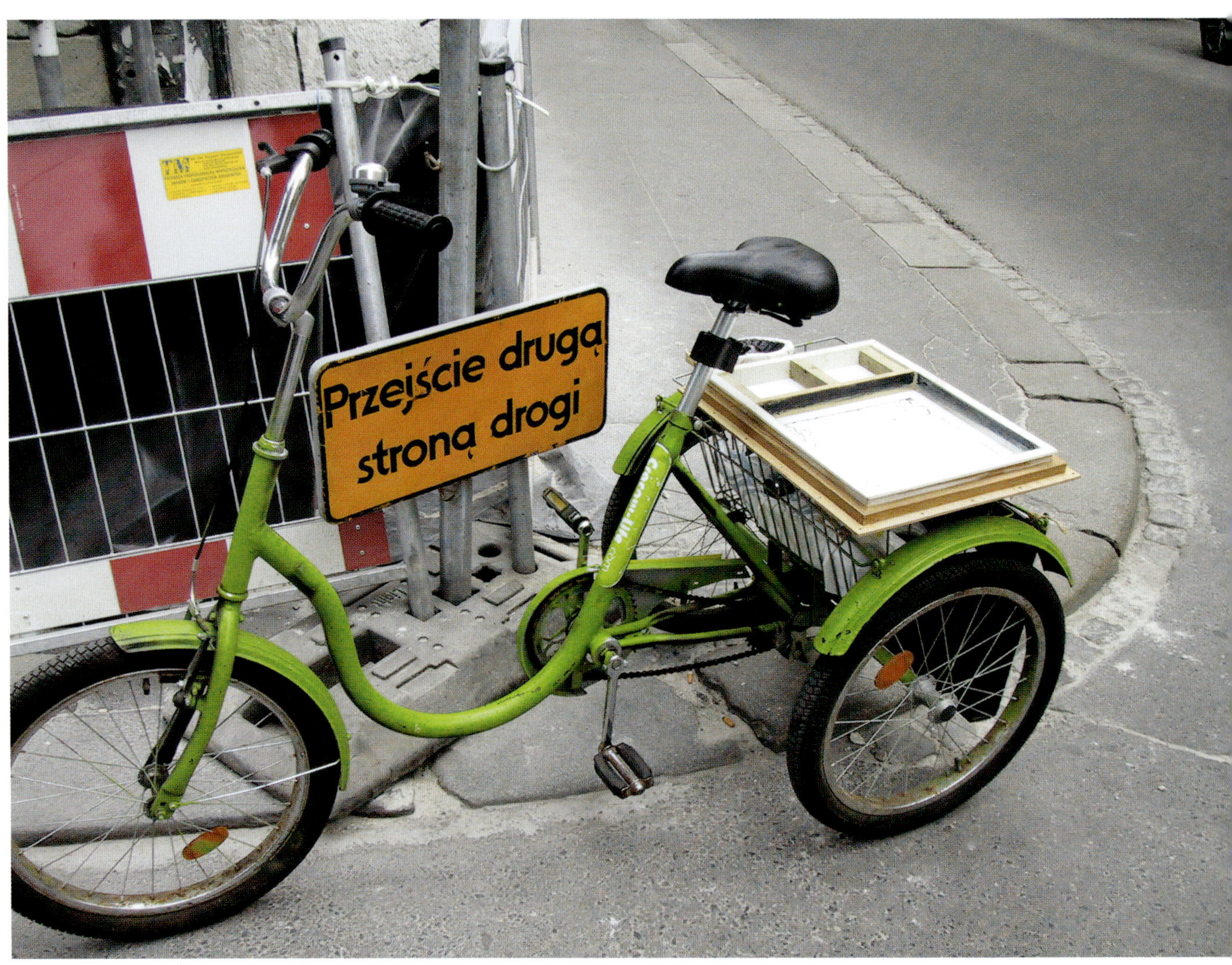

Klavs Weiss, *Modified tricycle used for Ball Print performance,*
Galerie Camelot, Kraków, Poland, 2006. No size.

Tthis book and its predecessor were researched and written during the first decade of the 21st century, and taken together they can be seen as a record of a personal journey through one area of the contemporary visual arts during that time. The two books feature the work of almost 100 individual artists from many parts of the world. And yet, while they offer a wide and representative sample of the excellent work that is being done, that only hope to be a partial picture of the global visual arts scene. When I started out on the journey in November 2002 I could not have foreseen where it would take me, or what I would find. But these things are certain – the world of contemporary printmaking is not limited; it cannot be completely defined or circumscribed, and there is no easy way to sum up the huge variety of work being undertaken; and it is still evolving. This is as it should be in a world in which constant change is the driving force for so many of the social and political developments that affect the way we live and interact with each other.

The world of printmaking thrives on collaboration as well as on international gatherings and competitions, and it is encouraging that initiatives continue to extend the challenge and excitement of contemporary printmaking into new locations. There follows a selection of those initiatives, all of which show promise for being developed further and for stimulating dialogue between artists and print mediums, and between printmaking and the public.

'The mission of contemporary art is to push the boundaries of the senses, exploring new grounds that in turn open up people's minds, revealing new   experiences that are sensual, intellectual, and connected to the essence of being human.'

NY Arts online, in reference to Yoko Ono, October 2009

ARTIST GROUPS

CHHAAP, India:

Situated in the city of Vadodara in Gujarat in the northwest of India, CHHAAP, the Baroda Printmaking Workshop, was founded as a cooperative in 1999 to create and promote a wider appreciation of original prints and printmaking techniques. Printmaking in India has a long history of traditional techniques connected to religious images, fabrics and miniatures, and in a rapidly developing country it has the potential for considerable further evolution. Kavita Shah and her colleagues at CHHAAP have set up a programme of workshops in a range of techniques, and also put on artist talks and exhibitions, which have widened the understanding of what printmaking can achieve. A number of small print portfolios containing work by local artists have been produced, and have proved to be popular. An important further development has been Shah's determination to expand into international projects. Through her contributions to international conferences she has created much interest in Indian printmaking, and in 2008 she set up an international folio of prints based on Ganjifa playing cards, resulting in a collection of 54 prints by international artists that has been seen in a number of venues. With initiatives like this one, there is no doubt that India will become a major contributor to international contemporary printmaking.

Go Block, Malaysia:

Printing from wooden blocks is a central part of the traditional arts and crafts of Southeast Asia, but in the hands of this group of artists from Malaysia it is being taken into completely new areas of artistic expression. Painting, based on the Western tradition of modernism, played the major role in the development of post-independence art in the country, leaving printmaking in a very subordinate position. But between them Juhari Said, Kim Ng, Izan Tahir, Zulkifli Yusoff and Shahrul Njamili are producing a range of work, from lyrical to conceptual that, although derived from traditional techniques, is as innovative and challenging as anything produced in Europe or North America. A major exhibition of their work at the prestigious Galeri Petronas in Kuala Lumpur in 2009 established beyond doubt that printmaking in its wider sense as a major part of the contemporary visual arts had found its place in Malaysia. The ambition of the group, beyond the development and exhibition of their work as individual artists, is to bring the contemporary printmaking of their country to the attention of a wider international audience. The freshness and individual integrity of their work is certainly worthy of that attention.

Toi Whakataa, New Zealand:

The traditional art forms of the Māori people are carving and weaving, as well as tattoo; there is no comparable tradition in printmaking. However, in common with artists in many other parts of the world, there is a desire to use printmaking techniques as a form of expression that ties in with the other forms of contemporary art that currently exist in New Zealand and further afield. Toi Whakataa is the Māori printmaking collective that was formed in 2006. The name means 'to make an impression', and relates not only to the technique but also to the spirit of the group. The confirmation of cultural identity is clearly an important issue, as is the need to establish the ways in which a non-traditional medium can be incorporated into the range of forms by which the culture is defined. The network that has been established by the work of the collective is strengthening the individual and group identity through support and nurture, and through exhibitions, gatherings and workshops. The opportunities include international as well as national initiatives, and through these the identity of contemporary Māori art can be enhanced, and make a valuable and important contribution to the arts of the region.

Printmaking in the United Arab Emirates:

To set up a programme of printmaking in a country that is less than 40 years old, and in which the cultural tradition is in written rather than visual form, is indeed to work at the edge. This is what Karen Oremus has been actively involved with since 2003 when she was appointed Assistant Professor in the Department of Art and Design at Zayed University. Born in Canada, educated there and in Italy and the UK, she has worked in art education across North America, Europe and the Middle East. Her efforts to establish a teaching programme in printmaking have resulted in many students learning for the first time the ways in which print techniques can be used to produce editions of images that relate to this young country. As she has commented the recent initiatives that will bring branch museums of the Louvre and Guggenheim to Abu Dhabi are going to bring about a major shift in public awareness of international arts and art forms. It is her hope that printmaking will continue to be taught, and that this will lead to the growth of a community-based printmaking workshop. In addition, as the presence of the UAE as Guest Country at the 2007 Lessedra Printmaking Exhibition in Bulgaria shows, she has already established an international role for printmaking from the UAE. There is still some way to go, but the steps taken so far have been positive, and in the right direction.

This small selection offers some indications of the work that is going on in many parts of the world to explore the ways in which printmaking can be redefined and repositioned in the world of the contemporary arts. Printmakers have always been pioneers, leading new movements in the visual arts rather than following them. At the same time there has always been the danger of the pioneers becoming the establishment. But if the artists who use printmaking can stay light on their toes, there is no reason why further generations of pioneers cannot keep the wheels spinning. The adventurous journey across new frontiers of expression and exploration, merging tradition and experiment with human creativity, may yet prove to be more fascinating than ever before.

INTERNATIONAL EXHIBITIONS AND COMPETITIONS

Estampa, Spain: Estampa 09,

The International Print and Contemporary Art Editions Fair, was the 17th edition of this increasingly international annual event, staged at the end of October at the IFEMA Trade Fairs venue on the outskirts of Madrid. In 2005 a decision was taken to broaden the scope of the fair from fine-art prints to other mediums, and it now encompasses fine books, photography, video and other forms of multiple art. It is a major event, occupying a vast hall and attracting galleries from across Spain and its islands, as well as from other European countries. In addition space is given to the numerous arts institutions and foundations that are based on the work of a single artist or group of artists, some of whom are regrettably not sufficiently known outside Spain. A visit to this fair not only gives a broad overview of Spanish printmaking within a European context but also allows for an insight into the directions in which printmaking is developing in a number of countries. This is assisted by the 'Tentaciones' section, which gives space for young artists to exhibit new work, allowing this to be seen alongside galleries showing the best examples of printmaking across the ages, from Old Masters to emerging contemporary artists.

Guanlan Print Base, China:

This unusual development is situated in the 300-year-old Dashuitan village in the vicinity of the new metropolis of Shenzhen. Inspired by the success of the Dafen Oil Painting Village in Longgang, Guanlan aspires to provide an international base for printmaking. The village, in which traditional Hakka houses and buildings have been converted to provide accommodation and working space, as well as spaces for meetings and discussions, provides residencies for artists from all over the world, enabling them to develop new work in a stimulating context, with full support from assistants and interpreters. The Belgian artist Ingrid Ledent was one of the first to benefit from a residency there, and found the experience extremely valuable. The base also stages the Guanlan International Print Biennial – the first was held in 2007 – which has achieved remarkable success in a short time, attracting printmakers from China and all over the world, with prizes going to a wide range of artists. The long history of printmaking in China, and its role in establishing many traditions, is well-known. The Guanlan project will build on these strengths, and aims to establish an international forum for print development and a major world centre for both traditional and innovative printmaking.

Ingráfica, Spain:

This new festival was first held in Autumn 2008 in the UNESCO World Heritage Site city of Cuenca, in Castilla La Mancha, southeast of Madrid. The ambition of the first Ingráfica was considerable, but during the six weeks of exhibitions, events and an important conference, the great appetite for printmaking in Spain was proved beyond doubt. The conference, at which there were speakers from Great Britain, Germany, Poland, Romania and Slovenia as well as from Spain, encouraged all those present to discuss the role of printmaking in the 21st century, and in particular its condition and future in Spain. The range of exhibitions was very wide, from international masters such as Picasso, Juan Gris and Robert Motherwell, to lesser-known Spanish masters, and a wide range of young artists from Spain and further afield. Cuenca has the advantage of being the location of a number of important foundations, many of them based in historic buildings, which provided an excellent range of idiosyncratic spaces in which the exhibitions could be staged. The 2009 Ingráfica built on the success of the first, and added an important programme of events centred on the local community, including the Transversal project, which used local buses and bus shelters as carriers for specially commissioned graphic works. This festival provides an excellent model upon which festivals elsewhere could be based.

The International Experimental Engraving Biennial, Romania:

The 3rd edition of this biennial was staged in Mogoşoaia in Romania in the spring of 2008. IEEB was founded by Ciprian Ciuclea as a forum for discussing and exhibiting new tendencies in image-multiplication techniques. In common with many other young artists across the world Ciuclea had become concerned at the way in which processes for traditional engraving (and other printmaking techniques) were being accorded more interest and value than the results themselves. He felt that the idea of experimenting with techniques and forms, and of seeking out new means for expression, was not being given sufficient attention. The exhibitions and associated events of this biennial have included a very wide range of works and techniques from across the full spectrum of reproducible means. It is entirely logical that this programme should have emerged in Romania: despite the dark days of the Ceauşescu regime the country has a reputation for avant-garde art that stretches back to Brancusi. The artists whose work was shown in the 3rd edition came from across the world, and the exhibitions, staged in historic buildings, provided spaces that lent themselves to the intervention of challenging works in a range of mediums. As in the past, Romania once again provides the context for a valuable contribution to the international printmaking dialogue.

BIBLIOGRAPHY

Benjamin, Walter, *Illuminations*, trans. Harry Zorn (London: Pimlico/Random House, 1999).

Spalding, Julian, *The Eclipse of Art* (Munich, Berlin, London, New York: Prestel, 2003).

Marioni, Tom, *Beer, Art and Philosophy* (San Francisco: Crown Point Press, 2003).

Nuttall, Jeff, *Art and the Degradation of Awareness* (London: Calder Publications, 2001).

Cleveland, William, *Art and Upheaval* (Oakland, CA: New Village Press, 2008).

Websites

Art for Humanity
www.afh.org.za

CHHAAP
www.chhaap.org

Estampa
www.estampa.org

Guanlan Biennial
www.guanlanprints.com/b/

Ingráfica
www.ingrafica.org

International Experimental Engraving Biennale
www.experimentalproject.ro

Printeresting
www.printeresting.org

Southern Graphics Council
www.southerngraphics.org

Toi Whakataa
http://toiwhakataapress.weebly.com

Tradigital
http://tradigitalprintmaking.blogspot.com

INDEX